THE DEBATE
OVER CHRISTIAN
RECONSTRUCTION

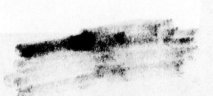

Other books by Gary DeMar

God and Government:
  A Biblical and Historical Study, 1982

God and Government:
  Issues in Biblical Perspective, 1984

God and Government:
  The Restoration of the Republic, 1986

Ruler of the Nations:
  Biblical Blueprints for Government, 1987

The Reduction of Christianity:
  A Biblical Response to Dave Hunt, 1988
  (with Peter J. Leithart)

*Surviving College Successfully: A Complete
  Manual for the Rigors of Academic Combat*, 1988

*Something Greater is Here: Christian
  Reconstruction in Biblical Perspective*, 1988

THE DEBATE OVER CHRISTIAN RECONSTRUCTION

Gary DeMar

DOMINION PRESS • FT. WORTH, TEXAS

AMERICAN VISION PRESS • ATLANTA, GEORGIA

Copyright © 1988 by American Vision, Atlanta, Georgia.

First printing, September 1988

American Vision is a Christian educational and communication organization providing materials to help Christians develop a biblical worldview. American Vision publishes a monthly magazine, *The Biblical Worldview*, which is edited by Gary DeMar. For a year's free subscription, write: American Vision, P.O. Box 720515, Atlanta, Georgia 30328.

Typesetting by Thoburn Press, Tyler, Texas

Printed in the United States of America

Unless otherwise noted, all Scripture quotations are from the New American Standard Version.

ISBN 0-915815-07-9 American Vision edition

ISBN 0-930462-33-5 Dominion Press edition

To Dr. Steven F. Hotze

TABLE OF CONTENTS

FOREWORD

by Dr. Greg L. Bahnsen

The recent "debate" over Christian Reconstruction has been going on for over ten years now. The debate in contemporary Christian circles could actually be pushed back to the early 1970s, with the publication or general recognition of certain probing theological works by R. J. Rushdoony. (Of course, to the extent that Reconstructionist theology is true to God's Word, the debate has been carried on throughout redemptive history, since the time of the fall!) The active and open criticism of Reconstructionist distinctives as such, however, surfaced about a year following the publication of *Theonomy in Christian Ethics* (1977) — and ironically, surfaced within the context of that theological tradition which has given historical impetus to the Reconstructionist perspective: the circles of Presbyterian and Puritan conviction. The school of thought, however, which most conspicuously and naturally stands opposed to Reconstructionist theology is dispensationalism.

Reconstructionism contradicts the dispensationalist view of the Old Testament (which emphasizes discontinuity with Old Testament ethics) as well as the dispensationalist view of the millennium (which emphasizes discontinuity with the present church age). Therefore, dispensationalism most clearly and diametrically opposes Reconstructionist distinctives. The first public debate between a Reconstructionist and a dispensationalist took place at the annual Evangelical Theological Society meeting, held in Toronto in 1981.[1]

---

1. "The Bahnsen-Feinberg Debate." Available from Covenant Tape Ministry, Box 4134, Reno, Nevada 89510, tape #00340.

This was an important and insightful interchange between two trained theologians. But I believe that the debate held seven years later, which is the subject of this book, may prove to be more significant, both because the issues are self-consciously becoming more clear today and because of the broader audience and appeal of the most recent debate.

Of the many pastors and teachers who are publishing materials written from a "Reconstructionist" perspective today, our finest author is, in my opinion, Gary DeMar. His books and articles are clearly written, soundly researched, and politely expressed. For these reasons Mr. DeMar's publications have proven to be the most helpful summaries of Reconstructionist thought we can offer to those willing to learn about the position. He pursues cogent theological polemics, rather than creative innovations and imaginative interpretations; accordingly, he has gained a reputation for reliability. He expresses himself in a well-tempered fashion, which has brought him a reputation as a Christian gentleman.

Therefore, those wishing to study "Christian Reconstruction" seriously and carefully are advised to read this and other works by Gary DeMar. This particular book, *The Debate over Christian Reconstruction*, arises from a specific interchange with certain critics of Reconstruction (Dave Hunt and Tommy Ice) at a public debate April 14, 1988. Previous to this occasion, Mr. DeMar (along with Peter Leithart) had already replied to, and interacted extensively with, critic Dave Hunt in the book, *The Reduction of Christianity*. That book is perhaps the best presentation of the transformational world-and-life-view known as "Christian Reconstruction" which has been published to date, and it would do the careful reader well to study it along with (maybe, before) the present work.

It is evident that Dave Hunt and Tommy Ice did not do so adequately prior to their public debate with Gary DeMar and Gary North. This lapse severely crippled any effort on their part to set forth a serious or accurate critique of Christian Reconstruction—which is disappointing, of course, for anyone who wished to see the theological issues competently engaged in the debate. Hunt and Ice did not address the integrated theological perspective (the total worldview) of Christian Reconstruction, but targeted only one element of it: its victorious millennial eschatology. This one *faux pas* alone precluded their winning the debate because the question being debated was whether Christian Reconstruction is a "deviant theology," and millennial eschatology has never in the history of the evangelical Christian church been made a creedal point of orthodoxy which defines heresy or apostasy. All Christians of good will who profess "the holy catholic [universal] church" (the Apostles' Creed) recognize that others who hold millennial interpretations different from their own are nevertheless their Christian brothers and sisters in the Lord. They may be mistaken, but to accuse them of "deviant" theology is an altogether different—and very serious—charge. Hunt and Ice were incapable (perhaps unqualified) to substantiate such a grave charge. Heresy-hunters bear a heavy responsibility for theological proficiency, and (like all Christian teachers) will come under greater judgment for their inaccuracies (James 3:1).

Even more, as the present book demonstrates, Hunt and Ice left themselves open to ready refutation on the particular points of eschatology they addressed, from the exegesis of Matthew 24 to the biblical concepts of victory and dominion. Their historical claims were equally flimsy. The reader can explore this general observation for himself. I wish to point out but one particular and conspicuous defect in the argumentation of the Reconstructionist critics and comment upon it: their penchant for misrepresentation of what they were called upon to criticize. It is especially because of this (and not simply the academic shortcomings) that we must judge, ethically, that critics Hunt and Ice lost the debate. Repeatedly we encounter allegations and critical assumptions about Reconstructionist eschatology which are misleading, false portrayals of it— for instance, the suggestion that a preterist interpretation of the Olivet Discourse is essential to it, or that it is an innovation from theological liberalism which claims no Biblical support, or that it has affinity with the positive confession movement or Manifest Sons of God, or that it promotes dominion "over people" (tyranny?), or that it does not allow Christ to rule over His earthly kingdom, etc.

None of this is even remotely accurate. And that fact is highly significant if we are sensitive to Biblical ethics.

Of course, this is not the first time by any means that Reconstructionist thought has suffered abuse from those who have not responsibly studied the issues or bothered to be fair in how they depict its distinctives. The faulty scholarship has been witnessed over and over again, from minor points to thundering accusations. Ten years ago at a faculty forum on theonomic ethics at Reformed Theological Seminary (Jackson, Mississippi), one professor publicly criticized the author of *Theonomy in Christian Ethics* for the scholarly shortcoming of failing to interact with Delling's treatment (in Kittel's *Theological Dictionary of the New Testament*) of "fulfill" from Matthew 5:17, only to be informed to his embarrassment that Delling's treatment was rehearsed and rebutted on page 64 of the book he was criticizing! This may seem a minor point, and relative to others it is.

In that same year, Evangel Presbytery (of the Presbyterian Church in America) publicly declared that ministerial candidates holding a theonomic view were unacceptable to the church. More remarkable than this harsh judgment, however, was the fact that it was *after* the decision to promulgate it that the presbytery determined to appoint a committee to study the matter! A year later the study committee recommended a reversal of the previous judgment, acknowledging that it "was taken without proper study and deliberation." The committee's report said: "We admit that many of our minds were made up before we began this study. . . . The vast majority of us . . . had never seen, much less read a copy of the book [*Theonomy in Christian Ethics*]."

In 1978 Aiken Taylor, as editor of the *Presbyterian Journal*, wrote in criticism of the theonomic (or Reconstructionist) position that it was contrary to the Westminster Confession of Faith,[2] even as others had hastily declared that it was not part of mainstream Reformed theological thinking. Such claims were readily refuted by

---

2. Aiken Taylor, "Theonomy Revisited," *The Presbyterian Journal* (December 6, 1978); Taylor, "Theonomy and Christian Behavior," *The Presbyterian Journal* (September 13, 1978).

historical research, however.[3] Indeed, a severe critic of theonomic ethics, Meredith Kline, subsequently conceded that the theonomic outlook was indeed the position of the Westminster Standards.[4] This concession did not deter Kline, however, from railing against the theonomic view as "a delusive and grotesque perversion of the teaching of Scripture." Yet in the very place where this thundering condemnation is found, Kline adduced not one exegetical argument against the position, *but* there were no less than fifty places in the book he was criticizing which stood contrary to his representations of the theonomic position![5] In a circulated but unpublished paper written against theonomic ethics in 1980, Paul Fowler falsely alleged that the position allows nothing unique about Israel's civil order, and then arrogantly insisted that his characterization could not be mistaken—even though it directly flew in the face of numerous things taught in the book he was criticizing.[6] Critics like Robert Strong,[7] Gary Long,[8] Walter Chantry[9] and others have used epithets like "Judaizing" or "legalism" of the position, when over and over again Reconstructionists have shown as clearly as anyone could expect that they are committed to salvation by God's grace alone. In a feature article in *Christianity Today*, Rodney Clapp made the outlandish mistake of pitting Reconstructionist political theory against democratic procedures, a portrayal which runs counter to everything in the Presbyterian and Puritan historical background for the position![10] Examples

---

3. See, for instance, Gary North, ed., *Journal of Christian Reconstruction*, Symposium on Puritanism and Law, Vol. 5, No. 2 (Winter 1978-79).

4. Meredith Kline, "Comments on an Old-New Error," *Westminster Theological Journal*, Vol. 41, No. 1 (Fall 1978), pp. 172-189.

5. See Greg L. Bahnsen, "M. G. Kline on Theonomic Politics," *Journal of Christian Reconstruction*, Symposium on Puritanism and Society, Vol. 6, No. 2 (Winter 1979-80), pp. 195-221.

6. Paul Fowler, "God's Law Free from Legalism" (unpublished paper, 1980).

7. "Theonomy: Expanded Observations" (privately distributed, 1978).

8. Gary D. Long, *Biblical Law and Ethics: Absolute and Covenantal* (Rochester, NY: Backus Book Publishers, 1981).

9. Walter J. Chantry, *God's Righteous Kingdom* (Edinburgh: Banner of Truth Trust, 1980).

10. Rodney Clapp, "Democracy as Heresy," *Christianity Today*, Vol. 31, No. 3 (February 20, 1987), pp. 17-23.

could go on and on.[11]

Over the last decade I have witnessed more slurs and misrepresentations of Reconstructionist thought than I have the heart or ability to count, and I am thinking here only of the remarks made by Christians in positions of leadership: elders, pastors, instructors, writers—those who bear the "greater accountability" since they lead Christ's sheep as teachers. This has forced me as an educated believer to stand back and look more generally at what is transpiring in the Christian community as a whole with respect to its scholarly integrity. And I am heart broken. It is difficult enough for us to gain a hearing in the unbelieving world because of its hostility to the Lord Jesus Christ and its preconception of the lowly intelligence of His followers. The difficulty is magnified many times over when believers offer public, obvious evidence of their inability to treat each other's opinions with careful accuracy. Our "scholarship" is justly ridiculed by those who have been educated in institutions which have no commitment to Christ or His Word, but who have the ethical integrity to demand as a prerequisite to acceptable scholarship that a student represent his opponent fairly before proceeding to criticize or refute him. To use a Pauline expression, "even the Gentiles" know better than to permit imprecision and erroneous portrayals in a serious intellectual discussion. Yet Christians (I include all of us) often seem to care little for that minimal standard of scholarly respectability. How, then, can we be taken seriously? How can we take ourselves seriously?

That holy and inspired Word of God, to which all of us swear allegiance as followers of Christ (whether Presbyterians or Baptists or charismatics or dispensationalists or Reconstructionists or whatever), is *profitable* to us "for correction, for instruction in righteousness" (2 Timothy 3:16). From it we should learn not to speak carelessly: "See a man who is hasty in his words? There is more hope for a fool than for him" (Proverbs 29:20). We should learn to speak cautiously about others (e.g., Matthew 5:22; Psalm

---

11. See the Preface to the expanded edition of my *Theonomy in Christian Ethics* (Phillipsburg, NJ: Presbyterian and Reformed, [1977] 1984).

116:11; James 3:5-18), not wresting people's words or reviling them (Psalm 50:20; 56:5; 1 Corinthians 5:11; 6:10). We should interpret them in the best light afforded by the facts (cf. Acts 24:8), rather than with evil suspicion (1 Timothy 6:4). "He who would love life and see good days, let him refrain his tongue from evil and his lips that they speak no guile" (1 Peter 3:10).

God's Word directs us to study a matter before we presume to speak critically regarding it: "He who gives an answer before he hears, it is a folly and shame to him" (Proverbs 18:13). Scripture teaches us to avoid slander, if we would dwell with Jehovah (Psalm 15:3). We must then be scrupulous to speak the truth about others, even those we would criticize. "A man who bears false witness against his neighbor is a maul, and a sword, and a sharp arrow" (Proverbs 25:18). When we witness against our neighbors "without a cause," we become guilty of "deceiving" with our lips (Proverbs 24:28). The exhortation of Paul is inescapably clear: "Therefore, putting away falsehood, speak the truth each one with his neighbor, for we are members one of another" (Ephesians 4:25). All of this is an extended commentary on the fundamental command of God's law: "You shall not bear false witness against your neighbor" (Exodus 20:16)—reiterated by Christ (Matthew 19:18), who indicts us further by showing that false witness comes from the heart and defiles us (Matthew 15:19-20).

When we engage in theological debate with each other as fellow believers, then, it is ethically imperative that we honor our common Lord (who is the Truth, John 14:6) by being cautious to speak the truth about each other's positions. We are "members" together of the body of Christ.

Theological correction, of course, must be given where necessary; there is no disputing that. However, before presuming to correct one another, we must give the intellectual and personal effort necessary to portraying each other's views correctly. Only then are we ethically qualified to offer a critique. Only then will our critiques bring theological health and unity to the Christian community. If we refuse to speak accurately of each other, we have settled for uncharitable prejudices and party-spirit, and a watching world has little reason to take seriously our claims to being born again with hearts enabled to love each other as God intends.

Over the last decade we have seen some extremely strong words of condemnation uttered about Reconstructionist theology. Those condemnatory words, however, have repeatedly proven to be tied to gross misrepresentations of the Reconstructionist perspective. When those counterfeit portrayals are laid aside, the cautious student will find that not one substantial line of refutation or criticism has been established against the *fundamental distinctives* of Reconstructionism — a transformational worldview embracing theonomic ethics, postmillennial eschatology, and presuppositional apologetics. These theological underpinnings can be shown to be sound and reliable.

That should not be taken to mean that Reconstructionist *writers* (i.e., those who subscribe to the theological distinctives listed here) can be defended regarding every particular aspect of their own personal theological method or regarding every doctrinal conclusion they have ever drawn. There is continuing need for correction and reform at particular points, and Reconstructionism is not above hearing constructive criticism. This has become evident in recent assessments of particular Reconstructionist writers for their hermeneutical excesses and for their harsh or uncharitable way of speaking. (I have particular examples in mind, but they need not be mentioned here.) It is a mark of spiritual health and wisdom that such examinations of our flaws are issued and heeded. Such criticisms do not, however, belie the underlying strength of the Reconstructionist perspective.

The claim made by Dave Hunt and Tommy Ice that the Reconstructionist position is "a deviant theology" simply inaugurated one more rotation of the polemical cycle which we have witnessed over the last ten years: High rhetoric and harsh criticism met and thoroughly undermined by sober research and theological analysis which shows how critics of Reconstructionist theology have not produced a clear Scriptural refutation, have been led into positions which stand contrary to well-established Biblical teaching, or end up in ambiguity or self-contradiction regarding their own worldview and ethic.

We are grateful to Gary DeMar for one more turn of this wheel. May his fine *Debate over Christian Reconstruction* lead further students of the Scripture to consider the challenge, the cogency, and the benefit of the Reconstructionist worldview.

INTRODUCTION

Controversy for controversy's sake is sin, but controversy for truth's sake is biblical and vital to the church.[1]

The debate over Christian Reconstruction held in Dallas, Texas, on April 14, 1988, between Tommy Ice and Dave Hunt (representing dispensational premillennialism) and Gary North and Gary DeMar (representing Christian Reconstruction) was historic. This public debate pitted dispensational[2] premillennialists, representing a recent school of biblical interpretation, against Christian Reconstructionists, fully in the tradition of the historic Protestant faith.

Who won? You must decide.

---

1. Walter Martin, noted cult expert and author of *Kingdom of the Cults*, quoted in *Christian Research Journal* (May 1988), p. 3.

2. For evaluations and critiques of dispensationalism see the following books: Millard J. Erickson, *Contemporary Options in Eschatology: A Study of the Millennium* (Grand Rapids, MI: Baker Book House, 1977), pp. 109-181; Robert G. Clouse, ed. *The Meaning of the Millennium: Four Views* (Downers Grove, IL: InterVarsity Press, 1977); Oswald T. Allis, *Prophecy and the Church: An Examination of the Claim of Dispensationalists that the Christian Church is a Mystery Parenthesis which Interrupts the Fulfillment to Israel of the Kingdom Prophecies of the Old Testament* (Philadelphia, PA: Presbyterian and Reformed, 1945); Vern S. Poythress, *Understanding Dispensationalists* (Grand Rapids, MI: Zondervan/Academie Books, 1987); Clarence B. Bass, *Backgrounds to Dispensationalism: Its Historical Genesis and Ecclesiastical Implications* (Grand Rapids, MI: Baker Book House, [1960] 1977); John H. Gerstner, *A Primer on Dispensationalism* (Phillipsburg, NJ: Presbyterian and Reformed, 1982); William E. Cox, *Why I Left Scofieldism* (Phillipsburg, NJ: Presbyterian and Reformed, n.d.); *An Examination of Dispensationalism* (Philadelphia, PA: Presbyterian and Reformed, 1963). For a critique of dispensationalism by two former dispensationalists who attended Dallas Theological Seminary, see Curtis I. Crenshaw and Grover E. Gunn, III, *Dispensationalism Today, Yesterday, and Tomorrow* (Memphis, TN: Footstool Publications, 1985).

1

The debate question was: Is Christian Reconstruction a deviant theology? As *The Debate Over Christian Reconstruction* will show, the basic tenets of Christian Reconstruction are thoroughly orthodox. The April 14th debate did nothing to change the long-standing and authoritative opinions of other studies on Christian Reconstruction.

Let's look at four independent studies on the orthodoxy of Christian Reconstruction and the narrower topic of biblical law, which is one of Christian Reconstruction's major distinctives.

The Presbyterian Church in America

The General Assembly of the Presbyterian Church in America[3] made the following recommendations on the issue of theonomy (biblical law), a basic tenet of Christian Reconstruction:

1. That since the term "theonomy" in its simplest definition means "God's Law," the General Assembly affirms the *Westminster Confession of Faith*, Chapter 19, and the *Larger Catechism*, Questions 93-150, as a broad but adequate definition of theonomy.

2. That no further study of the subject of theonomy be undertaken at the General Assembly level at this time, but that individual Christians, sessions, and presbyteries having particular interest be encouraged to study the subject in a spirit of love, kindness, and patience.

3. That the General Assembly affirm that no particular view of the application of the judicial law for today should be made a basis for orthodoxy or excluded as heresy.

4. That the General Assembly encourage pastors and sessions to instruct their people in the Law of God and its application in a manner consistent with our confessional standards.[4]

---

3. The Presbyterian Church in American (PCA) was created in 1973 as a conservative Presbyterian alternative to the liberal mainline Presbyterian churches. In the past 15 years, the PCA has grown from 240 congregations and 40,000 members to 1046 churches and 160,000 members. In short, the PCA is not a radical fringe denomination. These statistics are drawn from Frank Trexler's June 13, 1988, Religious News Service report on the 1988 PCA General Assembly.

4. "Report on Theonomy," Minutes of the Seventh General Assembly of the Presbyterian Church in America, 1979, p. 195.

A Reformed Presbyterian Critic

Meredith Kline, a Presbyterian critic of Christian Reconstruction, states that theonomic ethics "is in fact a revival of certain teachings contained in the Westminster Confession of Faith—
at least in the Confession's original formulations."[5] The men who
drafted the Westminster Confession of Faith (1643-48) held that
the moral standards of the laws outside the Ten Commandments
(what are typically called "case laws" since the Ten Commandments are a "summary" of the whole law) were still binding in the
New Testament age. This is obvious from the proof texts in the
Larger Catechism's exposition of the sins and duties covered by
the Ten Commandments. The Westminster Confession and Catechisms are the historic doctrinal standards of Reformed Christians around the world.

Christian Research Institute

A paper prepared by Robert M. Bowman, Jr., of Walter Martin's Christian Research Institute, had this to say about Christian
Reconstruction:

> "Reconstructionism" is a Christian movement which has
> arisen in the past decade or so from within the Reformed or Cal-
> vinistic tradition within Protestant Christianity. As such, it is
> thoroughly orthodox on all of the essential teachings of the Bible,
> including the Trinity, the person and work of Christ, salvation by
> grace through faith, etc. Considered as a whole, the movement is
> neither cultic nor heretical nor aberrational.[6]

---

5. Meredith G. Kline, "Comments on an Old-New Error," *The Westminster
Theological Journal*, Vol. 41, No. 1 (Fall, 1978), p. 174. Greg L. Bahnsen, in a reply
to Kline's critique of his *Theonomy in Christian Ethics*, tells us that the "American
revision pertained only to a subsection of the chapter on the civil magistrate,
aiming to reinforce disestablishment and the rejection of Erastianism (see *Theonomy*, pp. 527-537, 541-543). There was no revision of the declaration about the
law of God or its use in catechisms (i.e., the strictly theonomic elements of the
Confessional Standards)." Bahnsen, "M. G. Kline on Theonomic Politics: An
Evaluation of His Reply," *The Journal of Christian Reconstruction: Symposium on Puritanism and Society*, ed. Gary North, Vol. VI, No. 2 (Winter 1979-80), p. 201.
6. Robert M. Bowman, Jr., "Reconstructionism," Christian Research Institute (P.O. Box 500, San Juan Capistrano, California 92693), p. 1.

Christian Research Journal

Mr. Bowman makes a more detailed assessment of Christian Reconstruction in the Winter/Spring 1988 issue of the *Christian Research Journal*, entitled "The New Puritanism: A Preliminary Assessment of Reconstructionism."

In a related article in the same issue of *Christian Research Journal*, Bowman writes that "it is unfortunate that almost every critique of K[ingdom] T[heology] has treated K[ingdom] T[heology] and Reconstruction as two strands of the same teaching. While there is some overlap of terminology, ideas, and activities, the two movements are largely distinct."[7] Kingdom Theology is an easy target.[8] The critics of Christian Reconstruction have purposely linked Kingdom Theology with Christian Reconstruction, because by condemning one, the other sinks in its wake.[9] As you will notice in the debate, Dave Hunt still refuses to make clear distinctions between Kingdom Theology and Christian Reconstruction.[10]

In a brief footnote to his article on Christian Reconstruction, Bowman offers the following:

> Christian Research Institute and Walter Martin, the publisher of this journal, view Reconstructionism as an orthodox though very controversial movement. The primary purpose of this article is to explain the reasons for this position. Beyond this basic discernment of the movement's relationship to orthodoxy, CRI takes no official position. However, it seemed appropriate to

---

7. Robert M. Bowman, Jr., with Craig S. Hawkins and Dan R. Schlesinger, "The Gospel According to Paulk: A Critique of 'Kingdom Theology,'" *Christian Research Journal* (Winter/Spring 1988), p. 14. You can order the *CRJ* from Christian Research Institute, P.O. Box 500, San Juan Capistrano, California 92693.

8. The authors of "The Gospel According to Paulk" write that "In Part II of this article we will set out in detail the theology of Earl Paulk with extensive documentation, leaving no doubt concerning the nature of Paulk's doctrine. We shall then offer a biblical critique of K[ingdom] T[heology] as found in the representative writings of Bishop Paulk" (p. 14).

9. Dave Hunt tried to do this on Peter Waldron's "Contact America" show, but to no avail. See Gary DeMar and Peter J. Leithart, *The Reduction of Christianity: A Biblical Response to Dave Hunt* (Ft. Worth, TX: Dominion Press/Atlanta, GA: American Vision, 1988), p. 20.

10. For these distinctions, see *ibid.*, pp. xiv (note 5), 24-37, 76-83, 166, 335-36.

the editors that in this article some further observations and comments be made concerning Reconstructionism's most distinctive beliefs. Therefore, the opinions expressed herein as to the soundness or acceptability of these beliefs are the author's and should not be attributed to CRI or Walter Martin.[11]

Bowman takes the reader through three of the distinctives of Christian Reconstruction: Presuppositionalism, Theonomy, and Postmillennialism. None of these is described as heretical. As Peter Leithart and I have shown in *The Reduction of Christianity*, all three positions have been held throughout church history by some of the most highly respected biblical theologians.[12] This assessment alone sets Bowman's article apart from every other analysis I have seen on Christian Reconstruction. While the author does not always agree with reconstructionists, he does offer a fair and accurate analysis of each distinctive. Mr. Bowman and the *Christian Research Journal* should be commended on an excellent research job. They have done the church a great service, and their work should be held up as a model for all of those who believe they have something to say about "aberrational theologies." Before you go on the attack, *make sure you do your homework!*

Mr. Bowman ends his article with this "Challenge":

> Reconstructionism is an orthodox though highly controversial movement. Much of what they say is open to serious question. Whether Christians agree with their answers or not, however, the Reconstructionists are certainly asking the right questions. What is the proper relationship between church and state? Is a Christian culture possible? If a culture were to be converted to faith in Christ, how would their institutions change? What would be the basis of such a culture's laws? Does the Bible have the answers to society's problems, and if so, what are those answers? If Reconstructionism does nothing else than to force the church to reexamine these questions and deepens its understanding of these issues, it will have served the church well.[13]

---

11. Robert M. Bowman, "The New Puritanism," *Christian Research Journal* (Winter/Spring 1988), p. 23.

12. DeMar and Leithart, *Reduction of Christianity*, pp. 30-42, 229-70.

13. Bowman, "The New Puritanism," p. 27.

This book will show that Christian Reconstruction is far from a deviant theology. Tommy Ice and Dave Hunt want to view all of theology in terms of a dispensational premillennial theological system, a system that is beginning to disintegrate as a viable method of understanding the Bible. This brings us to the next point.

Dispensationalism: A Deviant Theology?

In light of a preponderance of evidence to the contrary, why did Dave Hunt and Tommy Ice (who formulated the debate topic) label Christian Reconstruction a "deviant theology"? The answer is: From the perspective of their brand of dispensational premillennial theology, Christian Reconstruction *is* deviant. This, then, is the counter question: Is their brand of dispensational premillennialism deviant? The lively debate raised the possibility that it might be, and this book considers it in more formal biblical and historical terms.

The Debate over Christian Reconstruction interacts with the comments of two of dispensationalism's most ardent supporters in an attempt to answer the question of who holds the deviant position. Of course, this was not the original purpose of the debate or this book. Keep in mind the charges made by Dave Hunt and Tommy Ice and the implications for the church today. They want you to believe that the Christian Reconstruction perspective is deviant in light of the following definition:

> Christian Reconstructionists believe that God's law — which Paul called holy, just, and good (Romans 7:14) — applies to every area of life and that God will sovereignly win the victory over His enemies *before* Jesus returns to deliver the kingdom to His Father.

Their assessment of these fundamental Christian doctrines would exclude many Christians from the orthodox faith, since history is filled with outstanding men who have believed that God's law does apply in today's world (witness the Westminster Confession of Faith) and that postmillennialism is the correct biblical position on eschatology. Simply put, Tommy Ice and Dave Hunt are attempting to make their own views the standard for orthodoxy.

The Limitations of Debates

Debates are frustrating. There is never an opportunity to answer all the points raised by the opposition. Nearly anything can be said by the person who gets to make the final statement because the opposition cannot respond. The last word is usually remembered. This is why some of the most outlandish, irrelevant, and insupportable charges were made by Tommy Ice and Dave Hunt against Christian Reconstruction at the summary point in the debate: There was no opportunity to answer their misrepresentations.

Moreover, there was no occasion to question the remarks made by the opposing side. The format of the debate — four participants instead of two — made cross-examination impossible. Both sides felt the frustration.

The Debate over Christian Reconstruction is an attempt to answer what could not be answered during the debate. Not every point will be discussed, but only those issues where we believe an answer is needed. The footnotes will offer additional information that will help you study the issues further. Again, you must decide based on what Scripture says (Acts 17:11).

One last point needs to be made before the critique begins. Peter Leithart and I wrote *The Reduction of Christianity*, an extensive evaluation of the literature that has come out against Christian Reconstruction, to put the issue of eschatology into biblical and historical perspective. Please note that during the debate, Dave Hunt and Tommy Ice did not interact with the book. They continued to misrepresent the Reconstructionists' position in spite of the detailed work of *Reduction*.

How to Read This Book

The Debate over Christian Reconstruction is divided into two parts. Chapters one through ten are a brief and popular apologetic for Christian Reconstruction. For those of you who find detailed argumentation hard going, these chapters will give you the essence of Christian Reconstruction.

Chapters eleven through seventeen follow the debate as it was presented on April 14, 1988, in Dallas, Texas. I suggest that you listen to the tapes[14] and then read my evaluation and critique. The chapters are clearly marked as to the topics they cover. Chapter eleven is an expanded and footnoted version of my presentation at the debate, representing the Christian Reconstruction position. It serves as an overview of the Reconstructionist position. Chapters twelve through fifteen follow the presentations of Tommy Ice and Dave Hunt in sequence. Chapter sixteen analyzes the answers given by Dave Hunt and Tommy Ice to a series of questions from the audience. Chapter seventeen evaluates the concluding remarks of Dave Hunt and Tommy Ice.

There are three appendixes. Appendix A, "The Abomination of Desolation: An Alternative Interpretation," is an attempt to make better sense out of the relationship between Daniel 9:24-27, Matthew 24:15, and 2 Thessalonians 2:1-12. Appendix B answers two questions. First, what have postmillennialists said about the future of Israel? Second, how do Reconstructionists answer the charges made by some that Christian Reconstruction is "antisemitic"? Appendix C is a letter from a Jewish Christian pastor who also is a Christian Reconstructionist.

A Word to Dispensationalists

The Debate over Christian Reconstruction was not originally conceived to be a critique of dispensationalism. Since Tommy Ice and Dave Hunt made *their brand* of dispensationalism an issue in the debate, it became necessary to evaluate the basic tenets of their system, as well as traditional dispensationalism, in order to make sense out of their critique of Christian Reconstruction. This debate, therefore, cannot be understood without first understanding dispensationalism. I do not assume that those who read this book understand dispensationalism. This is why I present the dispensational position along with my evaluation.

The debate over Christian Reconstruction is certainly not new. The issues have been debated for centuries. More recently the de-

---

14. You can order a set of tapes from American Vision, P.O. Box 720515, Atlanta, Georgia 30328 or Dominion Press, 7112 Burns Street, Ft. Worth, Texas 76118. See the order form in the back of this book.

bate has been renewed within traditional Reformed circles.[15] The debate will not end with this book, and the debate should not end here. Much more work needs to be done.

At this point, a further word needs to be said about dispensationalism. First, Tommy Ice is not a standard dispensationalist. He has been strongly influenced by Confessional Reformed theology, as expressed in the Westminster Confession of Faith, and Reformed Baptist thought. He says that he is a Calvinist as well as a presuppositionalist.[16] At various times, Ice has called himself a Reconstructionist.[17] His own philosophy, therefore, is a mixture of a number of theological traditions.

Second, Dave Hunt is not a standard dispensationalist. His view of the millennium is shared by few if any standard dispensationalists. Also, Hunt is in the more popular dispensational school of thought whose most well-known spokesman is Hal Lindsey. To my knowledge, Lindsey's views have never been popular at Dallas Theological Seminary. His books are rarely quoted by dispensational scholars.[18]

Dallas Theological Seminary was founded by Presbyterians (e.g., Lewis Sperry Chafer) and episcopalians (e.g., Griffith Thomas), not by Plymouth Brethren. The seminary was set up to be a more moderate articulation of dispensational belief and to keep dispensationalism within the orthodox tradition.

---

15. Gary Scott Smith, ed., *The Bible and Civil Government* (Phillipsburg, NJ: Presbyterian and Reformed, 1989). This book is a compilation of position and response papers representing four Reformed views on how the Bible applies to civil government: Theonomy (Dr. Greg L. Bahnsen), Christian America (Dr. Harold O. J. Brown), Principled Pluralism (Dr. Gordon J. Spykman), and National Confession (Dr. William Edgar).

16. For definitions see DeMar and Leithart, *Reduction of Christianity*, pp. 30-37.

17. Many Christian Reconstructionists came out of the dispensational camp. Gary North describes his "exodus" in *The Journal of Christian Reconstruction: Symposium on the Millennium*, Vol. III, No. 2 (Winter 1976-77), pp. 3-4. Some of the most vocal critics of dispensationalism are now Reconstructionists: Curtis I. Crenshaw and Grover E. Gunn, III, *Dispensationalism Today, Yesterday, and Tomorrow* (Memphis, TN: Footstool Publications, 1985).

18. For an evaluation of dispensationalism today, see Timothy P. Weber, *Living in the Shadow of the Second Coming: American Premillennialism, 1875-1982* (enl. ed.; Grand Rapids, MI: Zondervan, 1983), pp. 204-44.

In the course of this book it will not always be possible to make the necessary distinctions between traditional and non-traditional dispensationalists.[19] I have tried, however, to separate traditional dispensational beliefs from the more hybrid dispensational views of Tommy Ice and Dave Hunt. At the same time, in spite of some of these differences in style and belief, there is a community of people who share a belief in the pretribulational rapture and in an Israel-Church separation. Because of this, there is really no other word to use for them than "dispensationalists." In arguing against dispensationalism in general, and Hunt and Ice in particular, I am aware that these two men do not always speak for standard dispensationalism.

Finally, a critique of a theological system is not an evaluation of the character of those people who hold to that system. Dispensationalists have honored God and His Word for decades when many mainline churches were apostatizing. Dispensationalists have been vigorous in evangelism and missions. Not all dispensationalists have said "we don't polish brass on a sinking ship." Christian Reconstructionists respect this.

*   *   *   *   *

I would like to thank Grover E. Gunn III, Kenneth Gentry, Curtis I. Crenshaw, James B. Jordan, and Peter J. Leithart for their valuable contributions to this work. The conclusions and assessments, however, are mine alone.

---

19. For an elaboration of these distinctions, see James B. Jordan, "Christian Zionism and Messianic Judaism," in *The Sociology of the Church: Essays in Reconstruction* (Tyler, TX: Geneva Ministries, 1986), pp. 175-86.

Part I

AN INTRODUCTION TO CHRISTIAN RECONSTRUCTION

1

TURNING THE WORLD UPSIDE DOWN

For nearly 2000 years the church has believed in the life-transforming power of the gospel, the regenerating power of the Holy Spirit, the sufficiency of Scripture as "an Instruction Book on how to live,"[1] the Sovereignty and Providence of God in time and in history, the subjection of Satan to the finished work of Christ and the church (Matthew 16:18; Romans 16:20; Colossians 1:13; 2:15; Revelation 12:7-9; Mark 3:27; Luke 10:18; 11:20; John 14:30; 16:11; 1 John 3:8; 5:18; James 4:7), the discipling of the nations (Matthew 28:18-20), and the ultimate victory of God's kingdom that will one day be delivered up by Jesus to His Father (1 Corinthians 15:20-28; cf. Luke 11:20; Colossians 1:13 23).

This was the faith of the early church, a faith that prompted those outside of Christ to acknowledge that in a short span of time these Christians had "turned the world upside down" (Acts 17:6). What a testimony! These few rag-tag disciples of Christ, with little if any money, no national television ministries, and no publishing houses or newsletters, had turned the world upside down.

How did they do it?

They took with them the Word of God, "sharper than any two-edged sword" (Hebrews 4:12-13) and able to equip us "for every good work" (2 Timothy 3:16-17), the gospel which is "the power of God for salvation to every one who believes" (Romans 1:16), and the Holy Spirit who equips us "in every good thing to do His will"

---

1. Martin and Deidre Bobgan, *Psychoheresy: The Psychological Seduction of Christianity* (Santa Barbara, CA: Eastgate Publishers, 1987), p. 11.

13

(Hebrews 13:21). And, yes, faith in God that *He* would accomplish all that *He* had promised. Oh, there is one other thing: obedience to God's revealed will.

There really isn't anything new in any of this. God's people have "by faith conquered kingdoms" and "performed acts of right-eousness, obtained promises, shut the mouths of lions, quenched the power of fire, escaped the edge of the sword, from weakness were made strong, became mighty in war, put foreign armies to flight" (Hebrews 11:33-34).

But you say, "Well, that was under the *Old* covenant." Yes, that's true. But don't we have a *better* covenant, with a *better* High Priest, and *better* promises? We should *at least* expect God to do for His people under the New Covenant what He did for His elect under the Old Covenant. If God poured out blessings for His elect under the Old Covenant, why should we expect anything less under the *New* and *Better* Covenant? But we know that God is doing far more for His *New* Covenant people. God is "able to do exceedingly abundantly beyond all that we ask or think, according to the power that works within us, to Him be the glory in the church and in Christ Jesus to all generations forever and ever" (Ephesians 3:20-21).

How can this be? Why should we expect the transformation of our world through the preaching of the gospel and the application of God's Word to every area of life? The Bible tells us that "something greater than the temple is here" (Matthew 12:6). "Something greater than Jonah is here" (v. 41). "Something greater than Solomon is here" (v. 42). I think you get the idea. *Something Greater is here!*

2

A CITY ON A HILL

Jesus calls us to reconstruct broken foundations, not to become revolutionaries for a misguided political faith or escapists from the world that God gave us as a possession. Our vision should be like that of John Winthrop and his "Model of Christian Charity," penned in 1630 aboard the *Arabella* as it sailed to New England.

> The Lord will be our God and delight to dwell among us as His own people. He will command a blessing on us in all our ways, so that we shall see much more of His wisdom, power, goodness, and truth than we have formerly known. We shall find that the God of Israel is among us, and ten of us shall be able to resist a thousand of our enemies. The Lord will make our name a praise and glory, so that men shall say of succeeding plantations: "The Lord make it like that of New England." For we must consider that we shall be like a City upon a Hill; the eyes of all the people are on us.

This was Israel's task (Deuteronomy 4:1-8) and it has now fallen upon us, the true Israel of God, to be a "city set on a hill" (Matthew 5:14), to give "the people who are sitting in darkness . . . a great light" (Matthew 4:16; cf. Isaiah 9:2).

There is no indication in Scripture that this task has been postponed or awaits a millennial reign of Christ. The Bible tells us that as a city set on a hill, we are to be an example of righteousness to the world. The church's ethical witness attracts the world, acting as a light to the nations.

15

A Continuing Reformation

Cotton Mather wrote a history of early New England which he entitled *Magnalia Christi Americana*, or *The Great Works of Christ in America*. "The sum of the matter," he explained, "is that from the beginning of the Reformation in the English nation, there had always been a generation of godly men, desirous to pursue the reformation of religion, according to the Word of God. . . ." But in England, there were others with "power . . . in their hands" who desired "not only to stop the progress of the desired Reformation but also, with innumerable vexations, to persecute those that most heartily wished well unto it."[1]

These Puritan disciples of Christ were driven to America to "seek a place for the exercise of the Protestant religion, according to the light of conscience, in the deserts of America." Their purpose was nothing less than to complete the Reformation, believing "that the first reformers never intended that what they did should be the absolute boundary of reformation. . . ."[2]

There are those in our day who would want to set limits on God's Reformation of the world. For some reason these modern-day skeptics believe that God has set a boundary for reformation. Such limitations on God's providence and sovereignty are a denial of the Bible and of all history.

We're being told that the devil controls the world, that he orchestrates the movements of history. This, too, is an unbiblical idea. The Bible says that Satan is defeated, disarmed, and spoiled (Colossians 2:15; Revelation 12:7ff.; Mark 3:27), "fallen" (Luke 10:18), and "thrown down" (Revelation 12:9). He was "crushed" under the feet of the early Christians (Romans 16:20). He has lost "authority" over Christians (Colossians 1:13) and has been "judged" (John 16:11). He cannot "touch" a Christian (1 John 5:18). His works have been "destroyed" (1 John 3:8). He has "nothing" (John 14:30). He "flees" when "resisted" (James 4:7) and is "bound" (Mark 3:27; Luke 11:20; Revelation 20:2).

---

1. Cotton Mather, *The Great Works of Christ in America*, 2 vols. (Edinburgh: The Banner of Truth Trust, [1702] 1979), vol. 1, p. 26.
2. *Idem.*

The early Christians understood the place of the devil and the sovereignty of God. Our forefathers worked in terms of God as the Ruler of the kings of the earth, not in terms of Satan as the "ruler of this world," because "the ruler of this world" has been "cast out" (John 12:31). They took the Bible seriously when it said, "And Thou hast made them to be a kingdom and priests to our God; and they will reign upon the earth" (Revelation 5:10; compare 1 Peter 2:9-10).

"A Christian Nation"

In 1892, the United States Supreme Court determined, in the case of *The Church of the Holy Trinity vs. United States*, that America was a Christian nation from its earliest days. The court opinion, delivered by Justice Josiah Brewer, was an exhaustive study of the historical and legal evidence for America's Christian heritage. After examining hundreds of court cases, state constitutions, and other historical documents, the court came to the following conclusion:

> Our laws and our institutions must necessarily be based upon and embody the teachings of the Redeemer of mankind. It is impossible that it should be otherwise; and in this sense and to this extent our civilization and our institutions are emphatically Christian. . . . This is a religious people. This is historically true. From the discovery of this continent to the present hour, there is a single voice making this affirmation. . . . We find everywhere a clear recognition of the same truth. . . . These, and many other matters which might be noticed, add a volume of unofficial declarations to the mass of organic utterances that this is a Christian nation.[3]

The first principle in the Biblical blueprint for government is that the foundation upon which a nation is built is a reflection of the god that the nation worships.

---

3. Decision of the Supreme Court of the United States in the case of *The Church of the Holy Trinity v. The United States* (143 United States 457 [1892]).

Our forefathers understood that, in the words of Benjamin Franklin, "God governs in the affairs of men." Any nation that refuses to acknowledge that God is the "chief cornerstone" in the building of a nation, including the United States, will succeed no better than the builders of Babel.

The rich Christian heritage of America is evidence that we began as a Christian nation, cognizant of the fact that God is truly the ruler of the kings of the earth. Any nation that rejects God as its sovereign will be broken "with a rod of iron" and will certainly "perish in the way" (Psalm 2:9, 12).

Libraries are filled with the histories of men and nations which sought to overrule the "King of kings and Lord of lords" (Revelation 19:15). There is no hope for those who "take counsel together against the LORD and against His Anointed" (Psalm 2:2).

3

BY WHAT STANDARD?

What's the real issue in the debate concerning Christian reconstruction? The first issue, and the most basic one, is the question of ethics. How are Christians to determine what is right and wrong? What is our standard? How do we make ethical decisions in our personal lives? How do we know the right way to treat our spouse and children? How do we know how to deal with a sinful brother in the church? How do we know how to treat our employers or our employees? How do we know what laws are just?

Most Christians would agree that the Bible is our standard for personal morality, for family morality, for the church, and perhaps for business ethics. But many would stop short of saying that the Bible is the standard for civil justice. We need to emphasize this, not because we believe that politics is the most important thing, but because this is an area where many Christians become confused and inconsistent.

If we don't use the Bible as our standard of civil justice, what shall we use? We cannot make our final appeal to reason, because our minds are tainted by the effects of sin. We cannot make our final appeal to the majority, because the majority often enacts laws that perpetuate self-interest. Nor can we make our final appeal to some elite, because they too are prone to error and sin. If we want to please God in our political action, we need to be obedient to the Word of God.

This doesn't mean that it's always easy to decide what the Bible teaches about a certain issue. We need to do our homework, studying both the Bible and our situation, if we want to find God-honoring policies and laws.

19

But when we have done all our homework, we must finally ask, What does the Bible say? And, when we discover what the Bible teaches, we are left with the question: Will we obey God?

It is also important that we recognize the *entire* Bible as our standard. The New Testament provides the fullest revelation of God's will and of His character, but the Old Testament is just as much God's Word as the New. And, along with the New, the Old Testament provides wisdom for making Godly decisions in every area of life.

This was Paul's point in 2 Timothy 3:16-17: "All Scripture is God-breathed and useful." That is the bottom-line: The Old Testament, which is the immediate focus of Paul's comment, is "useful." Moreover, it is useful to equip the Christian "for every good work." We should, of course, broaden this statement to include the "other Scriptures" of the New Testament.

The Bible as a whole, then, both Old and New Testaments, is useful for every good work. It provides all we need as believers to direct us in every area of life; it tells us everything we need to know to live a life pleasing to God.

Unless we affirm a sphere of neutrality in which God is not Lord and King, then Paul's statement implies that the Bible is useful for the Christian in his social and political duty, as much as in his personal life of devotion to the Lord. The laws are useful for the Christian parent, the Christian businessman, the Christian minister, the Christian statesman.

The Christian husband should be searching the Scriptures for wisdom to direct him in his relationship with his spouse and in the training of his children. Should he spank his children? What should he do if he has an argument with his wife? Does he have any responsibility for teaching his children?

The Christian businessman should be seeking wisdom for running his business: Should he go into debt to expand his business? Should he cheat on his income tax, or engage in a tax revolt? How much of his income should he give to the Lord? How should he treat his employees?

Pastors and other leaders in the church should search the Scriptures to teach them how to worship, how and when to discipline their members, what kinds of things he should teach from the pulpit, whether women should be ordained as ministers, whether children should be baptized and take communion.

The Christian statesman also seeks wisdom from the Bible, the whole Bible, to understand what justice entails. Is it just to give homosexuals civil rights? Is it just to permit abortion on demand? What penalties are just? Should the State exercise the death penalty? What is the role of the civil government in society? Isn't this Paul's point when he tells us that "rulers are not a cause of fear for good behavior, but for evil"? (Romans 13:3). How do rulers know the difference between "good" and "evil"?

All of these issues are addressed, directly or by implication, in the Scriptures of the Old and New Testaments. In short, if the Christian walks in the law of the Lord, he will be blameless (Psalm 119:1).

This does not mean, of course, that the Christian cannot learn anything from a source outside the Bible. It doesn't mean that he cannot learn anything from an unbeliever. But, however much he may learn from outside sources, the Bible must be the final judge of good and evil. Whatever he learns from outside sources, the Christian's duty will always be an application of Scripture.

On the other hand, the life, death, resurrection, and ascension of Jesus have transformed the world. Everything is different. Everyone who is in Christ is a new creation; the old has gone, the new has come (2 Corinthians 5:17). There has been a revolution in the heavens and on the earth. Satan has been cast out; Jesus Christ, the God-Man, sits on the throne at the Father's right hand. Unbelieving Israel has been cast out and has been replaced by the international church, those whom Jesus purchased with His own blood "from every tribe and tongue and people and nation" (Revelation 5:9).

In principle, everything has been renewed and the curse has been reversed by the death and resurrection of Jesus Christ. In a sense, everything is new, or renewed. This means that we need to consider the work of Christ when we try to decide how the Old Testament applies today.

This is what Christian reconstructionists are saying: The Bible, the whole Bible, is our final standard for every area of life. Everything is under Christ's Lordship. Everything we do must be done in obedience to Him.

4

HEAVENLY AND EARTHLY REWARDS

When we obey God's commandments, He will bless us. This was true under the Old Covenant, as Deuteronomy 28 and Leviticus 26 show. Obedience to God brings blessing, and disobedience to God brings curses. Ultimately, of course, none of us can obey God perfectly. We receive God's blessing only because Jesus Christ has obeyed perfectly and shares His blessings with us. But even in the New Testament, we are taught that God blesses His church as it is faithful to Him.

Paul encouraged children to obey parents with the promise that "you shall live long on the *earth*" (Ephesians 6:3). Elsewhere, Paul told the Corinthians that in Christ they possess not only "things to come," but "the world" and "things present" (1 Corinthians 3:22). As the true children of Abraham, we are with him heirs of the *world* (Romans 4:13).

Jesus promised that those who seek His kingdom above all will receive all the earthly things that they need (Matthew 6:33), and claimed that the meek would inherit the *earth* (Matthew 5:5). On the other hand, He threatens to punish rebels against Him with earthly punishments (Psalm 2:10-12). Putting these two considerations together, we conclude that, in general, God's people receive earthly blessing and success, and the unrighteous receive earthly judgment.

Several qualifications are needed to avoid a misunderstanding of what has just been said. First, this does not mean that every individual Christian will be successful in his lifetime, or that spirituality is measured in financial or material terms. But faithful

Christian peoples and nations will, in general, be more economically successful than non-Christian peoples and nations.

Of course, God may raise up non-Christian nations, such as the Islamic nations in the Middle Ages and today, to act as a scourge against His church. In the short run, moreover, Christian cultures may not enjoy earthly blessing. But in the long run and on a general cultural scale, Christians will receive God's blessing.

Even on an individual level, faithful obedience to the commands of Christ tends to lead to relative earthly prosperity. The Bible tells us to avoid debt; the Bible teaches us not to live beyond our financial means. As Christian financial advisor Ron Blue says, if you spend less than you earn, and do it for a long period of time, you will be financially successful. At least, a faithful Christian will be more successful than someone with a similar income who has no self-restraint and borrows heavily.

Second, the fact that God promises earthly rewards does not mean that we are motivated solely or even primarily by our hope for material rewards. God made us in such a way that the expectation of reward motivates us to action. There is nothing necessarily sinful about that; this seems to be the situation even before the fall: Adam was promised the reward of life if he would be faithful, and threatened with death if he was unfaithful. God has graciously promised to make us *sons* and "fellow-heirs with Christ" (Romans 8:16-17).

But this is not our most important motivation. Above all, we should seek God's glory and good pleasure. A Christian should be satisfied with pleasing God, with being a doorkeeper in the house of the Lord, a mere servant in our Father's house, with hearing the Master say, "Well done, thou good and faithful servant." If need be, we should be ready to give up our lives, and all our resources for the good of His Kingdom. This is what it means to "seek first the Kingdom of God" (Matthew 6:33).

So, while our primary motivation for being faithful to God is to please Him, God has given many promises that provide a secondary motivation for obedience and faith.

Finally, this does not mean that the Christian life is not a life under the cross. Nor does it mean that Christians who are suffering sickness, financial difficulties, vocational frustrations, or other problems are necessarily suffering because they lack faith. That may be the case in some instances, but it is not the case in every instance.

Many of the biblical characters who exercised the strongest faith were also the most sorely pressed with manifold difficulties: Joseph, Moses, Job, David, Nehemiah, Paul, and Jesus Christ Himself, to name but a few. The faith praised in Scripture is not one that is able to avoid suffering, but one that perseveres *through* suffering. Jesus is said to have learned obedience through what He suffered (Hebrews 5:8), and the same pattern applies to us (cf. Psalm 119:71).

Yet even this truth must also be seen from the ultimate perspective of victory. This can be understood in several different ways. First, God delivers us out of affliction — be it sickness, persecution, or something else — bringing greater glory to Himself.

But obviously not every Christian is delivered out of his or her affliction. Still, suffering is not defeat, but victory because our afflictions strengthen our faith; our faith overcomes our afflictions. As Paul said in one of the most rhapsodic passages in the Bible:

> Who shall separate us from the love of Christ? Shall tribulation, or distress, or persecution, or famine, or nakedness, or peril, or sword? Just as it is written, "For Thy sake we are being put to death all day long; we were considered as sheep to be slaughtered." But in all these things we overwhelmingly conquer through Him who loved us. For I am convinced that neither death, nor life, nor angels, nor principalities, nor things present, nor things to come, nor powers, nor height, nor depth, nor any other creature shall be able to separate us from the love of God, which is in Christ Jesus (Romans 8:35-39).

In other words, there is a sense in which we are victorious even *in the midst* of suffering.

Also, we need to recognize the continuing power of sin in the life of a believer. We already possess the new life of the Kingdom, but we still are engaged in an internal war between our flesh and the Spirit (Romans 6-7). God's blessings should humble us, reminding us again and again of how utterly undeserving we are. All of this is well summarized in Mark 10:29-31. Jesus promises several things to His faithful disciples, those who have left everything to follow Him.

First, He promises them earthly prosperity and enjoyment of blessing. That these blessings are not merely future and heavenly is indicated by several facts: Not only does Jesus say that His disciples will receive a hundred-fold reward "in the present age," but the blessings He lists are very concrete and earthly: houses, wives, children, farms. In short, Jesus is here promising earthly rewards.

Second, Jesus promises that persecution will accompany these blessings. His faithful disciples should therefore expect both.

Finally, Jesus promises that our reward will be fully realized in the future age, in heaven. We should never let God's blessings in this world blind us to our ultimate hope and our final rest, which is in heaven. Abraham became a wealthy man, but he continued to look for a heavenly city, made without hands.

Jesus saw no contradiction in laying these three themes side-by-side: earthly reward, persecution, heavenly reward. He promises all three, and we need to emphasize all three equally strongly.

5

THE NEUTRALITY MYTH

One Christian writer maintains that "Government is not based on special revelation, such as the Bible. It is based on God's general revelation to all men."[1] Nations, whether Christian or non-Christian, establish governments. Does this mean that nations are free to establish the standard by which they will rule? What are the limits of power? How much tax should be collected? Should the State control education? Is homosexuality a crime? If it is, what should the punishment be if two men are caught in the act, are tried, and are found to be guilty? Is bestiality wrong? How about abortion? It's convenient to say that "government is not based on special revelation," but it is not much help when you must deal in particulars. General revelation does not give answers to specific ethical dilemmas.

But what if the Bible is available to a nation as an ethical standard for civil legislation? Is it inappropriate to use it as a blueprint for governance? Should those who rule trust the fallen "light of reason" or the Word of God that "is a lamp to my feet, and a light to my path"? (Psalm 119:105). The assumption of those who choose the "light of reason" over "special revelation" is that man's sense of justice is greater than God's revealed will relating to justice. Israel's obedience to the law was to be an enticement to follow its directives: "So keep and do them, for that is your wisdom and your understanding in the sight of the peoples who will hear

---

1. Norman L. Geisler, "A Premillennial View of Law and Government," *The Best in Theology*, gen. ed., J. I. Packer (Carol Stream, IL: Christianity Today/ Word, 1986), vol. 1, p. 259.

all these statutes and say, 'Surely this great nation is a wise and understanding people.' For what great nation is there that has a god so near to it as is the LORD our God whenever we call on Him? Or what great nation is there that has statutes and judgments as righteous as this whole law which I am setting before you today?" (Deuteronomy 4:6-8).

Some Christians would tell us to put the Bible away! Why? The writer quoted above, who maintains that "Government is not based on special revelation," rejects the Bible as a standard for civil legislation because "the unregenerate cannot live out the demands of God's law." I can just hear my children telling me that my standards for their behavior should not be obeyed because they are *unable* to obey them. A criminal could use this defense when accused of a crime listed in the Bible. "I'm not a Christian, so I am unable to live out the demands of God's law." The purpose of civil government, as a minister of justice, is to punish external acts of disobedience that the Bible describes as criminal. If any of us could keep the law perfectly, then there would be no need for the civil magistrate. Moreover, punishment is designed to restrain evil in all people. The law and its attendant punishment are designed to protect law-abiding citizens from anarchy.

I'm sure that this same author believes that murder is wrong and that common sense, the laws of nature, natural rights, natural conscience, reason, principles of reason, and the light of reason would also lead a judge to conclude that murder, for example, is wrong. Adherents to a natural law ethic want to maintain that if it's in the Bible then we cannot use it.

There are many non-Christians who never murder, commit adultery, or practice sodomy. Much of their restraint comes from the fear of punishment. Let us keep in mind that the civil magistrate can only punish *public* acts of disobedience. It does not deal with sins of the heart, nor does it compel the unregenerate to become Christians. If the above writer wants to say that the unregenerate cannot keep the law in its demands on the heart, then I will agree. But the civil magistrate does not have jurisdiction over the heart.

A law system that is formulated on the basis of the "principles of reason common to all men" fails to account for man's fallen nature, especially the noetic effects of sin, that is, sin as it affects the mind. Fallen man "suppresses the truth in unrighteousness" (Romans 1:18). Are we to trust fallen man with determining what "natural laws" we are to follow? This is the height of subjectivism.

There are two areas where the "principles of reason" cannot match biblical laws. First, the Bible has them all written in one place. The "laws of nature" must be hunted down by finite, fallible, and fallen creatures. While it is true that these same finite, fallible, and fallen creatures must interpret the Bible, at least the hunting process is taken care of. The laws are there for *all* to see. Second, the "principles of reason" are not specific enough. The Bible is a detailed ethical blueprint.

The Bible or the Bayonet

When the world is crying out for answers, why is it that some leaders in the Christian community are saying the Bible is a book that was only designed to show you how to get to heaven? We're often told that the Bible is not a blueprint for life beyond the family and church. There is tyranny in the Soviet Union, Cuba, El Salvador, South Africa, Chile, and numerous other countries around the world. They all have two things in common: First, Jesus Christ is not seen as the only mediator between God and rebellious sinners. In fact, the problems of tyranny and oppression are not seen as fundamentally religious. Rather, it is believed that reconciliation must come between man and man without any need of Jesus' redemptive work.

Second, the Bible is rejected as a blueprint for living. The Bible is ridiculed. Even many Christians do not take the Bible seriously. They reject its solutions for the homeless, the rising incidence of sodomy and AIDS, the poor, teenage promiscuity, foreign affairs, and the threat of a nuclear holocaust. It's no wonder that tyranny is replacing freedom around the world.

On May 28th, 1849, Robert C. Winthrop addressed the Annual Meeting of the Massachusetts Bible Society in Boston. His words are no less true today:

All societies of men must be governed in some way or other. The less they may have of stringent State Government, the more they must have of individual self-government. The less they rely on public law or physical force, the more they must rely on private moral restraint. Men, in a word, must necessarily be controlled, either by a power within them, or by a power without them; either by the word of God, or by the strong arm of man; either by the Bible, or by the bayonet. It may do for other countries and other governments to talk about the State supporting religion. Here, under our own free institutions, it is Religion which must support the State.

The bayonet rules in those nations which reject Jesus Christ and His word. Iran is a perfect example. The major news magazines show the leadership of the Iranian ecclesiocracy holding the inscribed Bible aloft in obvious ridicule. The United States is moving in a similar direction. As the Bible ceases to govern in the hearts of the people, and those who rule reject the Bible as a standard of civil righteousness, you will see more of the glistening steel of the sharpened bayonet rule in America.

•

6

ONE STANDARD FOR ALL

It's time that Christians begin to understand what's at stake. A battle is raging. In many cases, the fire is coming from within the camp. Millions of Christians say they believe the Bible is the Word of God, that it's inerrant and infallible. But when it comes to using the Bible as a blueprint for living, they begin to take out their scissors. You've heard the objections:

- The Old Testament doesn't apply in the church age.
- You can't put a non-Christian under Biblical law.
- We're under grace, not law.

These objections are myths, or at best, dangerous half-truths. Just try to understand the New Testament without the Old Testament. Paul says that pastors are to be paid, and he supports this from a seemingly obscure verse from the Old Testament: "For the Scripture says, 'You shall not muzzle the ox while he is threshing,' and 'The laborer is worthy of his wages'" (1 Timothy 5:18; see Deuteronomy 25:4; Leviticus 19:13).

Read what the Bible says about the alien in Israel. The alien was required to keep the law just like the covenant-bound Israelite: "There shall be one standard for you; it shall be for the stranger as well as the native, for I am the LORD your God" (Leviticus 24:22; cf. Exodus 12:49). The alien was given "equal protection under the law." Aliens could acquire property and accumulate wealth (Leviticus 25:47). They were protected from wrong-doing and treated like the "native" Israelite (Leviticus 19:33-34). A

31

native-born Israelite could "not wrong a stranger or oppress him" (Exodus 22:21; 23:9). If the alien was bound to keep the law of God, then the law of God was the standard for protecting him against injustice as well (Deuteronomy 1:16; cf. 24:16; 27:19). John the Baptist saw no restriction attached to him when he confronted King Herod and his adulterous relationship with Herodias, the wife of his brother Philip: "For John had been saying to Herod, 'It is not lawful for you to have your brother's wife' " (Mark 6:18; cf. Leviticus 20:21; Exodus 20:14).

One of the most mis-quoted verses in the whole Bible is Romans 6:14: "For sin shall not be master over you, for you are not under law, but under grace." Paul is not talking about the law as a standard of righteousness. In chapter 3, the apostle makes it clear that the justified sinner is not free from keeping the law: "Do we then nullify the Law through faith? May it never be! *On the contrary, we establish the law*" (Romans 3:21). The Christian is no longer under the *condemnation* or *curse* of the law: "Christ redeemed us from the *curse of the Law*, having become a curse for us—for it is written, 'CURSED IS EVERY ONE WHO HANGS ON A TREE' " (Galatians 3:13).

We all follow some law. We can make up our own law apart from Scripture. The church can determine what is lawful apart from Scripture. Experts in natural law can determine what is lawful. Even the State can determine what is law. In all of these choices there is the rejection of God as the Law-giver. Jesus was very clear in His warning to those who reject Scripture as the final authority in law-keeping: "Neglecting the commandment of God, you hold to the tradition of men. . . . You nicely set aside the commandment of God in order to keep your tradition" (Mark 7:8-9).

At a time when the world is looking for firm ground, Christians should be ready, willing, and able to turn people to the Bible as the blueprint by which we can build a Christian civilization.

Many Christians are still locked into the conviction that the Bible speaks to a very narrow slice of life. Of course, all Christians believe that the Bible has some very specific things to say about prayer, Bible reading, worship, and evangelism. But many Christians are not convinced that the Bible has some very definite things to say about civil government, the judicial system, economics, indebtedness, the punishment of criminals, foreign affairs, care for the poor, journalism, science, medicine, business, education, taxation, inflation, property, terrorism, war, peace negotiations, military defense, ethical issues like abortion and homosexuality, environmental concerns, inheritance, investments, building safety, banking, child discipline, pollution, marriage, contracts, and many other world-view issues.

7

THINKING GOD'S THOUGHTS AFTER HIM

Because of the distortions of sin, we need a reliable standard to evaluate all of life. We cannot trust ourselves, the opinion of experts, the wishes of the majority, or "natural law" to be that standard. The Bible is our set of corrective lenses for all of life. Man simply cannot be trusted. John Calvin said it well:

> Just as old or bleary-eyed men and those with weak vision, if you thrust before them a most beautiful volume, even if they recognize it to be some sort of writing, yet can scarcely construe two words, but with the aid of spectacles will begin to read distinctly; so Scripture, gathering up the otherwise confused knowledge of God in our minds, having dispersed our dullness, clearly shows us the true God.[1]

All Christians must remove their blinders and widen their scope of ministry to include the world. This will mean the development and implementation of a comprehensive Biblical World View. Put simply, a world view is the way you and I look at things. How did we get here? How did the world get here? How does it run? Who or what runs it? What laws govern us and the world? What role, if any, do we have in the government of the world? What does God think of the world? How does He want it to run? Whom has He put in charge of the world? What are His plans for the world? Basically, the Christian's worldview should be

---

1. John Calvin, *Institutes of the Christian Religion*, John T. McNeill, ed. (Philadelphia, PA: Westminster Press, 1960), Book I, chapter 2, section 1.

the same as God's worldview, the creature thinking the thoughts of the Creator.[2]

Is God's view of the world comprehensive? Is He concerned about every nook and cranny of creation? Did He give His life for the "world"? Is He Lord of "all things"? To all of these questions we would answer "Yes!" Then, why should Christians limit their scope of the world? Why should Christians have a lower view of the world than God does? Why should humanists have a higher view of the world than we do? George Grant writes:

> One of the basic demands of Christian discipleship, of following Jesus Christ, is to change our way of thinking. We are to "take captive every thought to make it obedient to Christ" (2 Corinthians 10:5). We are "not to be conformed to this world but [are to] be transformed by the renewing of our minds" (Romans 12:2). In other words, we are commanded to have a Biblical worldview. All our thinking, our perspective on life, and our understanding of the world around us, is to be comprehensively informed by Scripture.
>
> God's condemnation of Israel came because "their ways were not His ways and their thoughts were not His thoughts" (Isaiah 55:8). They did not have a Biblical worldview. When we begin to think about the law, or bio-medical ethics, or art, or business, or love, or history, or welfare, or anything else apart from God's revelation, we too have made ourselves vulnerable to condemnation. A Biblical worldview is not optional. It is mandatory.[3]

How does the Christian begin to develop a Biblical worldview? Of course, the first place to start is with the Bible. The Bible is the blueprint for life. Just like a builder turns to his blueprints to build a house, the Christian turns to the Bible to build a civilization that includes every area of life.

---

2. Johannes Kepler (1571-1630) wrote: "O God, I am thinking thy thoughts after thee." Cited by Charles Hummel, *The Galileo Connection: Resolving Conflicts between Science and the Bible* (Downers Grove, IL: InterVarsity Press, 1986), p. 57.

3. George Grant, *Bringing in the Sheaves: Transforming Poverty into Productivity* (Atlanta, GA: American Vision Press, 1985), p. 93.

Martin and Deidre Bobgan write that "God has given an Instruction Book on how to live."[4] Why is the Bible sufficient for explaining "why people behave the way they do and how they change,"[5] but it is not sufficient for law, economics, education, and politics? The Bobgans go on to write that "the Bible claims divine revelation" while "psychotherapy claims scientific substantiation."[6] Their point is obvious: Why would we want to go anywhere else for answers to life's most perplexing problems? Substitute any discipline where you see the word "psychotherapy." The Bible claims divine revelation while (law, economics, education, and politics) claim scientific substantiation.

It should be pointed out that Dave Hunt wrote the Foreword to this fine book. The Bobgans are saying what Reconstructionists have been saying for years: The Bible is a blueprint for living.

---

4. Martin and Deidre Bobgan, *Psychoheresy: The Psychological Seduction of Christianity* (Santa Barbara, CA: Eastgate Publishers, 1987), p. 11.

5. *Idem.*

6. *Idem.*

8

THE SECULARIZATION OF LIFE

A lack of a comprehensive biblical world view has left Christians open to a blind-side attack from humanists who have developed a comprehensive secular[1] world view. Non-Christians have no problem secularizing law, economics, ethics, journalism, education, politics, foreign affairs, and environmental issues. The sad thing is that many Christians believe that the steady secularization of every area of life is inevitable and that Christians should not involve themselves in the "Christianization" of every area of life. We, therefore, have witnessed the steady decline of the family, politics, education, and law, to name just a few.

Let's take a brief look at education. In our own nation one of the first acts performed in the New World was the establishment of schools whose purpose was to further the gospel of Christ in all disciplines.

> Regardless of the vocation for which a student was preparing, the colonial college sought to provide for him an education that was distinctly Christian. At Harvard the original goal of higher learning was "to know God and Jesus Christ which is eternal life (John 17:3), and therefore to lay Christ in the bottom as the only foundation of all sound knowledge and learning." Yale in the early

---

1. The adjective secular comes from the Latin *saeculum*, which means "time" or "age." "To call someone secular means he is completely time-bound, totally a child of his age, a creature of history, with no vision of eternity. Unable to see anything in the perspective of eternity, he cannot believe God exists or acts in human affairs." James Hitchcock, *What is Secular Humanism?* (Ann Arbor, MI: Servant Publications, 1982), pp. 10-11.

1700s stated as its primary goal that "every student shall consider
the main end of his study to wit to know God in Jesus Christ and
answerably to lead a Godly, sober life."[2]

The Puritan educational system was comprehensive in its
espousal of a comprehensive Biblical world view. It was designed
to train men for every vocation. The emphasis, however, was to
train men so that future generations would not be left with "an il-
literate ministry." The curriculum of Harvard, for example, emphasized the study of biblical languages, logic, divinity
(theology), and skills in communication (public speaking and
rhetoric). Churches expected their ministers to read the Scriptures in the original languages. At Princeton, even those who did
not enter the gospel ministry, were expected to know their Bible
"from cover to cover."

Since civil government was a major concern in the colonies,
courses in ethics, politics, and history also were required. Many
of the 18th-century framers of the Constitution had been steeped
in basic Bible doctrines. These biblical concepts formed our Constitutional political system (e.g., decentralized political power,
checks and balances, a republican form of government, abhor-
rence of mob-rule democracy, jurisdictional separation of family,
church, and State, a design for stability in the rule of law, private
property, the gold standard, the keeping of the Lord's Day, and
the protection of Christian worship).

Courses in law and medicine also were offered, along with as-
tronomy, physics, botany, other sciences, and mathematics. During the colonial period, from 1636 when Harvard was established
to 1769 when Dartmouth was founded, nearly all colleges were organized as Christian institutions. In time, however, emphasis
shifted from a staunchly biblio-centric education to a "Common
Sense Realism" philosophy which put reason on an equal level
with special revelation. Of course, this shift did not occur overnight. Harvard moved from its original Calvinist foundation to

---

2. William C. Ringenberg, *The Christian College: A History of Protestant Higher
Education in America* (Grand Rapids, MI: Eerdmans, 1984), p. 38.

Arminianism, then during the 18th century even beyond Arminianism to Unitarianism. "The takeover of Harvard in 1805 by the Unitarians is probably the most important intellectual event in American history—at least from the standpoint of education."[3]

Nearly every educational institution of the early colonies has been taken over by those who denied the Bible. These schools of higher education now train millions of young people who influence every sphere of American life. Compare the educational pursuits of Harvard in 1636 with the Harvard of today:

> Every child in America entering school at the age of five is mentally ill, because he comes to school with certain allegiances toward our founding fathers, our elected officials, toward his parents, toward a belief in a supernatural Being, toward the sovereignty of this nation as a separate entity. It's up to you teachers to make all of these sick children well by creating the international children of the future.[4]

Where Christ had been considered the foundation of all knowledge, believing in "a supernatural Being" now constitutes mental illness. Dr. Pierce understands the importance of education, however; it is to mold "the international children of the future," in terms of a man-centered world view. The humanists have captured the vision of the Christians.

God's Zion

Both religious and political persecution motivated our forefathers to leave the shores of England and to start a "Christian Commonwealth" in the New World. "The purpose of the New England colonies was, with respect to church and state, twofold: First, to establish the true and free church, free of the *control* of the state, free to be a co-worker in terms of the Kingdom of God, to

---

3. Samuel Blumenfeld, *Is Public Education Necessary?* (Old Greenwich, CT: The Devin-Adair Company, 1981), p. 30.

4. Chester Pierce, Professor of Education in the faculty of Medicine and Graduate School of Education, Harvard University.

establish God's Zion on earth; second, to establish godly magistrates, i.e., a Christian state, magistrates as ordained by God."[5]

The separation of Christianity from the workings of the State was never in the minds of these early settlers. Christianity was the foundation of our great Republic. Consider the following:

1. The Ten Commandments hang over the head of the Chief Justice of the Supreme Court.

2. In the House and Senate chambers appear the words, "In God We Trust."

3. In the Rotunda is the figure of the crucified Christ.

4. On the walls of the Capitol dome, these words appear: "The New Testament according to the Lord and Savior Jesus Christ."

5. On the Great Seal of the United States is inscribed the phrase *Annuit Coeptis*, "God has smiled on our undertaking."

6. Under the Seal is the phrase from Lincoln's Gettysburg address: "This nation under God."

7. President Eliot of Harvard chose Micah 6:8 for the walls of the nation's library: "He hath showed thee, O man, what is good; and what doth God require of thee, but to do justly, and to love mercy, and to walk humbly with thy God."

8. The lawmaker's library quotes the Psalmist's acknowledgment of the beauty and order of creation: "The heavens declare the glory of God, and the firmament showeth His handiwork" (Psalm 19:1).

9. Engraved on the metal cap on the top of the Washington Monument are the words: "Praise be to God." Lining the walls of the stairwell are numerous Bible verses: "Search the Scriptures," "Holiness to the Lord," and "Train up a child in the way he should go, and when he is old he will not depart from it."

10. The crier who opens each session of the Supreme Court closes with the words, "God save the United States and the Honorable Court."

---

5. Rousas J. Rushdoony, *This Independent Republic* (Nutley, NJ: The Craig Press, 1964), pp. 97-98.

11. At the opposite end of the Lincoln memorial, words and phrases from Lincoln's Second Inaugural Address allude to "God," the "Bible," "providence," the "Almighty," and "divine attributes."

12. The plaque in the Dirksen Office Building has the words "IN GOD WE TRUST" in bronze relief.

13. *The Connecticut Constitution* (until 1818): "The People of this State . . . by the Providence of God . . . hath the sole and exclusive right of governing themselves as a free, sovereign, and independent State . . . and forasmuch as the free fruition of such liberties and privileges as humanity, civility, and Christianity call for us, as is due to every man in his place and proportion . . . hath ever been, and will be the tranquility and stability of Churches and Commonwealth; and the denial thereof, the disturbances, if not the ruin of both."

14. *The Delaware Constitution* (1831): ". . . no man ought to be compelled to attend any religious worship. . . ." It recognizes "the duty of all men frequently to assemble together for the public worship of the Author of the Universe." The following oath of office was in force until 1792: "I . . . do profess faith in God the Father, and in Jesus Christ His only Son, and in the Holy Ghost, one God, blessed for evermore; I do acknowledge the Holy Scriptures of the Old and New Testaments to be given by divine inspiration."

15. *The North Carolina Constitution* (1876): "That no person who shall deny the being of God, or the truth of the Protestant religion, or the divine authority of the Old or New Testaments, or who shall hold religious principles incompatible with the freedom and safety of the State, shall be capable of holding any office or place of trust or profit in the civil department within this State."

16. In the Capitol Building a room was set aside by the Eighty-third Congress to be used exclusively for the private prayer and meditation of Members of Congress. In this specially designated room there is a stained-glass window showing George Washington kneeling in prayer. Behind Washington a prayer is etched: "Preserve me, O God, for in Thee do I put my trust" (Psalm 16:1). The two lower corners of the window each show the Holy Scriptures and an open book and a candle, signifying the light from

God's law: "Thy Word is a lamp unto my feet and a light unto my path" (Psalm 119:105).

17. Franklin's appeal to Congress during the drafting of the Constitution reads in part: "In the beginning of the contest with Britain, when we were sensible of danger, we had daily prayers in this room for Divine protection. Our prayers, Sir, were heard — and they were graciously answered. All of us who were engaged in the struggle must have observed frequent instances of a superintending Providence in our favor . . . . And have we now forgotten that powerful Friend? Or do we imagine we no longer need its assistance? I have lived, Sir, a long time, and the longer I live the more convincing proofs I see of this truth, that God governs in the affairs of men. And if a sparrow can not fall to the ground without His notice, is it probable that an empire can rise without His aid?

"We have been assured, Sir, in the sacred writings, that 'except the Lord build the house, they labor in vain that build it' [Psalm 127:1]. I firmly believe this and I also believe that, without His concurring aid, we shall succeed in this political building no better than the builders of Babel. . . ."[6]

18. The Supreme Court narrowly defined the legal protections of the First Amendment to exclude polygamy on the grounds that the practice was out of accord with the basic tenets of Christianity: "It is contrary to the spirit of Christianity and the civilization which Christianity has produced in the Western world."[7] A year earlier the Court declared that "Bigamy and polygamy are crimes by the laws of all civilized and Christian countries. . . . To call their advocacy a tenet of religion is to offend the common sense of mankind."[8]

19. The highest office in our land demands the greatest wisdom. King Solomon learned this early in his political career.

---

6. Benjamin Franklin, "Motion for Prayers in the Convention," *The Works of Benjamin Franklin*, Federal edition, ed. John Bigelow (New York and London: The Knickerbocker Press, 1904), II:337-338.

7. *Late Corporation of the Church of Jesus Christ of Latter Day Saints v. United States*, 136 U.S. 1 (1890).

8. *Davis v. Beason*, 133 U.S. 333, 341-342 (1890). Cited in John Eidsmoe, *The Christian Legal Advisor* (Milford, MI: Mott Media, 1984), p. 150.

American Presidents have had a high regard for the Bible because they knew that its wisdom was greater than what any man could offer.

John Quincy Adams: The first and almost the only Book deserving of universal attention is the Bible.

Abraham Lincoln: All the good from the Saviour of the world is communicated through this Book; but for the Book we could not know right from wrong. All the things desirable to man are contained in it.

Andrew Jackson: Go to the Scriptures . . . the joyful promises it contains will be a balsam to all your troubles.

Calvin Coolidge: The foundations our society and our government rest so much on the teachings of the Bible that it would be difficult to support them if faith in these teachings would cease to be practically universal in our country.

Woodrow Wilson: The Bible . . . is the one supreme source of revelation of the meaning of life, the nature of God and spiritual nature and need of men. It is the only guide of life which really leads the spirit in the way of peace and salvation.

America was born a Christian nation. America was born to exemplify that devotion to the elements of righteousness which are derived from the revelations of Holy Scripture.

Harry Truman: The fundamental basis of this nation's law was given to Moses on the Mount [Sinai]. The fundamental basis of our Bill of Rights comes from the teachings we get from Exodus and St. Matthew, from Isaiah and St. Paul. I don't think we emphasize that enough these days. If we don't have the proper fundamental moral background, we will finally wind up with a totalitarian government which does not believe in rights for anybody but the state.

Those who deny that the world can be changed have ignored centuries of history. These skeptics are preoccupied with their own generation as if it is normative for all of history. This is a monumental mistake. The world has been changed, and it will be changed. Change will come in our generation or in some future generation.

9

TRUE AND FALSE SPIRITUALITY

Failure to develop a comprehensive world view often is related to a false view of spirituality. To be "spiritual" means to be governed by the Holy Spirit. For many, spirituality means to be preoccupied with non-physical reality. Therefore, to be spiritual means not to be involved with the material things of this world.

> The unbiblical idea of "spirituality" is that the truly "spiritual" man is the person who is sort of "non-physical," who doesn't get involved in "earthly" things, who doesn't work very much or think very hard, and who spends most of his time meditating about how he'd rather be in heaven. As long as he's on earth, though, he has one main duty in life: Get stepped on for Jesus. The "spiritual" man, in this view, is a wimp. A Loser. But at least he's a *Good* Loser.[1]

The devil and his demons are spiritual (non-physical) and evil: "And I saw coming out of the mouth of the dragon and out of the mouth of the beast and out of the mouth of the false prophet, three *unclean spirits* like frogs; for they are *spirits of demons*, performing signs, which go out to the kings of the whole world, to gather them together for the war of the great day of God Almighty" (Revelation 16:13-14). There are "deceitful spirits" (1 Timothy 4:1), "unclean spirits" (Revelation 18:2), and spirits of "error" (1 John 4:6). There is even "spiritual wickedness" (Ephesians 6:12).

---

1. David Chilton, *Paradise Restored: A Biblical Theology of Dominion* (Tyler, TX: Dominion Press, 1985), pp. 3-4.

On the other hand, Jesus has a body and He is good: "For David, after he had served the purpose of God in his own generation, fell asleep, and was laid among his fathers, and underwent decay; *but He whom God raised did not undergo decay*" (Acts 13:36-37). Jesus was raised with His body. He is "the Holy and Righteous One" (Acts 3:14). Spirituality is directly related to righteousness. The reason Jesus' body did not undergo decay was because He was without sin.

The word "spiritual" is often an adjective, describing the makeup of something. There is the "Holy Spirit" (e.g., Acts 13:2), a "spirit of truth" (1 John 4:6), "spiritual things" (1 Corinthians 9:11), "spiritual food" (10:3), a "spiritual body" (15:44), "spiritual sacrifices" (1 Peter 2:5), "spiritual wisdom and understanding" (Colossians 1:9), and "ministering spirits, sent out to render service for the sake of those who will inherit salvation" (Hebrews 1:14).

To be "spiritual" is to exhibit the "gifts of the Spirit" (Galatians 5:22). We are told to "walk in the Spirit" (5:16). But how does a Christian know when he or she is walking "in the Spirit"?

> To be Spiritual is to be guided and motivated by the Holy Spirit. It means obeying His commandments as recorded in Scriptures. The Spiritual man is not someone who floats in mid-air and hears eerie voices. The Spiritual man is the man who does what the Bible says (Rom. 8:4-8). This means, therefore, that we *are* to get involved in life. God wants us to apply Christian standards everywhere, in every way. Spirituality does not mean retreat and withdrawal from life; it means *dominion*. The basic Christian confession of faith is that *Jesus is Lord* (Rom. 10:9-10) — Lord of all things, in heaven and on earth.[2]

The commandments of God are the rules by which we measure our spirituality. We are told that the "Law is spiritual" (Romans 7:14). Notice also that the spiritual person "appraises [judges] *all things*" (2:15). The reason he can judge all things is because he has an inerrant, infallible, God-breathed Book (2 Timothy 3:16-17).

---

2. *Ibid.*, p. 4.

The Bible does not support the belief that Christians should abandon the world because the world is not "spiritual." Often, the word "world" has an ethical connotation; it refers to Satan's realm, not the material world as such. Christians are not to abandon the material world, but to transform the world through the power of the Spirit, using the spiritual Law of God as the standard of righteousness for appraising (judging) where regeneration and reconstruction are needed. Christians are to be "salt" and "light" *in* the world (Matthew 5:13-14). Salt is useless unless applied to a potentially decaying world. Light is not needed unless there is darkness to scatter (Matthew 5:15; Luke 2:32).

Without involvement in the world, salt and light are not needed. Christians are to be in the world, but they are not to be of the world (John 17:14-16). They are not to be squeezed into the world's mold (Romans 12:2). They are not to be led astray by the "elementary principles of the world" (Colossians 2:8). They are to keep themselves "unstained by the world" (James 1:27). They are warned not to get entangled in the "defilements of the world" (2 Peter 2:20). Nowhere are they told to abandon the world (cf. Matthew 28:18-20; John 3:16).

The "world" is corrupt because people are corrupt. Where corrupt people control certain aspects of the world we can expect defilement. But the world does not have to remain in decay. When individuals are redeemed, the effects of their redemption should spread to the society in which they live and conduct their affairs.

By denying the spirituality of God's created order, we neglect its importance and give it by default to those who deny Christ. *Worldliness* is to be avoided, not the world. The Bible warns

against worldliness *wherever* it is found [James 1:27], certainly in the church, and he [James] is emphasizing here precisely the importance of Christian involvement in *social* issues. Regrettably, we tend to read the Scriptures as though their rejection of a "worldly" life-style entails a recommendation of an "otherworldly" one.

This approach has led many Christians to abandon the "secular" realm to the trends and forces of secularism. Indeed, because of their two-realm theory, to a large degree, Christians have themselves to blame for the rapid secularization of the West. If political, industrial, artistic, and journalistic life, to mention only these areas, are branded as essentially "worldly," "secular," "profane," and part of the "natural domain of creaturely life," then is it surprising that Christians have not more effectively stemmed the tide of humanism in our culture?[3]

God created everything wholly good (Genesis 1:31). Man, through the fall, became profane, defiled by sin. Redemption restores things in Christ. Peter failed to understand the gospel's comprehensive cleansing effects. He could not believe the Gentiles were "clean": "What God has cleansed, no longer consider unholy" (Acts 10:15; cf. Matthew 15:11; Romans 14:14, 20). The fall did not nullify God's pronouncement that the created order "was very good" (Genesis 1:31). The New Testament reinforces the goodness of God's creation: "For everything created by God is good, and nothing is to be rejected, if it is received with gratitude; for it is sanctified by means of the word of God and prayer" (1 Timothy 4:4-5).

Scripture is our guide and not the Platonic view of matter as something less than good. God "became flesh and dwelt among us" (John 1:14). Jesus worked in his earthly father's shop as a carpenter, affirming the goodness of the created order and the value of physical labor. We do not, as Dave Hunt maintains, abandon heaven when we show a concern for the world.

---

3. Albert M. Wolters, *Creation Regained: Biblical Basics for a Reformational Worldview* (Grand Rapids, MI: Eerdmans, 1985), p. 54.

10

THE FUTURE IS OURS

When Israel was taken to the borders of the promised land, twelve spies were sent to survey the land and report to the nation (Numbers 13). Before choosing twelve representatives for the task, God *promised* the land would be theirs: "Send out for yourself men so that they may spy out the land of Canaan, which *I am going to give to the sons of Israel*; you shall send a man from each of their fathers' tribes, every one a leader among them" (v. 2). No matter what the spies encountered, the *promise* of God should have had priority and overruled any desire to retreat.

When the spies returned, ten brought back pessimistic (unbelieving) reports (vv. 28-29, 31-33). Two spies, Joshua and Caleb, returned with optimistic (faithful) reports because they believed God and not the circumstances they encountered (v. 30). It is important to note that Caleb never denied that there were "giants in the land"; he believed God was stronger than any army of giants. Why is this so? "You are from God, little children, and have overcome them; because greater is He that is in you than he who is in the world" (1 John 4:4).

The nation responded to the report without faith. In effect, they called God a liar: "Then all the congregation lifted up their voices and cried, and the people wept that night" (Numbers 14:1). Their refusal to believe the promise of God brought judgment upon the entire nation.

Israel did not enter the promised land until forty years passed and the unbelieving generation died (14:26-38). Their pessimistic perspective of the future affected their plans for the future. The

49

task of dominion was seen as too great for God, hence too great for man under God's providence. Instead of moving forward, they chose to retreat to the past: "Would that we had died in the land of Egypt! Or would that we had died in the wilderness! And why is the LORD bringing us into this land, to fall by the sword? Our wives and our little ones will become plunder; would it not be better for us to return to Egypt? So they said to one another, 'Let us appoint a leader and return to Egypt'" (Numbers 14:2-4).

A pessimistic faith ruins Christian dominion. Israel lost forty years of dominion because the nation trusted the words of men and the circumstances of the world more than the word of God. When Israel entered the land forty years later, Rahab told the two unnamed spies what the inhabitants were thinking: "For we have heard how the LORD dried up the water of the Red Sea before you when you came out of Egypt, and what you did to the two kings of the Amorites who were beyond the Jordan, to Sihon and Og, whom you utterly destroyed. And when we heard it, *our hearts melted and no courage remained in any man any longer because of you* (Joshua 2:10-11). The Canaanites looked upon the Israelites, at the time Israel was freed from Egyptian bondage over forty years before, as the giants. Forty years of dominion were wasted because Israel failed to trust the God who possesses the future (and controls the present in order to fulfill His plan for the future).

The Christian's view of the future determines how he lives and works in the present. If he believes the future to be bleak, his pessimism will be reflected in a variety of ways, usually in inactivity and unfaithfulness. The family will not be trained to consider the wider aspects of dominion as they relate to successive generations. Education will be present-oriented, with students obtaining an education merely to secure the necessary credentials for a job. While such Christians might establish schooling for children in grades 1-12, very little will be done to set up colleges, universities, and graduate schools to prepare *generations* of Christians to influence their professions, nation, and world for Christ. One reason students find it difficult to apply themselves in school is their inability to work for a purpose, which, in turn, is largely due to many

Christians' neglect of their divinely ordained duty of dominion: to create a Christian civilization.

A pessimistic view of the future, with the State embracing all other governments, fosters economic theory and practice that incite a buy-now-and-pay-later philosophy. Why worry about debt when there may not be a future, and I may not have to repay my loan? Moreover, why consider leaving an inheritance when there will be no earthly future to inherit?

For too long Christians have believed the future should be considered only in terms of heaven or the events that lead to the second coming of Jesus Christ. Events and concerns about the time "in between" have been considered of little real importance. Because of this false theology, many Christians abdicate their responsibilities toward economics, education, science, and civil government. This conception of the future has accelerated the debilitating doctrine that the end of all things is near, leading to further inactivity on the part of God's people. God instructed His people to influence the world:

> The apostle Paul had to rebuke some of the Thessalonians for ceasing to work simply because of the possibility that the Lord might return immediately (2 Thessalonians 3:10-12). Christians since then have often been notorious for embracing escapist attitudes toward work due to their eschatologies [doctrines of the last things]. Rather than aggressively moving forward to take dominion over the earth, the Church has all too often lapsed into an irresponsible passivity, approaching her commission with the attitude: "You don't polish brass on a sinking ship." Jesus, however, instructed us to take the opposite approach. In the parable of the ten minas (Luke 19:11-27), the master gave each of his servants money and told them, "*Do business with this* until I come back." In this story, Jesus commands us to take the offensive and "do business" until He returns.[1]

The biblical view of the future presents the truth that history is moving forward, and every Christian is responsible before God to

---

1. Joseph McAuliffe, "Do Business Until I Return," *New Wine* (January, 1982), p. 29.

show himself a good and faithful steward of his God-given gifts. God requires an accounting.

The kingdom of God has purpose because God directs its every movement. History is not bound by a never-ending series of cycles, with God powerless to intervene and govern. The future, as Nebuchadnezzar came to realize, is governed by God. Earthly sovereigns who fail to recognize God's absolute sovereignty will be destroyed: "You [Nebuchadnezzar] continued looking [at the statue] until a stone was cut out without hands, and it struck the statue on its feet of iron and clay, and crushed them. Then the iron, the clay, the bronze, the silver and the gold were crushed all at the same time, and became like chaff from the summer thresh-ing floors; and the wind carried them away so that not a trace of them was found. But the stone that struck the statue became a great mountain and filled the whole earth" (Daniel 2:34-35). The pagan idea of the future is a myth. The future belongs to God's people and Christians are not trapped in futile historical cycles.

The Christian's view of the future determines how he lives, plans, and works in the present *for the future*. Even during Israel's captivity under Babylonian rule, the nation's darkest hour, the people were told to plan and build for the future: " 'Build houses and live in them; and plant gardens, and eat their produce. Take wives and become the fathers of sons and daughters, and take wives for your sons and give your daughters to husbands, that they may bear sons and daughters; and multiply there and do not decrease. . . . For I know the plans that I have for you,' declares the LORD, 'plans for welfare and not for calamity to give you a future and a hope' " (Jeremiah 29:5-6, 11).

God's words seemed contrary to what people saw all around them. Destruction and captivity awaited the nation, yet God com-manded them to prepare for the *future*. In spite of every pessimistic view, God wanted the people's desires and hopes to be future-directed. Build for what will be. The psychological benefit of such a mind set does much to spur the church of Jesus Christ to greater kingdom activity. A preoccupation with defeat brings defeat by default. Why would anyone wish to build for the future when there is no earthly future hope? Who would invest in a losing proposition? Why should anyone work to establish a godly home, school, business, or civil government when all such institutions seem doomed despite our efforts?

"We must become *optimists* concerning the victory that lies before Christ's people, in time and on earth. We must be even more optimistic than Joshua and Caleb, for they were only asked to spy out the land of Canaan. They were called to give their report prior to Christ's sacrifice at Calvary. Why should we be pessimistic, like that first generation of former slaves? Why should we wander in the wilderness, generation after generation? Why should we despair?"[2] The hope of the future is real because the Christian knows that God governs the affairs of men and nations (Psalm 22:28; 47:8; Daniel 4:35).

Progress for the Godly

The Apostle Paul informs Timothy "that in the last days difficult times will come" (2 Timothy 3:1). The ungodly will manifest a variety of characteristics which evidence their opposition to God's purposes: "For men will be lovers of self, lovers of money, boastful, arrogant, evildoers, disobedient to parents, ungrateful, unholy, etc." (vv. 2-5). Timothy is told to "avoid such men as these" (v. 5).

Will the ungodly dominate culture? At first reading, 2 Timothy 3 would seem to indicate that the ungodly will prevail, and godly influence decline. Further study shows that the Apostle Paul offers a different conclusion. Paul compares the progress of the ungodly in Timothy's day with that of Jannes and Jambres, the Egyptian sorcerer-priests who opposed Moses (cf. Exodus 7:11): "But they will not make further progress; for their folly will be obvious to all, as also that of those two came to be" (2 Timothy 3:9). While it is true there is an *attempt* by the ungodly to dominate culture, the fact is, "they will not make further progress"; their

---

2. Gary North, *Unconditional Surrender* (3rd ed.; Tyler, TX: Institute for Christian Economics, 1988), p. 364.

fling with ungodliness is only temporary (cf. Romans 1:18-32). The Christian can remain optimistic even if ungodly actions increase. In time, if Christians remain faithful in influencing their world with the gospel, actions of the ungodly will be eliminated.

Paul, however, does not allow the Christian to remain passive as the ungodly self-destruct. Timothy has followed Paul's "teaching, conduct, purpose, faith, patience, love, perseverance, persecutions, [and] sufferings" (2 Timothy 3:10-11), and we are called to do the same (vv. 16-17). While the ungodly expend their spiritual capital in present-oriented living, and, therefore, have nothing saved for the future, the Christian is to develop future-oriented spiritual capital to replace the bankrupt culture of humanism with a Christ-centered society. Notice that the characteristics of the ungodly are all self-directed and short-lived, summarized by this phrase: "lovers of pleasure rather than lovers of God" (v. 4). Sin has its pleasure for a short period of time: "He who loves pleasure will become a poor man; he who loves wine and oil will not become rich" (Proverbs 21:17). The love of pleasure is no investment in the future.

The characteristics of the godly are future directed, foregoing the lure of present pleasures for the benefit of future productivity. Teaching, conduct, purpose, faith, patience, love, and perseverance take time and energy from the present, but result in future reward. For example, the farmer could consume all of his harvested grain in a year's time and have none to plant for the following year. By consuming just enough grain to feed his family and storing reserves for a potential poor crop along with some for planting, he guarantees his family security and a dominion status for the future. While the present-oriented consumer furiously looks for a way to feed his family, the future-oriented farmer spends his free time exercising godly dominion in his culture. Moreover, persecutions and sufferings should not deter the future-oriented Christian because "out of them all the Lord" delivers us (2 Timothy 3:11). In the same way, the future-oriented farmer can overcome the effects of a bad harvest because his store allows him to live until the next harvest. The effects of a bad harvest for the present-oriented consumer is disastrous. With no reserves, he possesses no hope for the future.

If the Christian looks only at present happenings he loses his hope of becoming a cultural influence, since he perceives the statement, "evil men and impostors will proceed from bad to worse, deceiving and being deceived" (2 Timothy 3:13) as something permanent. But we also must remember the previous words of Paul: "But they will not make further progress; for their folly will be obvious to all" (v. 9). In the short-term, it appears that the ungodly will prevail. Christians, however, must begin to think long-term; while the ungodly burn themselves out, the godly steadily influence their world: "You, however, *continue* in the things you have learned and become convinced of" (v. 14). In time, the effects of dominion will be seen: "And let us not lose heart in doing good, for in due time we shall reap if we do not grow weary" (Galatians 6:9).

Part II
THE DEBATE OVER CHRISTIAN RECONSTRUCTION

11

UNDERSTANDING
CHRISTIAN RECONSTRUCTION[1]

Christian Reconstructionists believe that the Word of God, that is, *"all* Scripture," should be applied to *all* areas of life. With such faithful application, Christian Reconstructionists expect that God will bless the efforts of His people in both "this age" and in the "age to come" (Mark 10:29-31). It's obvious that the "all Scripture" Paul mentions in 2 Timothy 3:16 is the *Old* Testament, since at the time of his writing, the New Testament canon had not been completely formulated. The "Scriptures" that circulated in the church was what we now call the "Old Testament." The Scriptures of the Old Testament did not pass away with the coming of Christ and the New Testament Scriptures. The Old Covenant order, with its types and shadows, did pass away. This vital distinction is often missed by today's Christians.

Paul tells us that these Scriptures are "God-breathed" and "profitable for teaching, for reproof, for correction, for training in righteousness." For what purpose? "That the man of God may be adequate, *equipped for every good work*" (v. 17). This verse should remind us of the Psalmist's words when he declares that those who

---

1. Each participant in the debate had fifteen minutes to present his position. This chapter is an expanded version of my presentation. Please keep in mind that this chapter does not go into great detail in defining and explaining sub points of the Reconstructionist position, evaluating the distinctive doctrines of dispensational premillennialism, and evaluating and criticizing the objections raised against Christian Reconstruction. The following chapters will offer a more comprehensive evaluation of the issues raised in this chapter.

delight in the "law of the LORD" will be "like a tree firmly planted by streams of water, which yields its fruit in its season, and its leaf does not whither; and *in whatever he does, he prospers*" (Psalm 1:3). Who can expect the benefits from God's inscripturated Word? Faithful individuals, families, and nations. There is a domino effect of good government, beginning with godly self-government under God and extending to family, church, and State.[2] Families, churches, business establishments, and the nation at large are simply a reflection of individuals, for either good or evil. There is also a domino effect of poor self-government (1 Timothy 3:1-7).

The Bible is filled with a "feedback" concept, both positive and negative. God tells us in Deuteronomy 28 that "all these blessings shall come upon you and overtake you, *if* you will obey the LORD your God" (v. 2). Deuteronomy 28 goes on to describe these blessings in individual, family, and national terms. They can be summed up with these verses:

> The LORD will make you abound in prosperity, in the off-spring of your body and in the offspring of your beast and in the produce of your ground, in the land which the LORD swore to your fathers to give you.[3] The LORD will open for you His good storehouse, the heavens, to give rain to your land in its season

---

2. Gary DeMar, *Ruler of the Nations: Biblical Principles for Government* (Ft. Worth, TX: Dominion Press/Atlanta, GA: American Vision, 1987), pp. 3-53.

3. Jesus tells us that *we* will "inherit the earth" (Matthew 5:5). Abraham is "heir to the world [*kosmos*]" (Romans 4:13). Is this promise limited to ethnic Israel? No! All "those who are of the faith of Abraham" share in the promise because he "is the *father of us all*, (as it is written, 'A FATHER OF *MANY NATIONS* HAVE I MADE YOU') in the sight of Him whom he believed, even God, who gives life to the dead and calls into being that which does not exist" (vv. 16-17). What is the scope of this promise? John Murray writes:

> It is defined as the promise to Abraham that *he* should be heir of the world, but it is also a promise to his seed and, therefore, can hardly involve anything less than the worldwide dominion promised to Christ and to the spiritual seed of Abraham in him. It is a promise that receives its ultimate fulfillment in the consummated order of the new heavens and the new earth. *The Epistle to the Romans*, 2 vols. (Grand Rapids, MI: Eerdmans, 1968), vol. 1, p. 142.

and to bless all the work of your hand; and you shall lend to many nations, but you shall not borrow. And the LORD shall make you the head and not the tail and you only shall be above, and you shall not be underneath, if you will listen to the commandments of the LORD your God, which I charge you today, to observe them carefully, and do not turn aside from any of the words which I command you today, to the right or to the left, to go after other gods to serve them (vv. 11-14).

But there is a flip side to the commandments. Those who fail to keep God's commandments remain under a curse that extends beyond the individual to the family, church, and nation (Deuteronomy 28:15-68). Keep in mind that this obedience is not an obedience unto salvation. God was addressing a redeemed community.

The Bible, because it is God's "Instruction Book" or "blueprint for living,"[4] outlines the basics of economic, legal, educational, and political action, as well as personal morality. There is nothing in the Bible that even hints at limiting the requirements of obedience and subsequent blessing to an exclusively *personal* benefit, a nebulous *spirituality*, or simply the life to come. Since all behavior is religious in nature, politics, law, education, and economics are also religious; they come under God's standard for righteousness. Economic and civil legislation are largely the product of a nation's faith — what the people believe and implement into law, declare as opinions, or express in behavior.[5]

It's no accident that Paul describes the civil magistrate as a "minister of God" (Romans 13:4), as someone who rules in God's

---

4. Martin and Deidre Bobgan, *Psychoheresy: The Psychological Seduction of Christianity* (Santa Barbara, CA: Eastgate Publishers, 1987), p. 11. Dave Hunt, author of *The Seduction of Christianity* and *Beyond Seduction*, though he criticizes Christian Reconstruction for its "blueprint" concept, wrote the Foreword to the Bobgans' book. The Bobgans understand that the Bible offers a comprehensive blueprint for Christian counseling. Christian Reconstructionists, following the Reformed writings of Jay Adams, concur. But we go beyond Christian counseling and conclude that the Bible is a blueprint for every endeavor under the sun.

5. Gary DeMar and Peter Leithart, *The Reduction of Christianity: A Biblical Response to Dave Hunt* (Ft. Worth, TX: Dominion Press/Atlanta, GA: American Vision, 1988), p. 300, note 1.

name, under His jurisdiction to do His will in *civil* affairs. The Bible makes it quite clear that the civil magistrate is to rule in terms of a God-ordained ethical standard, punishing the evil-doer and promoting the good. Who is *blessed* by this system? Scripture tells us that the civil magistrate is a minister of God *to us* for good (v. 4). The church directly benefits from the actions of a godly magistrate who "ministers" in God's name. This will mean that for goodness to flow from the magistrate's jurisdiction, the magistrate, and those who rule with him, must exhibit qualities of righteousness. "When the righteous increase, the people rejoice, but when a wicked man rules, people groan" (Proverbs 29:2; cf. 11:12; 28:12).

If you want to know how to rebuild or reconstruct your family, the Bible is the place to go. It's loaded with sound advice and instruction. How about running a business? There's no better book than the Bible to determine how a business ought to operate and how employers should treat employees. Matters of economic policy are also discussed in Scripture: just weights and measures, laws concerning theft and restitution, inflation, debt, and the gold standard. Simply put, the Bible is our standard for *everything*.

Reconstructionist Distinctives[6]

Reconstructionism is a distinctive blending of certain biblical doctrines. They are (1) personal regeneration, (2) the application of biblical law to all areas of life, and (3) the advance of the already-present kingdom in history through the preaching of the gospel and the empowering of the Holy Spirit (postmillennialism). The church, by and large, has neglected the place of the law in personal and cultural life and has relegated this world to inevitable destruction before Jesus returns.

All biblical doctrines are important. Nothing should be neglected. Evangelism is the church's priority. But Christian Reconstructionists ask this question: What do these newly converted people do if Jesus does not return in "their generation"?

---

6. These distinctives will be more fully developed in the following chapters.

The attacks against Christian Reconstruction center on two emphasized doctrines—biblical law and postmillennialism—while ignoring the comprehensive biblical system that includes all the doctrines of the faith. Such a procedure would make any theological system look out of focus. Reconstructionists do not cast aside prayer, evangelism, and worship. Instead, we *emphasize* long-neglected doctrines like the application of biblical law in the New Covenant order and the advance of God's kingdom in the world. Reconstructionists subscribe to the basics of the Christian faith: from the inerrancy of Scripture to a literal heaven and hell and everything in between.

While there are many "pillars of Christian Reconstruction," I have chosen three of the most prominent ones. There is an intimate and necessary relationship between regeneration, biblical law, and postmillennialism. There are other Reconstructionist distinctives. For a more complete analysis of Christian Reconstruction and its historical and theological setting, I encourage you to read *The Reduction of Christianity: A Biblical Response to Dave Hunt.*

Regeneration

Regeneration is the starting point for Reconstructionists. Society cannot change unless people change, and the only way people can change is through the regenerating work of the Holy Spirit. Those "dead in trespasses and sins" (Ephesians 2:1) must have a "new heart" and a "new spirit." The "heart of stone" must be removed and a "heart of flesh" substituted. This is God's work. God's Spirit must be in us *before* we can walk in His statutes (Romans 8:3-4, 7). The result will be that we "will be careful to observe" His "ordinances" (Ezekiel 36:26-27). The New Testament summarizes it this way: "If any man is in Christ, he is a new creature; the old things passed away; behold, new things have come" (2 Corinthians 5:17).

There is no way to change our world unless people are given the will to change (1 Corinthians 2:14). The instrument of that change is the preaching of the gospel, not political involvement, imposing biblical law on an unwilling citizenry, or, as some have inaccurately said concerning Christian Reconstruction, "taking over the government." We will have a better world when we have better people. Better people are the result of changed hearts and minds. Only God can do this. He *will* do this. This is why evangelism is a priority.

Rousas J. Rushdoony, a noted Reconstructionist scholar, says it this way:

> The key to remedying the [modern] situation is *not* revolution, nor any kind of resistance that works to subvert law and order. The New Testament abounds in warnings against disobedience and in summons to peace. *The key is regeneration, propagation of the gospel, and the conversion of men and nations to God's law-word.*[7]
> Clearly, there is no hope for man except in regeneration.[8]
> . . . true reform begins with regeneration and then the submission of the believer to the whole law-word of God.[9]

Tommy Ice and Wayne House, in a forthcoming book, try to link Reconstructionists with those who are working toward "the corrupted goal of bringing in a man-made kingdom." They tell us that this "is consistent with a general postmillennialist vision."[10]

---

7. R. J. Rushdoony, *The Institutes of Biblical Law* (Phillipsburg, NJ: Presbyterian and Reformed, 1973), p. 113.

8. *Ibid.*, p. 449.

9. *Ibid.*, p. 627. See also pages 122, 163, 147, 308, 413, 780.

10. In a letter to me, dated April 25, 1988, Tommy Ice wrote that he and co-author Wayne House do not "even come close to making statements which would support" my contention that their understanding of Christian Reconstruction is a "'gross and unfair misrepresentation.'" The following is from their forthcoming book on Christian Reconstruction. (The book is to be published by Multnomah Press under the title *Dominion Theology: Blessing or Curse? An Analysis of Christian Reconstructionism.*):

> Much of the New Deal and the Great Society of liberalism the last 60 years has had the corrupted goal of bringing in a man-made Messianic kingdom. This certainly does not flow out of a premillennialist, or even an amillennial view of the kingdom, but it is consistent with a general postmillennial vision. (From manuscript page 29, "Heat and Light," *Christian Reconstruction*, February 1, 1988, 11:52 PM).

For Tommy Ice and Wayne House, postmillennialism is similar to the "corrupted goal of bringing in a man-made Messianic kingdom." This is far from the truth.

This is a grossly unfair misrepresentation, especially in the light of the publication of *The Reduction of Christianity* wherein the goals of Christian Reconstructionists are plainly set forth. First, Christian Reconstructionists believe the kingdom was inaugurated by Jesus Christ. We do not "bring in the kingdom." Second, the kingdom is not "man-made." The Bible tells us that it's the "kingdom of *God*." Third, entering the kingdom comes through regeneration. Jesus tells Nicodemus that he cannot even "see the kingdom" until he is "born from above," that is, "born again" (John 3:3).

Biblical Law

The second Reconstructionist distinctive is biblical law. I've made it abundantly clear in my three-volume *God and Government* series and in *Ruler of the Nations* that civil government is just one government among many governments. The State is just as responsible to keep God's law as the individual. Many dispensational premillennialists deny that God's law is applicable for today's world, especially in the area of civil government. The dispensational system, if it is consistent with its own interpreting methodology, will have nothing to do with the Old Testament law in spite of the New Testament's own validation of it. Paul describes it as "God-breathed . . . and profitable for teaching, for reproof, for correction, for training in righteousness; that the man of God may be equipped for every good work" (2 Timothy 3:16-17). Paul declares that we confirm the Law by faith (Romans 3:31).

But what standard can the dispensational premillennialist appeal to when he denies the validity of biblical law? General revelation? Natural law? Look at nature, we're told, and we can then determine an ethical system for civil government. This is what Norm Geisler says, who is a dispensationalist and an ardent opponent of Christian Reconstruction. He contends, "Government is not based on special revelation, such as the Bible. It is based on God's general revelation to all men. . . . Thus, civil law, based as it is in the natural moral law, lays no specifically religious obligation on man."[11]

---

11. "A Premillennial View of Law and Government," *The Best in Theology*, gen. ed. J. I. Packer (Carol Stream, IL: Christianity Today/Word, 1986), vol. 1, p. 259.

But can nature be our standard if it is fallen and distorted? Fallen man is not adequately equipped to establish an ethical system apart from a fixed law code. He "suppresses the truth in unrighteousness" (Romans 1:18). In fact, unbelievers choose the "unnatural" while repudiating the "natural" (v. 26). So then, even if a natural law/general revelation moral code could be developed to handle *specific* points of law, those outside of Christ would still reject it (vv. 21-23).

How can we maintain that a fallen created order is any more suitable for deriving a moral code that can be used to govern nations when fallen man cannot be trusted with what is "evident" (v. 19)? Who is to determine what nature is saying to us? What does nature tell us about ethics? Well, the strong prey on the weak. Is this natural or unnatural? How do we know that it's "unnatural" for the strong to kill the weak? Maybe this is the way it should be; it's an observation from nature. The idea of an independent "natural law" that can clearly guide civil governments in the area of law-making is a myth. There's no specificity. We might learn that murder is wrong, but general revelation cannot show us how to distinguish between murder, self-defense, war, and executing a capital offender. J. I. Packer shows why it would be impossible to construct an ethical system based on observations from nature:

> One of the most revolting things I ever saw was one of our children's hamsters eating its young. Abortion, whereby a mother-to-be uses medical personnel as her agents "eats up" the small person of whom she gets rid, is the human equivalent.[12]

Is it any wonder in a day when God's law is despised and ridiculed, that abortion is legalized with few if any restrictions? There is nothing "unnatural" about abortion, since the "natural order" shows us that it's "natural" for a mother to kill her young and for a herd to reject its weakest members. And yet, natural law is the best that some dispensationalists can offer. I'm convinced that ad-

---

12. J. I. Packer, "It's Wrong to Eat People," *Christianity Today* (April 8, 1988), p. 11.

vocates of natural law are viewing this system through biblical lenses. Greg L. Bahnsen lists the options that the civil magistrate can draw on to establish a law code and concludes that biblical law is the only real option:

> [T]here must be *criteria* or a standard for this judgment (i.e., a law the magistrate is responsible to obey). If this law is *not* God's law, then it must be one of five alternatives. It might be *natural law*, but this is simply a projection of autonomy and satisfaction with the status quo. It might be the *people*, but then abortion, or racism, and any number of other things could be voted in by the population. It might be taken as the *politician's own* law to which he attributes absolute authority, but this is simply autonomy writ large. . . . Others have gone on to maintain that *natural revelation* will be the standard of judgment. However, this either amounts to preferring a sin-obscured edition of the same law of God or to denying the unity of natural and special revelation (and being willing to pit the one against the other). Not only this, but in fact natural revelation is suppressed in unrighteousness by the sinner, and this should dissuade us from thinking that it can be the recognized, functional measure of his ethical obligation. Finally, someone might suggest that the civil magistrate rules by means of continuing *special revelation*, each decision being founded upon the closed nature of the canon, but even if it were not it would fail to eliminate the necessity for having the state obey God's law since every new revelation must be judged, says Deuteronomy 13:1-4, as to its harmony with the *previous* revelation and law of God.[13]

Autonomous man likes options as long as those options do not force him to be accountable to a fix standard. "There is no alternative but to maintain that the civil magistrate is responsible to the entire law of God as a direction for his government and judging."[14]

All of God's laws were given for our good and for the good of the nations:

---

13. Greg L. Bahnsen, *Theonomy in Christian Ethics* (2nd ed.; Phillipsburg, NJ: Presbyterian and Reformed, [1977] 1984), p. 400.
14. *Idem.*

And now, Israel, what does the LORD require from you, but to
fear the LORD your God, to walk in all His ways and love Him,
and to serve the LORD your God with all your heart and with all
your soul, and to keep the LORD's commandments and His statutes which I am commanding you today for your good (Deuteronomy 10:12-13).[15]

So keep and do them, for that is your wisdom and your
understanding in the sight of the peoples who will hear all these
statutes and say, "Surely this great nation is a wise and understanding people." For what great nation is there that has a god so
near to it as is the LORD our God whenever we call on Him? Or
what great nation is there that has statutes and judgments as
righteous as this whole law which I am setting before you today?
(Deuteronomy 4:6-8).

Righteousness exalts a nation, but sin is a disgrace to any
people (Proverbs 14:34).

But we know that the Law is good, if one uses it lawfully,
realizing the fact that law is not made for a righteous man, but
for those who are lawless and rebellious, for the ungodly and sinners, for the unholy and profane, for those who kill their fathers
or mothers, for murderers and immoral men and homosexuals
and kidnappers and liars and perjurers, and whatever else is contrary to sound teaching (1 Timothy 1:8-10; cf. 4:8; Matthew 6:33;
Romans 13:1-4).

Postmillennialism

The third Reconstructionist distinctive is postmillennialism,
the victorious advance of God's established kingdom throughout
history. Dave Hunt wants us to believe that the Christian's *immediate* hope is the rapture, an event in dispensationalism that is separated by 1007 years from the judgment seat of Christ. It is only

---

15. Some would counter that these verses apply strictly to Israel as an ethnic
people. But the Bible tells us that the church, made up of Jews and Gentiles, is
now "a chosen race, a royal priesthood, a holy nation, a people for God's own
possession" (1 Peter 2:9). Jesus described it this way: "The kingdom of God will
be taken away from you [unbelieving Jews], and be given to a nation producing
the fruit of it [believing Jews and gentiles]" (Matthew 21:43; cf. Mark 12:1-12;
Luke 20:9-19).

after this lengthy period (plus two thousand years of history since Jesus' birth) that Jesus will be victorious. He understands the rapture as the "rescue of the church" rather than as the more biblical doctrine of the ascension of the saints. The rapture is the prelude to the return of Christ to deliver up the kingdom that was given to Jesus at His first coming (1 Corinthians 15:20-28). The rapture is not separated from the final return of Christ by a seven year tribulation period or a thousand year millennial reign of Jesus on the earth.

To support his view that the rapture is simply a "rescue," Mr. Hunt refers us to Lot and his wife and daughters being "raptured" out of Sodom, and to Israel's being "raptured" out of Egypt.[16] This is strained biblical interpretation at best, and hardly in keeping with dispensational literalism. Weren't the Jews also "raptured" *out of* Israel *into* pagan Babylon? Must we see the rapture in every geographical movement of God's people? In fact, Israel was led out of Egypt and brought to the *land* of Canaan to take dominion over it. In the New Testament, Jesus tells us that we are the "salt of the *earth*" and the "light of the *world*" (Matthew 5:13-14). Jesus prays to His Father on behalf of the disciples not "to take them *out of the world*" (John 17:15),[17] a clear contradiction of the rapture as rescue. If there is any given priority of order in Scripture, it is that the lost will be taken first in judgment, since the tares are gathered and burned before the wheat is gathered (Matthew 13:30).[18]

---

16. Post-tribulational futurists point out that Israel was *protected from* the plagues upon Egypt while still in the land. This was especially true of the tenth plague. And the emphasis in Revelation is upon *sealing* the tribulation saints. If the tribulation saints are sealed and thus protected from God's wrath, then church saints do not have to be removed from planet earth to avoid God's wrath. The context of 1 Thessalonians 5:9 does not logically require even a futurist to be pretribulational.

17. The Greek in John 17:15 is almost identical to Revelation 3:10, one of the few pretribulational rapture proof texts: "*keep* them *from* evil one" and "*keep from* the hour of testing."

18. In the first edition of the *Scofield Reference Bible*, Scofield reverses the order: "The gathering of the tares into bundles for burning does not imply immediate judgment. At the end of this age (v. 40) the tares are set apart for burning, but first the wheat is gathered into the barn (John 14.3; 1 Thes. 4.14-17)" (p. 1016, note 1). Matthew 13:30 reads: "*First* gather up the tares. . . .

The Apostle Paul tells us that "to live is Christ, and to die is gain" (Philippians 1:21). He explains that "to live in the flesh" will mean "fruitful labor" to him for the sake of the church (v. 22). He finds himself in a dilemma, however. He has the desire "to depart and be with Christ, for that is very much better; *yet to remain on in the flesh is more necessary for your sake*" (v. 24). His desire is to "remain and continue" with them for their "progress and joy in the faith" (v. 25).

The Bible is very clear about the advance of Christ's kingdom. All authority "in heaven and in *earth*" has been given to Jesus (Matthew 28:18). His kingdom is represented by the stone that is cut without hands that becomes a mountain that fills the whole earth (Daniel 2:34, 44-45). This follows immediately after the destruction of the fourth kingdom, Rome. In order for the dispensational eschatological scheme to work, a revived Roman empire, cut off from Jesus' day by at least two thousand years, must be reconstituted. There's always a revived kingdom, a rebuilt temple, a two-thousand-year parenthesis,[19] or a kingdom-postponement theory to ensure that their end-time system will not fall apart under close scrutiny.

---

19. In my estimation, the parenthesis doctrine, that is, a two thousand year division between the 69th and 70th week described in Daniel 9:24-27 is one of the weakest elements in the dispensational system. There is certainly *nothing* in the text that hints at such a breaking point between the 69th and 70th weeks. There is nothing in the New Testament that harkens back to the passage in Daniel that would allow an interpreter to inject a parenthesis. The postponed kingdom is an inference that grows out of other dispensational doctrines and is then mistakenly read into the text.

Some dispensationalists might want to point to the forty year postponement at Kadesh-barnea where the land promise was postponed because of disobedience, and a forty year wilderness parenthesis was injected, as support for their parenthesis theory (Numbers 13:26-35). But this example proves the point that what the dispensational system asserts in Daniel 9:24-27 is unnatural. First, the Bible tells us about the forty year wilderness wandering. We know that it's there. There's a lengthy description of it. In fact, much of Israel's post-exodus history is recounted in this forty year period. Second, it's for *forty years*, not two thousand years. Third, there is a forty year period in the New Testament that is a more exact parallel to the circumstances described in Numbers 13: God postponed His judgment upon apostate, Messiah-rejecting Israel until A.D. 70, forty years after Jesus gave His Olivet Discourse describing the judgment (Matthew 22:32-24:34).

Clearly, the Bible tells us that "the kingdom of God has come upon" us (Matthew 12:28). How do we know this? Because Jesus cast out demons. "But if I cast out demons by the finger of God, the *kingdom of God has come upon you*" (Luke 11:20). Both John the Baptist and Jesus tell us that the "kingdom of God is at hand" (Matthew 3:2; 4:17; 10:7; Mark 1:15).[20]

Conclusion

The dispensational premillennialist claims that a new temple must be rebuilt. But the Bible tells us that "something greater than the temple is here" (Matthew 12:6). The dispensational premillennialist maintains that an earthly throne must be established before there can be an earthly manifestation of God's kingdom, and yet the Bible informs us that "something greater than Solomon is here" (Matthew 12:42). The dispensational premillennialist asserts that the nations will not be converted and discipled before Jesus returns, yet Scripture assures us that "something greater than Jonah is here" (Matthew 12:41).[21] His name is Jesus. He is here. He promised to be with us always, "even to the end of the age" (Matthew 28:20).

The dispensational premillennialist insists that sacrifices must be made during the earthly millennium as a memorial to Jesus. According to Ezekiel 43:19, the Levitical priests are to be given "a young bull for a *sin offering*." J. Dwight Pentecost tells us that these sacrifices "*will be memorial* in character"[22] and that "the millennial sacrifices *will have no relation to the question of expiation.*"[23] But Ezekiel doesn't say that these sacrifices will be a memorial; these are *sin offerings* for atonement. Why not have blood sacrifices as memorials today? The Apostle Paul was horrified that some "Judaizers"

---

20. Matthew 26:18, 45-46; John 2:13; 7:2; Mark 14:42; 2 Timothy 4:6; 1 Peter 4:7; 2 Thessalonians 2:2; Philippians 4:5; Revelation 1:3; 22:10.

21. It was Jonah's preaching that led to the conversion of the Ninevites, who were Gentiles and thus representatives of the nations.

22. J. Dwight Pentecost, *Things to Come: A Study in Biblical Eschatology* (Grand Rapids, MI: Zondervan, [1958] 1964), p. 525.

23. *Ibid.*, p. 524.

wanted to saddle the church with the bloody rite of circumcision. What would he think of the revival of the entire sacrificial system instituted while Jesus is in the midst of His people? James H. Snowden writes:

> But this [memorial] interpretation cannot be allowed on pre-millenarian principles, because the command given to the priests in Ezekiel's temple is positive that "the priests" shall be given "a young bullock for a sin-offering. And thou shalt take of the blood thereof, and put on the four horns of it, and on the four corners of the ledge, an upon the border roundabout; thus shalt thou cleanse it and make atonement for it" (Ezekiel 43:19-20).[24]

In the original edition of his reference Bible, Scofield has the following footnote on Ezekiel 43:19: "Doubtless these offerings will be memorial, looking back to the cross, as the offerings under the old covenant were anticipatory, looking forward to the cross. In neither case have animal sacrifices power to put away sin (Heb. 10:4; Rom. 3:25)."[25]

The New Scofield Reference Bible attempts to clarify the issue regarding Ezekiel 43, but to no avail:

> A problem is posed by this paragraph (vv. 19-27). Since the N.T. clearly teaches that animal sacrifices do not in themselves cleanse away sin (Heb. 10:4) and that the one sacrifice of the Lord Jesus Christ that was made at Calvary completely provides for such expiation (cp. Heb. 9:12, 26., 28; 10:10, 14), how can there be a fulfillment of such a prophecy? Two answers have been suggested: (1) Such sacrifices, if actually offered, will be memorial in character. They will, according to this view, look back to our Lord's work on the cross, as the offerings of the old covenant anticipated His sacrifice. They would, of course, have no expiatory value. And (2) *the reference to sacrifices is not to be taken literally,* in view of the putting away of such offerings, but is rather to be re-

---

24. James H. Snowden, *The Coming of the Lord: Will it be Premillennial?* (New York: The Macmillan Company, 1919), pp. 216-17.
25. First edition, *Scofield Reference Bible,* p. 890.

garded as a presentation of the worship of redeemed Israel, in her own land and in the millennial Temple, using the terms with which the Jews were familiar in Ezekiel's day" (p. 888).[26]

The crucified, resurrected, and glorified Christ will not be enough during the millennium. Our eyes are to be diverted from the living and reigning Christ to bloody rituals that God's Word tells us are simply "shadows" (Hebrews 10:1). How could these "shadows" be necessary when the "substance"—even Christ—is physically present?! Animal sacrifices will be reestablished "looking back to the cross." Why not look up to the resurrected and glorified Christ, as Stephen did (Acts 7:55-56).

Dave Hunt even goes beyond traditional dispensational premillennialism by maintaining that the millennium is not even the kingdom of God. Even a physically present Christ cannot accomplish an earthly manifestation of the kingdom of God! According to Dave Hunt, not even Jesus is powerful or persuasive enough to thwart the will of man. Let me offer the following unbelievable quotation as evidence of his position:

> In fact, dominion—taking dominion and setting up the kingdom of Christ—is an *impossibility*, even for God. The millennial reign of Christ, far from being the kingdom, is actually the final proof of the incorrigible nature of the human heart, because Christ Himself can't do what these people say they are going to do.[27]

---

26. This is another instance where the hermeneutic methodology of dispensationalism falls apart. "These words convey a far-reaching concession on the part of dispensationalists. If the sacrifices are not to be taken literally, why should we take the temple literally? It would seem that the dispensational principle of the literal interpretation of Old Testament prophecy is here abandoned, and that a crucial foundation stone for the entire dispensational system has here been set aside!" Anthony A. Hoekema, *The Bible and the Future* (Grand Rapids, MI: Eerdmans, 1979), p. 204.

27. A taped interview with Peter Lalonde and Dave Hunt, "Dominion and the Cross," Tape #2 of *Dominion: The Word and New World Order*, distributed by the *Omega-Letter*, Ontario, Canada, 1987. There is a similar statement in Dave Hunt, *Beyond Seduction: A Return to Biblical Christianity* (Eugene, OR: Harvest House, 1987), p. 250. For a more extensive evaluation of Hunt's thesis, see DeMar and Leithart, *Reduction of Christianity, p. 157.*

But doesn't the Bible say that "with God all things are possible"? (Matthew 19:26). Doesn't the New Testament picture Christ as at the right hand of God Almighty ruling until His enemies become a footstool? (Acts 2:34-35; Romans 8:34; 1 Corinthians 15:24-25; Hebrews 1:13; 10:13). Doesn't Scripture tell us that our "God is in the heavens; He does whatever He pleases"? (Psalm 115:3). Should we excise Isaiah 46:9-10 and Daniel 2:20 and 4:34 from our Bibles?

The real issue, then, is not eschatology, but ethics, faithfulness, and the sovereignty of God. For Hunt's brand of dispensationalism, sinful man is powerful enough to frustrate God's own will, for Jesus could not take dominion even if He wanted to. Of course, as the Bible clearly shows, Jesus already has dominion: "Now to Him who is able to keep you from stumbling, and to make you stand in the presence of His glory blameless with great joy, to the only God our Savior, through Jesus Christ our Lord, be glory, majesty, *dominion and authority, before all time and now and forever.* Amen" (Jude 24-25).

Do we believe the Bible when it tells us that those who oppose Christ "will not make further progress," that their "folly will be obvious to all"? (2 Timothy 3:9). Dave Hunt says that these are people, who, like the two sorcerer high priests who opposed Moses and Aaron with magical powers, have limits on what they can do with their Satanic-inspired magical arts. Here is the definitive verse to destroy the entire dispensational system: Even when unbelieving men call on all the powers of hell, they cannot thwart the advance of Christ's kingdom. This is why Jesus tells us that "the gates of Hades" cannot stand against the advancing church of the Lord Jesus Christ (Matthew 16:18). The Bible promised the first-century Christians that God would "soon crush Satan" under their feet (Romans 16:20). Why is the church still waiting for it to happen instead of living in terms of its reality?

12

PUTTING ESCHATOLOGY INTO PERSPECTIVE

Eschatology is a fascinating topic. We all want to know about the future. But the Christian faith is more than a study of the timing of the rapture or the duration of the millennium. The Christian life is more than eschatology as it is narrowly defined in our day. This is why it is a mistake to base an evaluation of a theological system on a narrowly focussed doctrine like eschatology.

The debate over Christian Reconstruction is broader than a debate over disputed areas of eschatology. Unfortunately, Dave Hunt and Tommy Ice chose to make eschatology the deciding factor in determining the orthodoxy of professed Christians who hold to a millennial position that differs from what they believe the Bible teaches. Such an emphasis can only do harm to the body of Christ. If we are going to make millennial issues the center of doctrinal debate, then the church will be grievously and continually divided. Disagreements over millennial issues are centuries old. Dialogue and debate are the proper first steps in understanding where there are disagreements and why. Maintaining that a highly respected view of eschatology (postmillennialism) is heretical flies in the face of centuries of sound biblical exposition.[1] Postmillennialists could just as easily assert that dispensationalism is heretical because it's a variety of premillennialism, and premillennialism is held by some of the major cult groups. This approach would cut off all healthy debate.

---

1. See Gary DeMar and Peter J. Leithart, *The Reduction of Christianity: A Biblical Response to Dave Hunt* (Ft. Worth, TX: Dominion Press/Atlanta, GA: American Vision, 1988), pp. 1-43 for a discussion of eschatology as a test of orthodoxy.

This chapter is designed to put eschatology into perspective since the debate overemphasized the topic. Those who hear the debate tapes may come away wondering why Dr. North and I did not deal with all the numerous eschatological points raised by Hunt and Ice. The answer is simple: We came to debate Christian Reconstruction, of which eschatology is one part. A careful analysis of the debate will show that our presentation was balanced, since it covered the main distinctives of Christian Reconstruction, while Ice and Hunt overemphasized the single distinctive of postmillennialism.

The Eschatological Pillar in Dispensationalism

After reading a lot of dispensational literature, one begins to see that eschatology is the focal point of the system.[2] Dispensationalists claim that once a Christian gets the dispensational brand of eschatology straight, every other doctrine falls in line. Now, all of Scripture can and should be seen through eschatological eyes. If you begin with an incorrect eschatology, then all other doctrines will be distorted. But dispensationalists equate eschatology with the millennial issue, ignoring the broader meaning of eschatology common among most evangelical theologians.

Some dispensationalists believe that eschatology should be placed on an equal par with doctrines that traditionally have been considered "tests of orthodoxy": an inerrant and infallible Bible, the deity of Christ, the Trinity, the virgin birth, the substitutionary atonement, justification by grace through faith alone, the bodily resurrection of Jesus, a literal heaven and hell, the return of Jesus, a final judgment, etc., each of which is tenaciously held by Reconstructionists. John F. Walvoord, a noted dispensationalist, writes that millennialism is "of comparable importance to the

---

2. In one sense this statement is true. All of life should be evaluated in terms of what happened or will happen as specified by biblical predictions. The dispensationalist, however, sees most of these predictive events as still future. The postmillennialist looks back to their fulfillment. He takes comfort and assurance in their fulfillment. The focus of eschatology for the dispensationalist is the rapture and the earthly millennium. For him, these are the central events of history. The postmillennialist sees the cross, resurrection, and ascension as the center of history.

doctrines of verbal inspiration, the deity of Christ, substitutionary atonement, and bodily resurrection."[3]

Of course, all biblical doctrines are important. In fact, as I've already noted, all biblical doctrines can be studied in the light of eschatology, but can we say that a particular view of the millennium is comparable to the study of verbal inspiration, the deity of Christ, the substitutionary atonement, and the bodily resurrection — especially since there are so many divergent views among solidly orthodox Christians? While we will study this more fully in the next chapter, it's curious that none of the church's earliest creeds made the millennial issue a test of orthodoxy. Louis Berkhof writes that up to the present time "the doctrine of the millennium has never yet been embodied in a single confession, and therefore cannot be regarded as a dogma of the Church."[4] A number of dispensational Bible schools and seminaries, however, have made adherence to a particular millennial position a requirement of graduation.

A Word of Caution

Revelation 20 is the only chapter in the Bible that speaks of a thousand year reign of Christ or "millennium." This thousand year reign is mentioned in this single chapter of this one book of Scripture, and its meaning is not crystal clear.[5] Moreover, the

---

3. John F. Walvoord, *The Millennial Kingdom* (Findlay, OH: Dunham Publishing Co., 1959), p. 16.

4. Louis Berkhof, *The History of Christian Doctrines* (London: The Banner of Truth Trust, [1937] 1969), p. 264.

5. C. H. Spurgeon, in his very worthwhile and informative book *Commenting and Commentaries*, writes the following introductory section on Revelation:

> The works upon REVELATION are so extremely numerous (Darling's list contains 52 columns), and the views entertained are so many, so different, and so speculative, that after completing our List we resolved not to occupy our space with it, but merely to mention a few works of repute. (London: The Banner of Truth Trust, [1876] 1969), p. 198

This was written over one hundred years ago. Consider how large that list would be today. Spurgeon goes on to enumerate "a fourfold manner of apprehending the Apocalyptic Prophecy": Preterists, Continuists, Simple Futurists, and Extreme Futurists. No single position is designated orthodox or heretical.

millennium has been a point of contention for centuries. Some of the greatest Bible scholars have avoided writing commentaries on the Book of Revelation because of its seeming obscurity.[6] Ken Gentry writes:[7]

> In order to illustrate the need for caution and to hold rein upon the interpretive imagination—for so much written on Revelation is just that—it may serve well to list observations from a variety of Revelation's numerous interpreters on the book's formidability. After all, as Reuss observed, "ideas of the Apocalypse are so widely different that a summary notice of the exegetical literature, mingling all together would be inexpedient."[8]

Although he never wrote a commentary on Revelation,[9] that master theologian and exegete Benjamin B. Warfield proffered the following observation regarding the book: "The boldness of its symbolism makes it the most difficult book of the Bible: it has always been the most variously understood, the most arbitrarily interpreted, the most exegetically tortured."[10] Milton Terry in his 1911 classic, *Biblical Hermeneutics* (which is still widely employed in seminaries today), noted that "no portion of the Holy Scripture has been the subject of so much controversy and of so many varying interpretations as the Apocalypse of John."[11] Eminent church historian Philip Schaff cautioned that "no book has been more misunderstood and abused; none calls for greater modesty and reserve in interpretation."[12]

---

6. John Calvin and Martin Luther are noteworthy examples.

7. Kenneth L. Gentry, Jr., "The Date of Revelation: An Exegetical and Historical Argument for a Pre-A.D. 70 Composition" (Ph.D. diss., Whitefield Theological Seminary, 1987), Part I, pp. 15-16. This work is forthcoming from the Institute for Christian Economics in late 1988. Footnotes 8-12 below are from Gentry's text.

8. Eduard Wilhelm Eugen Reuss, *History of the Sacred Scriptures of the New Testament* (Edinburgh: T & T Clark, 1884), p. 155.

9. He did write several important theological treatises on Revelation studies, such as his entry under "Revelation" in Philip Schaff, ed., *A Religious Encyclopedia: Or Dictionary of Biblical, Historical, Doctrinal, and Practical Theology* (New York: Funk and Wagnalls, 1883), vol. 3; his "The Apocalypse" (1886); "The Millennium and the Apocalypse" (1904); etc.

10. Benjamin B. Warfield, "Revelation" in *Religious Encyclopedia*, vol. 3, p. 2034.

11. Milton S. Terry, *Biblical Hermeneutics* (Grand Rapids, MI: Zondervan, [1893] 1974), p. 466.

12. Philip Schaff, *History of the Christian Church*, 8 vols. (Grand Rapids, MI: Eerdmans, [1910] 1979), vol. 1, p. 826.

But today we find that a single interpretation of the Book of Revelation is being used as a test of orthodoxy. This can only do damage to the already divided body of Christ. And it forces new converts to tackle a difficult area of theology when they have not had their "senses trained to discern good and evil" on the more basic doctrines of the Christian faith (Hebrews 5:14). There are many more clear and crucial doctrines that a young Christian should contemplate before he begins to study eschatology. As David Chilton has observed:

> Many rush from their first profession of faith to the last book in the Bible, treating it as little more than a book of hallucinations, hastily disdaining a sober-minded attempt to allow the Bible to interpret itself—and finding, ultimately, only a reflection of their own prejudices.[13]

The term "eschatology" means "study of the last things." It also should be among the last things studied by young Christians. And yet, we find that eschatology is usually a new convert's introduction to the Christian faith. The impending "rapture" is the hook to get people to come to Christ. There's more concern about "prophetic events" than holy living. When the world seems to be collapsing, all too many Christians are turning to Scripture to calculate how these events fit into the timetable of the end of the world. It seems that people will fill an auditorium more readily to hear about the Anti-Christ than about Jesus Christ. This is not the Bible's emphasis.

Cultic Overtones

Earthquakes, wars and rumors of wars, and false messiahs always seem to raise interest in the study of eschatology. Unfortunately, few Christians understand that these "signs" occurred prior to the destruction of Jerusalem in A.D. 70. They have nothing to do with the "last days" of the twentieth century or any future century. And yet, generation after generation of prophetic specu-

---

13. David Chilton, *Paradise Restored: A Biblical Theology of Dominion* (Ft. Worth, TX: Dominion Press, [1985] 1987), p. 153.

lators continue to use these prophecies to lead more and more people into inaction. Some have taken the end-times scenario altogether too seriously and sold their possessions. There is often a "cultish" feature among those obsessed with the rapture and the supposed threatening end of the world. This is not to minimize the evil and hardships we are facing. Christians should seek solutions, not a timetable for lift-off.

Some cults entice prospective members by spinning a scenario that includes the approaching end of the world and the return of Christ in judgment. The Jehovah's Witnesses have made this a part of their "evangelistic" strategy since 1914. Converts are attracted to cults that maintain that Jesus is coming back on a certain day, and that by joining with the bearers of the only true religion, they can avoid the impending judgment.[14] Here's an extreme example:

> The group known as "The Lighthouse Gospel Tract Foundation," led by Bill Maupin, was located in Tucson. He originally calculated that the Rapture would take place on June 28, 1981. Some members of the group quit their jobs and/or sold their houses. When that date passed, Maupin said that he had miscalculated by forty days, and predicted that the Rapture would take place on August 7, 1981. The Return of Christ is to occur May 14, 1988. Maupin calculated his dates on the basis of Daniel's seventy "weeks," and the founding of the State of Israel on May 15, 1948.[15]

---

14. In the July 1988 issue of *Charisma* magazine, an advertisement appeared with this headline: "88 Reasons Why the Rapture Could Take Place in the 3-day Period from September 11-13, 1988." It goes on to say: "At no time in the past or future will the Bible dates of Daniel, Ezekiel and Revelation fit except 1988-1995."

15. William Sanford LaSor, *The Truth About Armageddon: What the Bible Says About the End Times* (Grand Rapids, MI: Baker Book House, 1982), p. 103, note *a*.

Parents are constantly fighting this cultish dimension of eschatology. A group of parents from Delaware County, Pennsylvania, have watched their children move to South Carolina at the invitation of a self-styled evangelist in anticipation of "the end."

> They say the children, most in their 20s, have "been brainwashed into believing that the end of the world is at hand and are selling their possessions, often at cut-rate prices, to move to the evangelist's South Carolina farm." "Pa. Parents Fear Children Lost to Cult," *The Atlanta Journal/Constitution* (April 24, 1988), p. 10-A.

For a balanced treatment of what Christians should expect in terms of the "end times," the reader is encouraged to study DeMar and Leithart, *Reduction of Christianity*.

I want to make it clear that I do not believe that dispensationalism is a cult. But a *preoccupation* with an end times scenario is cultish when it leads the church to establish timetables that assure us as to the timing of the Lord's return and when it turns the church into a retreatist institution.

The Test of Orthodoxy

In order to be considered an "orthodox Christian," one has to believe in verbal inspiration, the deity of Christ, the substitutionary atonement, the bodily resurrection, and other doctrines of the biblical faith. But when we come to the millennial issue, we learn that Christians are categorized as holding four views of the nature and timing of the millennium: amillennialism, premillennialism,[16] dispensational premillennialism, and postmillennialism.

In the debate, Tommy Ice and Dave Hunt focused their attention on eschatology. For them, dispensational premillennialism is *the* litmus test for establishing the bounds of orthodoxy. This is one of dispensationalism's major flaws.[17] But the dispensationalist is

---

16. There is a great amount of disagreement within the premillennial camp over the timing of the rapture, an eschatological distinctive that separates historic premillennialists from dispensationalists (for the most part). Does the "rapture" occur before (pre), during (mid), or after (post) the "Great Tribulation"? See Gleason Archer, Jr., Paul D. Feinberg, Douglas J. Moo, and Richard R. Reiter, *The Rapture: Pre-, Mid-, or Post-Tribulational?* (Grand Rapids, MI: Zondervan/ Academie Books, 1984). If "moderation" and "a call for unity that allows for diversity and promotes toleration" on the timing of the rapture is promoted among premillennialists, then why can't the church do the same with millennial positions in general? (p. 44).

17. George Eldon Ladd, an historic premillennialist, in a response to Herman Hoyt's article on dispensationalism, makes the following observation:

Hoyt's essay reflects the major problem in the discussion of the millennium. Several times he contrasts nondispensational views with his own, which he labels "the biblical view" (pp. 69-70, 84). If he is correct, then the other views, including my own, are "unbiblical" or even heretical. This is the reason that over the years there has been little creative dialogue between dispensationalists and other schools of prophetic interpretation. George Eldon Ladd, "An Historic Premillennial Response," *The Meaning of the Millennium: Four Views*, ed. Robert G. Clouse (Downers Grove, IL: InterVarsity Press, 1977), p. 93.

stuck with such a conclusion since it follows from his basic premises: His view of interpreting the Bible (a "literal" hermeneutic),[18] the distinction between Israel and the church, an imminent pre-tribulational rapture followed by a seven-year tribulation, and a thousand year reign of Christ on the earth. Anyone who does not hold these fundamentals is not "rightly dividing the word of truth." How can anyone be considered "orthodox" if he does not interpret the Bible "literally"? How can anyone possibly be orthodox if he mixes the promises made to God's earthly people (physical Israel) with His heavenly people (the church)? How can anyone be orthodox if he denies the next great eschatological event: the secret pre-tribulational rapture of the church?

In fact, as this book will show, Dave Hunt has made the timing of the rapture *the* litmus test of orthodoxy. A denial of *his* timing of the rapture is the denial of orthodoxy. But even pre-tribulational

---

18. Actually, even the dispensationalist is not consistent in his "literal" hermeneutic. For example, Charles Ryrie, a noted dispensational scholar, has written of Revelation:

> How do we make sense out of all those beasts and thrones and horsemen and huge numbers like 200 million? Answer: Take it at face value. (Ryrie, *The Living End*, p. 37).

Later he gives an example of the usefulness of his "face value" hermeneutic in seeking the correct interpretation of Revelation 9:1-12 (the locusts from the abyss):

> John's description sounds very much like some kind of war machine or UFO. Demons have the ability to take different shapes, so it is quite possible that John is picturing a coming invasion of warlike UFOs. Until someone comes up with a satisfactory answer to the UFO question, this possibility should not be ruled out. (*Ibid.*, p. 45).

A literal interpretation would mandate that locusts would be locusts. Hal Lindsey makes the locusts "cobra helicopters."

> I have a Christian friend who was a Green Beret in Viet Nam. When he first read this chapter he said, "I know what those are. I've seen hundreds of them in Viet Nam. They're cobra helicopters!"
> That may just be conjecture, but it does give you something to think about! A Cobra helicopter does fit the composite description very well. They also make the sound of "many chariots." My friend believes that the means of torment will be a kind of nerve gas sprayed from its tail.
> Lindsey, *There's a New World Coming* (New York: Bantam Books, 1984), p. 124.

premillennialists (dispensationalists) do not insist on such a view. Paul D. Feinberg writes:

> The time of the Rapture is neither the most important nor the most unimportant point in Christian theology. For some the Rapture question is a bellwether; its surrender marks the first step on the proverbial slippery slope that leads one to the rocks of liberalism. But such is neither logically or actually the case. When one considers the whole spectrum of Christian theology, eschatology is only a small part of it. Moreover, the Rapture question constitutes only a small segment of eschatology.[19]

Matthew 24:1-34 and Revelation 20 support the edifice of the dispensational system. But as we will see, Matthew 24:1-34 had its fulfillment in A.D. 70 with the destruction of Jerusalem. George Eldon Ladd, a premillennialist, writes that the "strongest objection to millennialism is that this truth is found in only one passage of Scripture — Revelation 20. Non-millenarians appeal to the argument of analogy, that difficult passages must be interpreted by clear passages. It is a fact that most of the New Testament writings say nothing about a millennium."[20] This is a weighty argument. Why is so much of the church preoccupied with a doctrine that most of the New Testament does not even discuss?[21]

A Different Emphasis

Historically, the church has never made eschatology — that is, a particular millennial position — a test of orthodoxy. Christian Reconstructionists, as heirs of the Reformation, put the emphasis where the Bible puts it: The sovereignty of God, justification by grace through faith alone, and keeping the commandments of God out of love for God (John 14:15; cf. James 2:14-26).

---

19. Archer, et al., *The Rapture*, p. 47.
20. George Eldon Ladd, "Historic Premillennialism," in *Meaning of the Millennium*, p. 38.
21. William Masselink, *Why Thousand Years?, or Will the Second Coming be Pre-Millennial?* (Grand Rapids, MI: Eerdmans, 1930), pp. 196-208.

Our theology flows out of our view of God. God, rather than His plan for the last few years of history, is most basic to our theology. If God is not sovereign, then either man or the devil is sovereign. An individual's view of sovereignty has tremendous ramifications for eschatology and every facet of theology. Notice how Dave Hunt's view of God's sovereignty shapes his eschatology:

> In fact, dominion — taking dominion and setting up the kingdom of Christ — is an *impossibility*, even for God. The millennial reign of Christ, far from being the kingdom, is actually the final proof of the incorrigible nature of the human heart, because Christ Himself can't do what these people say they are going to do.[22]

The reason that postmillennialism is an impossibility for Dave Hunt is that he apparently believes that there is a limitation in *God*. Hunt implicitly denies the sovereignty of God, and his eschatology is affected. His method of interpretation is shaped by his understanding of God's sovereignty.

It's ironic that Dave Hunt rightly criticizes some in the "Positive Confession" movement for teaching that Christians become or are "little gods." And yet he seems to teach a "little *God*" theology. Hunt's understanding of God reminds me of the book by J. B. Phillips, *Your God is Too Small*.[23] For many Christians, God is a "Grand Old Man" and Jesus is simply "Meek and Mild." We teach our children to sing the following inappropriate verse, and too often we grow up never maturing beyond its sugary sentimentality:

> Gentle Jesus, meek and mild,
> Look upon a little child.

We see Jesus meek and mild while in His humiliation on earth. He is never seen as such elsewhere in the New Testament

---

22. From a taped interview with Peter Lalonde and Dave Hunt, "Dominion and the Cross," Tape #2 of *Dominion: The Word and New World Order*, distributed by the *Omega-Letter*, Ontario, Canada, 1987. There is a similar quotation in Dave Hunt, *Beyond Seduction: A Return to Biblical Christianity* (Eugene, OR: Harvest House, 1987), p. 250. For a more extensive evaluation of Hunt's thesis, see DeMar and Leithart, *Reduction of Christianity*, p. 157.

23. New York: Macmillan, 1960.

after "all authority" was given to Him. In our day of impotent Christianity, with God, not all things are possible. Hunt's view of God is not much different from Rabbi Harold Kushner's conception of a limited God. Kushner claims that "God would like people to get what they deserve in life, but he cannot always arrange it."[24] According to the Rabbi, "there are some things God does not control."[25] For Dave Hunt, there are some things that God just can't pull off.

If God says that "the earth will be full of the knowledge of the LORD as the waters cover the sea" (Isaiah 11:9), then this will happen, in spite of the giants that might be present in the land at this particular period in history (Numbers 13:30-33). Just as the ten spies had no faith in the sovereignty of God to destroy their enemies, so the Dave Hunts and Tommy Ices shrink back in terror at the "sovereignty" of Satan and the evil of men in the earth. May God deliver us from wandering in this present "wilderness" for a few generations until His church matures enough to conquer the lost with the penetrating sword of the gospel message (Hebrews 4:12-13).[26]

Conclusion

The church is at a critical point in history. In fact, history turns on the action or inaction of the church, subject, of course, to God's sovereign action in history. The degeneration of culture is laid at the feet of the people of God. Who expects humanism to bring revival? So then, why are Christians surprised when they see personal and societal decay all around them? The church, for the most part, has given the world over to those who despise Christ. Dave Hunt and Tommy Ice seem to believe that this is the

---

24. Harold S. Kushner, *When Bad Things Happen to Good People* (New York: Schocken, 1981), p. 43.

25. *Ibid.*, p. 45.

26. It's unfortunate that much of what the lost hear about Christ comes through slick television formats by men and women who present a warped view of the gospel. It's equally horrifying when the world identifies much of Christianity with superstar television evangelists. Moreover, for many non-Christians, Christianity is simply a religion of the future, while Socialism and Marxism are seen as "religions" of the present.

way it *should* be. Christian Reconstructionists say otherwise. Those opposed to Christ are usurpers who must hear the gospel message that comes from their Sovereign Lord and King. Is this deviant? The early church turned the world "upside down" (Acts 17:6). Should we do any less?

TOMMY ICE: A RESPONSE
Part I

Tommy Ice opened the debate with a discussion of the histori-cal roots of premillennialism and a brief exposition of Matthew 24:1-34. At no time did he define the distinctives of Christian Re-construction.[1] He left the impression that Christian Reconstruc-tion hinges on a particular interpretation of Matthew 24:1-34. But there are numerous Reconstructionists who are premillennial and who hold to Ice's view of Matthew 24:1-34.[2] John Eidsmoe, a dis-pensational premillennialist, considers himself a Reconstruction-ist,[3] as does David Schnittger.[4] We could describe these men and others like them as "operating" Reconstructionists — since they be-lieve that Christians do have an obligation to work for change in this world before Jesus returns — while not adopting all of the Reconstructionist distinctives.[5]

---

1. For a definition of terms see Gary DeMar and Peter Leithart, *The Reduction of Christianity: A Biblical Response to Dave Hunt* (Ft. Worth, TX: Dominion Press/ Atlanta, GA: American Vision, 1988), pp. 19-37.

2. Douglas Kelly, ed., *The Journal of Christian Reconstruction: Symposium on Chris-tian Reconstruction in the Western World Today* (Special Double Issue, 1982-83), Vol. IX, Nos. 1&2.

3. John Eidsmoe, "Can a Premillennialist be a Reconstructionist? Yes. If He Reads Luther." Paper presented at Convention of American Political Science Association, Washington, D.C., August 29, 1986. See Eidsmoe, *Christianity and the Constitution* (Grand Rapids, MI: Baker Book House, 1987), page 19, note 5 and page 31, note 6.

4. David Schnittger, *Christian Reconstruction from a Pretribulational Perspective* (Southwest Radio Church, Box 1144, Oklahoma City, Oklahoma, 1986). See DeMar and Leithart, *Reduction of Christianity*, pp. xxxv, 293-94, 338-41.

5. For these distinctives see *ibid.*, pp. 30-37, 68-93.

God is more interested in faithfulness to His commandments than the speculative belief in the nearness of the rapture. Moreover, there are numerous non-Reconstructionist Bible scholars who believe that Matthew 24:1-34 should be interpreted in terms of an A.D. 70 fulfillment.[6] Loraine Boettner, whose book on the millennium revived classical postmillennialism,[7] does not consider himself a Christian Reconstructionist. Boettner writes:

> No requirements from the Old Covenant are binding on the Christian except the moral principles that are repeated in the New Covenant. The Old Testament is our *history* book. It is *not* our *law book*.[8]

So then, an attack on postmillennialism does very little to damage the Reconstructionist's position. Moreover, an attack on postmillennialism and the present reality of God's kingdom advancing in the world is an attack on a broader theological movement that has no ties with Christian Reconstruction.[9]

Dave Hunt implies in his May 1988 *CIB Bulletin* that, at the debate, Gary North and I could not defend postmillennialism exegetically. This is far from the truth. We made our presentations based on the agreed upon debate topic which includes a number

---

6. J. Marcellus Kik, *An Eschatology of Victory* (Nutley, NJ: Presbyterian and Reformed, 1975); T. Boersma, *Is the Bible a Jigsaw Puzzle?: An Evaluation of Hal Lindsey's Writings* (Ontario, Canada: Paideia Press, 1978), pp. 76-90; R. Bradley Jones, *The Great Tribulation* (Grand Rapids, MI: Baker Book House, 1980), pp. 63-82; Ralph Woodrow, *Great Prophecies of the Bible* (Riverside, CA: Ralph Woodrow Evangelistic Association, 1971), pp. 52-100; Thomas Newton, *Dissertations on the Prophecies* (London: J. F. Dove, 1754), pp. 324-76. William R. Kimball, *What the Bible Says About the Great Tribulation* (Phillipsburg, NJ: Presbyterian and Reformed, [1983] 1984); Cf. R. T. France, *Jesus and the Old Testament: His Application of Old Testament Passages to Himself and His Mission* (Grand Rapids, MI: Baker [1971] 1982), pp. 227-239.

7. Loraine Boettner, *The Millennium* (rev. ed.; Phillipsburg, NJ: Presbyterian and Reformed, [1957] 1984).

8. Loraine Boettner, "A Postmillennial Response to Dispensational Premillennialism," in Robert G. Clouse, ed., *The Meaning of the Millennium: Four Views* (Downers Grove, IL: InterVarsity Press, 1977), p. 98.

9. Walter J. Chantry, *God's Righteous Kingdom: The Law's Connection with the Gospel* (Edinburgh: The Banner of Truth Trust, 1980).

of Reconstructionist distinctives: Biblical law, the sovereignty of God in salvation, presuppositional apologetics, the dominion mandate, covenant theology, *and* postmillennialism.[10] Ice and Hunt decided to debate a single pillar of Christian Reconstruction: Postmillennialism.[11] Since many people listening to the debate will get the impression that postmillennialism is *the* issue, I've decided to answer Tommy Ice and Dave Hunt point by point on the issue of postmillennialism.

This chapter will examine the eschatological view presented by Tommy Ice, specifically his contentions that postmillennialism cannot be supported by Scripture and that there is no hint of a preterist[12] view of prophecy among the early church fathers. Moreover, I shall explicate several topics related to eschatology, the foremost being the identification of historical premillennialism with modern-day dispensionalism. In Part II of my response to Tommy Ice, I shall address the prophetic time frame of Matthew 24:1-34, the identification of the abomination of desolation, the man of sin, and a number of related eschatological issues.

---

10. For a definition of a number of these terms, see DeMar and Leithart, *Reduction of Christianity*, pp. 19-43; and Robert M. Bowman, Jr., "The New Puritanism: A Preliminary Assessment of Reconstructionism," *Christian Research Journal* (Winter/Spring 1988), pp. 23-27.

11. Dave Hunt and Tommy Ice knew the parameters that defined Christian Reconstruction. *The Reduction of Christianity* spelled them out. This is why it was inexcusable to weight the debate so heavily on the side of eschatology.

12. The *preterist* view of prophecy can be defined in at least two ways: *First*, an interpretation of prophecy, and particularly the book of Revelation, which holds that the events depicted had already taken place. This definition of *preterist* would deny predictive prophecy. Postmillennialists are not *preterists* in this sense. *Second*, an interpretation of prophecy, and particularly the book of Revelation, that describes the present and near-future struggles of the Christian church and the victory of Christ over His enemies. "This approach has its strength in the fact that when the Revelation is thus understood, it becomes immediately and thoroughly relevant to the life and struggle of the early church." Everett F. Harrison, *Introduction to the New Testament* (Grand Rapids, MI: Eerdmans, 1982), p. 463. The second view of *preterist*, held by many postmillennialists, maintains the predictive element in prophecy. The use of preterist in this book simply means an A.D. 70 fulfillment of much of New Testament prophecy.

1. Postmillennialism and Scripture

Tommy Ice opened the debate by making this charge against postmillennialism: "The postmillennial position, as it is advocated by the reconstructionist movement, really doesn't have any passages that teach it." This assertion hinges on where in eschatological time you put the thousand years of Revelation 20. Some amillennialists (many prefer to be called "realized millennialists")[13] believe that the great millennial blessings embrace the entire church age. Those prophecies that are not fulfilled in the church age are fulfilled during the establishment of the "new heavens and new earth."[14] So then, Tommy Ice's charge is equally applicable to the amillennialist since the "millennium" of Revelation 20 is a *present* reality for him.

The "Thousand Years" in Postmillennialism

Postmillennialists assert that the millennial blessings refer *primarily* to a future era, although many are progressively manifested during the gospel or church age. Some believe that the thousand years of Revelation 20 and the millennial blessings set forth in Scripture are yet future, to be fulfilled in some type of "golden age." This seems to be the view of the Westminster Confession of Faith and other confessions of the seventeenth century.[15]

---

13. Jay E. Adams, *The Time is at Hand* (Nutley, NJ: Presbyterian and Reformed, 1970), pp. 7-11; Anthony A. Hoekema, "Amillennialism," in Robert G. Clouse, ed., *The Meaning of the Millennium: Four Views* (Downers Grove, IL: Inter-Varsity Press, 1977) pp. 155-56; and Hoekema, *The Bible and the Future* (Grand Rapids, MI: Eerdmans, 1979), pp. 173-74.

14. For a rehearsal of the major tenets of amillennialism, see the following books: Adams, *The Time is at Hand*; Everett I. Carver, *When Jesus Comes Again* (Phillipsburg, NJ: Presbyterian and Reformed, 1979); Hoekema, *The Bible and the Future*; William E. Cox, *Amillennialism Today* (Nutley, NJ: Presbyterian and Reformed, 1966); William Hendriksen, *The Bible on the Life Hereafter* (Grand Rapids, MI: Baker Book House, 1959); Hendriksen, *More than Conquerors: An Interpretation of the Book of Revelation* (Grand Rapids, MI: Baker Book House, [1940] 1982).

15. "As the Lord is in care and love towards his Church, hath in his infinite wise providence exercised it with great variety in all ages, for the good of them that love him, and his own glory; so, according to his promise, we expect that in

Other postmillennialists hold a view of the thousand years similar to the interpretation advocated by amillennialists. The "thousand years" is thought to be figurative of a "very long period of time," since "thousand" is often used in Scripture to mean more than a thousand (Exodus 20:6; Deuteronomy 1:11; 7:9; 32:30; Joshua 23:10; Judges 15:15; Psalm 50:10; 90:4; 91:7; 105:8; Ecclesiastes 6:6; Isaiah 30:17; 60:22; 2 Peter 3:8). This view is not inconsistent with the way numbers are used in the Book of Revelation or the Bible in general.[16]

We know that the thousand years began with the "binding of Satan." Jesus said, "How can anyone enter the strong man's house and carry off his property, unless he first *binds* the strong man? And then he will plunder his house" (Matthew 12:29). Jesus bound the strong man, Satan, through His sinless life, propitiatory death, resurrection, ascension, and exaltation. He overpowered Satan, taking from him all his armor on which he had relied, and distributed his plunder (Luke 11:22). This is why the demons were "subject to" the disciples and why Jesus could say, "And I was watching Satan fall from heaven like lightning" (Luke 10:18). Paul gives a very descriptive picture of the present status of Satan in the world: "God will *soon* crush Satan under *your* feet" (Romans 16:20). The assumption is that Satan has already been crushed under Jesus' feet. Notice that this crushing is to happen "soon,"

---

the latter days, Antichrist being destroyed, the Jews called, and the adversaries of the Kingdom of his dear Son broken, the Churches of Christ being enlarged and edified through a free and plentiful communication of light and grace, shall enjoy in this world a more quiet, peaceable, and glorious condition than they have enjoyed." *The Savoy Declaration of Faith and Order* (1658), "Of the Church," Chapter XXVI, paragraph V. Philip Schaff, *The Creeds of Christendom: With History and Critical Notes*, 3 vols. (6th rev. ed.; Grand Raids, MI: Baker Book House, [1931] 1983), vol. 3, p. 723.

16. "As we have found the number ten to symbolize the general idea of *fullness, totality, completeness*, so not improbably the number one thousand may stand as the symbolic number of manifold fullness, the rounded aeon of Messianic triumph . . . , during which he shall abolish all rule and all authority and power, and put all his enemies under his feet (1 Cor. xv, 24, 25), and bring in the fullness . . . of both Jews and Gentiles (Rom. xi, 12, 25)." Milton S. Terry, *Biblical Hermeneutics: A Treatise on the Interpretation of the Old and New Testaments* (Grand Rapids, MI: Zondervan, [1883] 1909), p. 390.

that is, soon after Paul wrote these prophetic words. If Satan is yet to be crushed under *our* feet, then "soon" ceases to mean anything. Where, then, is the literalism of dispensationalism when "soon" means later, much later?

Millennial Blessings

If the millennial blessings are still future, as in premillennialism, then the postmillennial position is wrong. Then there would be no verses to support it. But consider this argument: The premillennialist places certain "millennial" blessings in a future earthly thousand year period. If it can be demonstrated that these so-called premillennial blessings are actually present now, in the "church age," then postmillennialism does have verses to support it. The same verses, in fact, that the premillennialist uses, the postmillennialist uses. *It's a question of timing!*

In 1652 John Owen preached before the English House of Commons describing "The Advantage of the Kingdom of Christ in the Shaking of the Kingdoms of the World." "Therein he explained the kingdom of God as spiritual control of Christians resulting in obedient conformity to the word of Christ. The antichristian kingdoms being shaken will, according to Owen, be replaced with the triumph of Christ's reign, signalized by the conversion of the Jews. Certain things will characterize this time."[17]

> That God in his appointed time will bring forth the kingdom of the Lord Christ unto more glory and power than in former days, I presume you are persuaded. Whatever will be more, these six things are clearly promised:
> 1. *Fullness of peace* unto the gospel and the professors thereof, Isa. 11.6,7, 54.13, 33.20,21; Rev. 21.15
> 2. *Purity and beauty of ordinances* and gospel worship, Rev. 11.2, 21.3. The tabernacle was wholly made by appointment, Mal. 3.3,4; Zech. 14.16; Rev. 21.27; Zech. 14.20; Isa. 35.

---

17. Greg L. Bahnsen, "The *Prima Facie* Acceptability of Postmillennialism," *The Journal of Christian Reconstruction: Symposium on the Millennium*, ed. Gary North, Vol. III, No. 2, (Winter 1976-77), p. 84.

3. *Multitudes of converts*, many persons, yea, nations, Isa. 60.7,8, 66.8, 49.18-22; Rev. 7.9

4. *The full casting out and rejecting of all will-worship*, and their attendant abominations, Rev. 11.2

5. *Professed subjection of the nations* throughout the whole world unto the Lord Christ, Dan. 2.44, 7.26,27; Isa. 60.6-9; — the kingdoms become the kingdoms of our Lord and his Christ (Rev. 11.15), amongst whom his appearance shall be so glorious, that David himself shall be said to reign

6. *A most glorious and dreadful breaking of all that rise in opposition unto him*, Isa. 60.12 — never such desolations, Rev. 16.17-19.[18]

These blessings are not reserved for a yet future thousand-year earthly reign of Christ. There is an unfolding of "more glory" since the coronation of Christ, the proclamation of the gospel, and the outpouring of God's Holy Spirit on "all mankind" (Acts 2:17). Dispensational premillennialists relegate the promises outlined by Owen to a distant earthly millennium. But keep in mind that postmillennialists and dispensationalists *use the same verses to prove their point.* A postmillennialist has the same number of verses as the dispensationalist to "prove" his future earthly millennial kingdom.

A. A. Hodge, a prominent postmillennial scholar of the last century and the son of Charles Hodge, also a prominent postmillennialist, wrote the following description of the postmillennial position with attendant Scripture support:

> The Scriptures, both of the Old and New Testament, clearly reveal that the gospel is to exercise an influence over all branches of the human family, immeasurably more extensive and more thoroughly transforming than any it has ever realized in time past. This end is to be gradually attained through the spiritual presence of Christ in the ordinary dispensation of Providence, and ministrations of his church. — Matt. xiii. 31, 32; xxviii. 19, 20; Ps. ii. 7, 8; xxii. 27, 29; lxxii. 8-11; Is. ii. 2, 3; xi. 6-9; lx. 12; lxvi. 23; Dan. ii. 35, 44; Zech. ix. 10; xiv. 9; Rev. xi. 15.[19]

---

18. Quoted in Iain Murray, *The Puritan Hope: Revival and the Interpretation of Prophecy* (London: Banner of Truth Trust, 1971), p. 38.

19. A. A. Hodge, *Outlines of Theology* (London: The Banner of Truth Trust, [1860] 1972), p. 568.

Tommy Ice's assertion that the postmillennialist has no passages to support his millennial position is off the mark. Again, the issue is, Where in eschatological time do you fit the passages that speak of gospel prosperity?

2. Postmillennialism and History

Tommy Ice maintains that "there is absolutely *no one* in the early church that even gives a hint that they believe that the [events described in Matthew 24:1-34 and the Book of Revelation] were fulfilled in 70 A.D." J. Dwight Pentecost, from whom Tommy Ice seems to get his historical information on premillennialism and postmillennialism, is even stronger in his assertion that premillennialism was the only orthodox position of the early church. Let's look at the evidence.

The Ante-Nicene Fathers

The place to begin to evaluate the assertion of Ice and Pentecost (and the majority of premillennial scholars) that premillennialism was *the only view* of the early church would be to survey the writings of the Ante-Nicene Fathers.[20] Of course, this is beyond the scope of this book. Instead, I shall first deal with the obvious historical errors made by Ice in the debate. Second, I shall evaluate the prevailing but erroneous view that premillennialism was the adopted millennial position prior to the Council of Nicaea in A.D. 325, at least as it is articulated today. Third, I shall answer Ice's contention that the preterist interpretation of Matthew 24:1-34 was unknown prior to Nicea (fourth century).

Pentecost, Ice's historical source, has this to say about Justin Martyr's (c. 100-165) evaluation of non-premillennial views in the second century:

> Justin evidently recognized premillennialism as "the criterion of a perfect orthodoxy." In his Dialogue with Trypho, where he writes: "some who are called Christians but are godless, impious

---

20. Ante-Nicene has reference to the writings of the early church *prior* to the Council of Nicaea in A.D. 325.

heretics, teach doctrines that are in every way blasphemous, atheistical, and foolish," he shows he would include any who denied premillennialism in this category, since he included in it those that denied the resurrection, a companion doctrine.[21]

Unfortunately, Pentecost was quoting a secondary source and failed to check the original. Tommy Ice repeats his error. Just prior to the sentence that Pentecost quotes, Justin had written:

> I am not so miserable a fellow, Trypho, as to say one thing and think another. I admitted to you formerly, that I and many[22] others are of this opinion, and [believe] that such will take place, as you assuredly are aware; *but, on the other hand, I signified to you that many who belong to the pure and pious faith, and are true Christians, think other wise.*[23]

Tommy Ice and Pentecost overstate their case. In fact, there were some in the second century — Justin says "many" — who did not agree with Justin's eschatological perspective. Justin is charitable and wise enough to state that they too "belong to the pure and pious faith, and are true Christians."

The heretics that Justin describes are those "who say there is no resurrection of the dead."[24] Those who hold to a different millennial position are said to "belong to the pure and pious faith, and are true Christians." Those who deny the resurrection "are *called* Christians, but are godless, impious heretics."[25] It's obvious that Justin has two groups in mind: those who disagree on eschatology ("true Christians") and those who deny the resurrection ("*called* Christians, but are godless, impious heretics").

Charles Ryrie maintains that "Premillennialism is the historic

---

21. J. Dwight Pentecost, *Things to Come: A Study in Biblical Eschatology* (Grand Rapids, MI: Zondervan, [1958] 1974), p. 377.

22. Notice that he does not say "all."

23. Justin, "Dialogue with Trypho," chapter LXXX. In *Ante-Nicene Fathers*, 10 vols. (Grand Rapids, MI: Eerdmans, 1985), vol. 1, p. 239. Emphasis added.

24. *Idem.*

25. *Idem.*

faith of the Church."[26] But not all agree. Take, for example, a Master's Thesis presented to the faculty of the Department of Historical Theology of Dallas Theological Seminary, a dispensational premillennial school. The author writes:

> It is the conclusion of this thesis that Dr. Ryrie's statement is historically invalid within the chronological framework of this thesis. The reasons for this conclusion are as follows: 1). the writers/writings surveyed did not generally adopt a consistently applied literal interpretation; 2). they did not generally distinguish between the Church and Israel; 3). there is no evidence that they generally held to a dispensational view of revealed history; 4). although Papias and Justin Martyr did believe in a Millennial kingdom, the 1,000 years is the only basic similarity with the modern system (in fact, they and dispensational premillennialism radically differ on the basis for the Millennium); 5). they had no concept of imminency or a pretribulational rapture of the Church; 6). in general, their eschatological chronology is not synonymous with that of the modern system. Indeed, this thesis would conclude that the eschatological beliefs of the period studied would be generally inimical [i.e., contrary] to those of the modern system (perhaps, seminal amillennialism, and not nascent [i.e., emerging] dispensational premillennialism ought to be seen in the eschatology of the period).[27]

So then, it's *amillennialism* that shows up in the early church. As was noted earlier, amillennialism and postmillennialism are very similar in that many of the millennial blessings are mani-

---

26. Charles C. Ryrie, *The Basis of the Premillennial Faith* (Neptune, NJ: Loiseaux Brothers, 1953), p. 17.

27. Alan Patrick Boyd, "A Dispensational Premillennial Analysis of the Eschatology of the Post-Apostolic Fathers (Until the Death of Justin Martyr)" (Th.M. thesis, Dallas Theological Seminary, 1977), pp. 90-91. In a footnote, the author states the following:

> Perhaps a word needs to be said about the eschatological position of the writer of this thesis. He is a dispensational premillennialist, and he does not consider this thesis to be a disproof of that system. *He originally undertook the thesis to bolster the system by patristic research, but the evidence of the original sources simply disallowed this* (p. 91, note 2). Emphasis added.

fested during the "church age." Boyd continues by challenging his fellow-dispensationalists "to be more familiar with, and competent in, patristics,[28] so as to avoid having to rely on second-hand evidence in patristic interpretation." He suggests that "it would seem wise for the modern system [of dispensational premillennialism] to abandon the claim that it is the historic faith of the church (for at least the period considered). . . ."[29]

Another graduate of Dallas Theological Seminary comes to a similar conclusion relating to a pretribulation rapture, a major pillar of dispensationalism: "An intensive examination of the writings of pretribulational scholars reveals only one passage from the early fathers which is put forth as a *possible* example of explicit pretribulationalism."[30]

A "Hint" of Evidence

Where, then, is the historical evidence for premillennialism? What was once considered insurmountable evidence, has now turned out to be scant evidence. This conclusion is made even by scholars from within the dispensational camp.

Tommy Ice says that "there's *absolutely no one* in the early church that even gives a hint that they believe that things were fulfilled in 70 A.D." But according to Justin, there were people who did hold a *non*-premillennial position. This is at least a "hint" of something else, perhaps even the possibility of an A.D. 70 fulfillment.

---

28. Relating to the church fathers and/or their writings.

29. *Ibid.*, p. 92. In a footnote on this same page, Boyd questions the historical accuracy of the research done on the patristic fathers by George N. H. Peters in his much consulted three-volume work, *The Theocratic Kingdom* (Grand Rapids, MI: Kregel, [1884] 1988). Boyd sides with the evaluation of the amillennialist Louis Berkhof when he writes that "it is not correct to say, as Premillenarians do, that it (millennialism) was *generally* accepted in the first three centuries. The truth of the matter is that the adherents of this doctrine were a rather limited number." Berkhof, *The History of Christian Doctrines* (London: The Banner of Truth Trust, [1937] 1969), p. 262. Boyd goes on to disagree with the conclusion of the dispensational author John F. Walvoord that "The early church was far from settled on details of eschatology though *definitely premillennial.*" Walvoord, *The Rapture Question* (Grand Rapids, MI: Zondervan, 1957), p. 137.

30. William Everett Bell, *A Critical Evaluation of the Pretribulation Rapture Doctrine in Christian Eschatology* (School of Education of New York University, unpublished doctoral dissertation, 1967), p. 27. Emphasis added.

Since we do not have all the opinions of the church fathers, or of all the teachers and preachers of that period, it is impossible to be dogmatic concerning what the early church believed. We do know, however, that the early church was not unanimous in its view of the millennium, contrary to what Pentecost, Ice, and other dispensationalists might assert. In fact, we should not put too much confidence in the views of the early church since they were often mistaken on more fundamental doctrines. Boyd writes:

> It is this writer's conviction that historical precedent cannot be employed to disprove a system of belief, but only Biblical precedent. There is much error in the Fathers studied in other areas of theology (e.g., soteriology—incipient baptismal regeneration, a weak view of justification; ecclesiology—incipient sacerdotalism), so it should be no occasion for surprise that there is much eschatological error there.[31]

One last point needs to be made. Tommy Ice claims that no one in the early church believed in an A.D. 70 fulfillment of much of the prophetic literature, especially Matthew 24:1-34. This would indeed be a strong argument for a dispensationalist like Tommy Ice against postmillennialism if it could be proved to be true. Yet, Eusebius, who was present at the Council of Nicaea in A.D. 325, and "played a very prominent part,"[32] believed in a preterist interpretation of Matthew 24:1-34. This is an important point since, as we will see in the next section, Tommy Ice asserts that the Nicene Creed advocates premillennialism. Again, Ice overstates his case by maintaining that "there's absolutely *no one*" who held to an A.D. 70 fulfillment. Only one person has to be found to prove him wrong.

Eusebius, in recounting the writings of Josephus and his recounting of the destruction of Jerusalem by the Romans in A.D. 70, writes that

---

31. Alan Patrick Boyd, *A Dispensational Premillennial Analysis of the Eschatology of the Post-Apostolic Fathers*, p. 91, note 2.

32. Arthur Cushman McGiffert, *Prolegomena: The Life and Writings of Eusebius of Caesarea*, in *A Select Library of Nicene and Post-Nicene Fathers*, Philip Schaff and Henry Wace, eds. (Grand Rapids, MI: Eerdmans, [1890] 1986), p. 19.

it is fitting to add to these accounts the true prediction of our Saviour in which he foretold these very events. His words are as follows: "Woe unto them that are with child, and to them that give suck in those days! But pray ye that your flight be not in the winter, neither on the Sabbath day. For there shall be great tribulation, such as was not since the beginning of the world to this time, no, nor ever shall be."

The discerning reader will recognize that these verses are found in Matthew 24:19-21, verses that dispensationalists say are yet to be fulfilled. But Eusebius tells us that "these things took place in this manner in the second year of the reign of Vespasian,[33] in accordance with the prophecies of our Lord and Saviour Jesus Christ, who by divine power saw them beforehand as if they were already present, and wept and mourned according to the statement of the holy evangelists. . . ."[34] What statement of the holy evangelists? Eusebius quotes verses from Luke's description of the destruction of Jerusalem: Luke 19:42-44; 21:20, 23-24. The passages in Luke 21 parallel those in Matthew 24:1-34. We will take an extended look at Matthew 24:1-34 in the next chapter. But Eusebius's words prove that Tommy Ice is wrong. Of course, there are probably others who held the same position of Eusebius on this issue.

The Nicene Creed

If premillennialism was the unanimous belief of the early church fathers, then why don't the earliest creeds reflect this belief? The Nicene Creed (fourth century) does not support any single millennial position. It states: "And He shall come again, with glory, to judge both the quick and the dead; Whose kingdom shall have no end. . . . And I look for the Resurrection of the dead: And the Life of the world to come. Amen."[35] This "coming" refers to Jesus returning to *judge*, not to *reign*. Premillennialists, postmillennialists, and amillennialists can and do confess this creed.

---

33. September 8, A.D. 70.

34. These quotations from Eusebius are found in *The Church History of Eusebius*, "Predictions of Christ," Book III, Chapter VII. Many editions.

35. For the full text of the Nicene Creed see DeMar and Leithart, *Reduction of Christianity*, p. 345.

But Tommy Ice is not satisfied with the general eschatological view of the Nicene Creed. He is eager to have it read as a premillennial tract. He tells us that "their own written document interprets the final statement as a future kingdom." The following is quoted by Tommy Ice as a commentary on the Nicene Creed that he maintains was written by the creed's framers: [36]

> The world was made less on account of God's providence, for God knew beforehand that man would sin. For that reason we look forward to *new heavens and a new earth* according to the Holy Scriptures: the appearance in the Kingdom of our Great God and Savior, who will become visible to us. And as Daniel says, "The holy ones of the Most High shall receive the Kingdom." And there will be a *pure holy earth, the land of the living and not of the dead*, of which David, seeing with eye of faith, is speaking (Ps. 27:13): "I believe that I shall see the goodness of the Lord in the land of the living"—the land of the meek and humble. [37]

Let's suppose for a moment that this "commentary" on the Nicene Creed is official [38] and that it does teach premillennialism. The fact that the Creed itself avoids taking a position supports the contention of postmillennialists that other millennial positions operated and were considered orthodox in the early church period. If premillennialism had been the *only* orthodox position, the creeds themselves would express the position forthrightly. They do not.

But the question remains: Does this "commentary" on the

---

36. This material was included in a letter written by Tommy Ice to Pastor John A. Gilley, November 13, 1987.

37. Tommy Ice offers no bibliographical information for this quotation. Although there are a number of differences in translation, this quotation can be found in *Historia Actorum Concilii Niceni*, quoted in J. W. Brooks, *Elements of Prophetical Interpretation* (London: R. B. Seeley and W. Burnside, 1836), p. 55.

38. Philip Schaff writes: "Official minutes of the transactions [of the Council] were not at that time made; only the *decrees as adopted* were set down in writing and subscribed by all (comp. Euseb[ius] Vita Const[antine]. iii. 14). All later accounts of voluminous acts of the council are sheer fabrications (comp. Hefele, i. p. 249 sqq.)." *History of the Christian Church*, 8 vols. (Grand Rapids, MI: Eerdmans, [1910] 1979), vol. 3, p. 622.

creed teach premillennialism? Only if you're predisposed to pre-millennialism. Tommy Ice adds his own final remarks: "Notice that although the word 'millennium' is not used, it is clearly referring to a *future*, not present, kingdom; a *future*, not present-age resurrection." So what's to disagree with here? Since when do postmillennialists deny a future dimension to the kingdom? Scripture clearly teaches the *nearness* of the kingdom in Jesus' day (Matthew 3:2; 4:17, 23; Mark 1:14-15; Luke 4:16-30; 4:43; 8:1; 10:9; Colossians 1:13), a definitive or present manifestation of the kingdom through Jesus' work (Matthew 11:2-6; Luke 4:21; 11:20; 17:21), the continuing coming of the kingdom (Matthew 6:10), the progressive advance of the kingdom (Isaiah 9:6-7; Daniel 2:31-34, 44-45; 1 Corinthians 15:24; Matthew 13:31-33), and the consummation of the kingdom (Matthew 25; 1 Corinthians 15:23-24; Revelation 21).[39]

Since the last section of the Nicene Creed is confessing the last of the last things, we should expect it to present the *consummation* of the kingdom and not the present status of the kingdom. Notice Ice's admission that "the word 'millennium' is not used." The reason for this is obvious: *The millennium is not being discussed.* A "pure holy earth," that is, the "land of the living and not of the dead," is obviously a reference to the post-resurrection world, the final new heavens and new earth, not to a millennium where death is still present (Isaiah 65:20).

3. Dispensationalism and History

A pretribulational rapture is one of the hallmarks of dispensationalism. But it is absent from the writings from *every* document left to the church. Even dispensationalists admit this.

> It is freely admitted by pretribulationists that no trace of the doctrine is to be found in church history after the Ante-Nicene fathers until the nineteenth century. . . .[40]

---

39. For a comprehensive study of the kingdom, see DeMar and Leithart, *Reduction of Christianity*, pp. 149-228.

40. William Everett Bell, *A Critical Evaluation of the Pretribulation Rapture Doctrine in Christian Eschatology*, p. 27. Bell goes on to show that neither is there a trace of pretribulationalism in the Ante-Nicene writings.

Dispensationalism had its beginnings around 1830.[41] This in itself does not mean that dispensationalism is an unorthodox theological position. But Tommy Ice used the historical argument to support premillennialism over against postmillennialism. His argument may be summarized this way: Premillennialism has been around since the second century, and postmillennialism had its origins as a system in the sixteenth century, therefore premillennialism is the orthodox view. But this assumes too much. As we have already noted, there is little if any support in the early church for modern dispensational premillennialism. Even the type of premillennialism that operated in the early church fell out of favor with many after a time. It gained support only from fringe sects.

> In the course of time millenarian belief (or 'chiliasm' to give it its Greek name) was repudiated and relegated to sectarian versions of Christianity. [I]t is only fair to point out that in the second century, it did provide a kind of this-worldly hope for Christians in addition to their ultimate hope of heaven. . . . [T]he experience of persecution and the hostility of the all-powerful Roman Empire, left little room for hope for the historical future of human society. . . . As with late Jewish apocalyptic, Christian millennialism flourished in times of persecution, when there seemed no hope for human society without drastic divine intervention.[42]

Millennialism flourishes in times of trouble, persecution, and a general decline in the health of the church. It becomes an escapist eschatology as society seems to be disintegrating.

---

41. For a discussion of the origins of dispensationalism see the following: Murray, *Puritan Hope*, pp. 185-206; Timothy P. Weber, *Living in the Shadow of the Second Coming: American Premillennialism, 1875-1982* (enl. ed.; Grand Rapids, MI: Zondervan/Academie Books, 1983); Dave MacPherson, *The Incredible Cover-Up* (Medford, OR: Omega Publications, [1975] 1980); Charles Caldwell Ryrie, *Dispensationalism Today* (Chicago, IL: Moody Press, 1965); William E. Cox, *An Examination of Dispensationalism* (Nutley, NJ: Presbyterian and Reformed, 1963); Joseph M. Canfield, *The Incredible Scofield and His Book* (Asheville, NC: n.p., 1984); John Zens, *Dispensationalism: A Reformed Inquiry into its Leading Figures and Features*, reprinted from *Baptist Reformation Review* (Autumn 1973), Vol. 2, No. 3; Clarence B. Bass, *Backgrounds to Dispensationalism: Its Historical Genesis and Ecclesiastical Implications* (Grand Rapids, MI: Baker, [1960] 1977).

42. Brian Hebblethwaite, *The Christian Hope* (Grand Rapids, MI: Eerdmans, [1984] 1985), pp. 47-48.

As the early church began to supplant the decaying Roman Empire, however, the nature of eschatology changed. The church recognized its error, for prophetic passages that had been seen as having reference to a future earthly millennium were being fulfilled in the life of the church.[43] Premillennialism was soon supplanted by amillennialism and postmillennialism. Postmillennialism became the impetus for missionary zeal[44] and social transformation from the sixteenth through the nineteenth centuries.[45]

The Ultimate Test

To dismiss postmillennialism because the early church did not hold it (an unproved assertion made by dispensationalists) is no reason to label it aberrational or heretical. Charles Ryrie, a noted dispensationalist, writes:

> The ultimate test of the truth of any doctrine is whether it is in accord with the Biblical revelation. The fact that the church taught something in the first century does not make it true, and likewise if the church did not teach something until the twentieth century, it is not necessarily false.[46]

We agree that historical arguments are helpful and interesting, but they are not normative nor authoritative. The rallying cry today should be, *sola scriptura*, Scripture alone.

---

43. "There was a wave of eschatological expectation as the year 1000 approached: the calendar seemed to be showing the end of the thousand years of Revelation 20. This expectation was disappointed, but it arose again in the years 1200 and 1260, which coincided with computations based on eschatological prophecies in Daniel. Over and over again Christians have allowed themselves to be persuaded, sometimes by rather implausible arguments, that the 'signs of his coming' were fulfilled and that the return of Christ was imminent. During the 1970s, the detailed eschatological calculations of a layman, Hal Lindsey, sold millions of copies to Christians and non-Christians alike, even to Moslems." Harold O. J. Brown, *Heresies: The Image of Christ in the Mirror of Heresy and Orthodoxy from the Apostles to the Present* (Garden City, NY: Doubleday & Company, 1984), p. 447.

44. Murray, *Puritan Hope*.

45. George M. Marsden, *Fundamentalism and American Culture: The Shaping of Twentieth Century Evangelicalism, 1870-1925* (New York: Oxford University Press, 1980).

46. Ryrie, *Dispensationalism Today*, p. 14.

Dispensationalism, however, was not readily accepted in the nineteenth century. In fact, even premillennialism was considered aberrational. J. Gresham Machen, a staunch opponent of modernism, wrote:

> The recrudescence of "Chiliasm" or "premillennialism" in the modern Church causes us serious concern; it is coupled, we think, with a false method of interpreting Scripture which in the long run will be productive of harm.[47]

David Bogue, an eighteenth-century minister in the Church of Scotland and a great supporter of foreign missions, wrote of premillennialism:

> How wise and pious men could ever suppose that the saints, whose souls are now in heaven, should, after the resurrection of the body from the grave, descend to live on earth again; and that Jesus Christ should quit the throne of his glory above, and descend and reign personally over them here below, in distinguished splendour, for a thousand years, may justly excite our astonishment, since it is in direct opposition to the whole tenor of the doctrinal parts of the sacred volume. Such, however, have been the opinions of some great men. Happy will it be if we take warning from their aberrations.[48]

R. B. Kuiper of the newly organized Westminster Theological Seminary considered "Arminianism and the Dispensationalism of the Scofield Bible" to be "two errors which are so extremely prevalent among American fundamentalists." He went on to describe them as "anti-reformed heresies." John Murray, professor of Westminster Theological Seminary, regarded dispensationalism as "palpably inconsistent with the system of truth embodied in" the Westminster Confession of Faith and its Larger and Shorter Catechisms. He describes it as "heterodox from the standpoint of the

---

47. Machen, *Christianity and Liberalism* (Grand Rapids, MI: Eerdmans, [1923] 1981), p. 49.
48. Bogue, *Discourses on the Millennium* (1818), p. 17. Quoted in Murray, *The Puritan Hope*, p. 187.

Reformed Faith."[49] Their attack, however, was not on historic or classical premillennialism.

Dispensational Beginnings

Tommy Ice attributes the preterist view of eschatology to a Jesuit Catholic by the name of Lacunza who Ice says originated it in 1614. Supposedly, Lacunza fabricated the *preterist* interpretation of the Book of Revelation to prove that the Pope was not the antichrist. On this point, I believe, Tommy Ice is confused. (He must have meant Daniel Whitby [1638-1726].) Manuel De Lacunza (1731-1801), writing under the penname Rabbi Ben-Ezra — to give the illusion that he was a converted Jew — wrote *The Coming of the Messiah in Glory and Majesty.* It was published in 1812, eleven years after his death. A complete Spanish edition was published in London in 1816.

Now, if this is the same Lacunza mentioned by Ice in the debate, then his ties are with dispensational premillennialism and not postmillennialism. Edward Irving translated Lacunza's work into English and had it published in 1827 with an added "preliminary discourse of two hundred pages. . . . The prefatory material supplied by Irving contends for the premillennial advent with great persuasiveness. . . ."[50]

The prophetic speculation of Dave Hunt and modern dispensationalism can be found in the writings of Edward Irving, who was influenced by Lacunza, over 150 years ago. Irving believed that the end of the world was near, that the church was in apostasy, and that Jesus would return soon. He published a small prophetic work with the title *Babylon and Infidelity Foredoomed.* "Babylon was his term for all Christendom, and he declared that because of its infidelity it was doomed, judgment was soon to fall, and the coming of Christ was very near."[51]

---

49. Edwin H. Rian, *The Presbyterian Conflict* (Grand Rapids, MI: Eerdmans, 1940), pp. 235-36.

50. Murray, *Puritan Hope*, pp. 189, 190.

51. Arnold Dallimore, *Forerunner of the Charismatic Movement: The Life Of Edward Irving* (Chicago, IL: Moody Press, 1983), p. 76.

But let's continue with Ice's argument and overlook that he is mistaken about Lacunza. He asserts that by making the prophecies concerning the destruction of Jerusalem and the rise of antichrist a past event, that is, past in terms of the sixteenth century, Lacunza rescued the Pope from being labelled the predicted antichrist. But this argument cuts both ways. By making the prophecies fit a distant future, as Lacunza and others did, the papacy escapes just as easily. And it's not coincidental that the futurist interpretation arose from within the Catholic church for the same reason that Ice faults postmillennialists.

> In its present form (the futurist interpretation) it may be said to have originated at the end of the sixteenth century with the Jesuit Ribera, who moved . . . to relieve the Papacy from the terrible stigma cast upon it by the Protestant interpretation, and tried to do so by referring their prophecies to the distant future. . . .[52]

O. T. Allis makes the same charge in his critique of dispensationalism, *Prophecy and the Church*. "The futurist interpretation is traced back to the Jesuit Ribera (A.D. 1580) whose aim was to disprove the claim of the Reformers that the Pope was the Antichrist."[53] Ribera "claimed that the antichrist would be an individual who would rebuild Jerusalem, abolish the Christian Religion, deny Christ, persecute the church, and dominate the world for three and a half years."[54] This is modern-day dispensationalism!

52. H. Grattan Guiness, *The Approaching End of the Age* (London: Hodder & Stoughton, 1879), p. 100. Quoted in William R. Kimball, *The Rapture: A Question of Timing* (Grand Rapids, MI: Baker Book House, 1985), p. 30. See chapter 2 of Kimball's book for an historical overview of the origin of the pretribulational rapture idea.

53. Oswald T. Allis, *Prophecy and the Church: An Examination of the Claim of Dispensationalists that the Christian Church is a Mystery Parenthesis Which Interrupts the Fulfillment to Israel of the Kingdom Prophecies of the Old Testament* (Philadelphia, PA: Presbyterian and Reformed, 1945), p. 296, note 66.

54. Kimball, *The Rapture*, p. 31.

4. Dispensationalism and Classical Premillennialism

Throughout the debate, Tommy Ice gave the impression that *dispensational* premillennialism is the historic Christian position and that *dispensational* premillennialism is little different from *historic* premillennialism. This is a favorite tactic of dispensationalists.

> Dispensationalists have attempted repeatedly to demonstrate that both the chronology and method of dispensationalism may be traced back to the theology of the apostolic church. An example of this is found in *The Basis of the Premillennial Faith* by C. H. Ryrie. The author asserts that "premillennialism is the historic faith of the church," and he then proceeds to identify this historic belief in a premillennial return of the Lord with dispensationalism by asserting that "opponents of the premillennial system have attempted to obscure the main issues involved by inventing distinctives between historic premillennialists, pretribulationists, dispensationalists, and ultradispensationalists. Such distinctives are not warranted since differences are minor."[55]

Historic premillennialists would disagree with Ryrie. George Eldon Ladd, an historic premillennialist (non-dispensational), takes exception to the notion that the "differences are minor." He states that "we can find no trace of pretribulationism in the early church: and no modern pretribulationist has successfully proved that this particular doctrine was held by any of the church fathers or students of the Word before the nineteenth century."[56] A pre-

---

55. Bass, *Backgrounds to Dispensationalism*, p. 13.

56. George Eldon Ladd, *The Blessed Hope* (Grand Rapids, MI: Eerdmans, 1956), p. 31. The idea of "dispensations" is not unique to dispensationalism. Charles Ryrie lists the *sine qua non* of dispensationalism: "(1) A dispensationalist keeps Israel and the Church distinct. . . . (2) This distinction between Israel and the Church is born out of a system of hermeneutics which is usually called literal interpretation. . . . (3) A third aspect of the *sine qua non* of dispensationalism is a rather technical matter . . . that concerns the underlying purpose of God in the world. The covenant theologian in practice makes this purpose salvation, and the dispensationalist says the purpose is broader than that, namely, the glory of God." *Dispensationalism Today*, pp. 43-47.

The entire dispensational system stands or falls on the literal hermeneutic which even dispensationalists do not hold consistently. Ryrie's third point is discussed in DeMar and Leithart, *Reduction of Christianity*, p. 39, note 51.

tribulational rapture is essential to dispensationalism because it keeps the church-Israel distinction intact. This is a *major* difference between historic and dispensational premillennialists.

Dispensationalism has a number of unique doctrinal peculiarities that did not arise until the nineteenth century: the *rigidity* of dispensations;[57] a narrowly defined and inconsistently literal method of interpretation;[58] a strict dichotomy between Israel and the church; the church as a "mystery" not foreseen in the Old Testament; an earthly, distinctively Jewish millennial kingdom; a postponement of the kingdom from the time of Christ; a secret pre-tribulational rapture. Dispensationalism is a nineteenth-century premillennial hybrid.

5. Postmillennialism and Liberalism

Ice's implication that postmillennialism grows out of liberalism is quite unfair and is an attempt to prejudice the audience against Christian Reconstruction. Rushdoony writes:

> Since the publication of H. Richard Niebuhr's *The Kingdom of God in America* (1937), it has been widely assumed that postmillennialism led to the social gospel. . . . The heart of the problem,

---

57. Noted Bible scholars have divided the Bible into "dispensations," but no Bible scholar attached the meaning to these divisions that C. I. Scofield did in his "Reference Bible." The divisions of dispensationalism are more like the compartmentalizing of God's work in history. John Gerstner writes:

What is peculiar about the dispensational way of understanding is not its seeing different, unfolding stages of revelation but the way it sees those stages. Unlike traditional interpreters, dispensationalists "divide" these sections sharply into areas that *conflict with* one another rather than *unfold from* one another. Genuine biblical revelation is developmental; one stage unfolds naturally from another as the unfolding of the blossom of a flower. But for dispensationalists, these periods are sharply divided rather than integrated, and they conflict rather than harmonize. *A Primer on Dispensationalism* (Phillipsburg, NJ: Presbyterian and Reformed, 1982), p. 2.

58. Michael R. Gilstrap, "Dispensationalism's Hermeneutic: 'Literal, Except When Embarrassing,'" *Dispensationalism in Transition*, Institute for Christian Economics, P.O. Box 8000, Tyler, Texas 75711, Vol. I, No. 5 (May, 1988); Vern Poythress, *Understanding Dispensationalists* (Grand Rapids, MI: Zondervan, 1987).

however, has been a simplistic confusion in the minds of many that historical succession means necessary and logical connection and succession. Hence, it is held, because postmillennialism was the original kingdom of God idea in America, the social gospel idea of the kingdom of God is a logical and necessary product of postmillennialism. This "proves" too much. Niebuhr gives us three stages in the theological motive forces of American history: a) the kingdom of God, God as sovereign, a Calvinistic, postmillennial faith; b) the kingdom of Christ, Arminian, revivalistic, and concerned with soul-saving, amillennial and premillennial in eschatology; c) the social gospel kingdom of God, modernistic, humanistic, and socialistic (or statist). It is highly illogical and irrational to jump from "a" to "c"; if Calvinistic postmillennialism is the cause, then Arminianism and revivalism are also its logical products! Then too we must hold that Arminian revivalism led to the social gospel and to modernism! But history is not merely logical development; it involves rival faiths, and their rise and fall.[59]

Christian Reconstructionists have no ties with liberalism, and postmillennialism no more leads to liberalism than dispensational premillennialism leads to cultism.[60] All Reconstructionists believe

---

59. R. J. Rushdoony, "Postmillennialism Versus Impotent Religion," *The Journal of Christian Reconstruction: Symposium on the Millennium*, p. 122.

60. Some of the major cults are premillennial: Jehovah's Witnesses, Mormonism, Children of God, and The Worldwide Church of God (Armstrongism). Moreover, you can find elements of premillennialism in the Manifest Sons of God. In fact, most cults are premillennial in their eschatology. Here's an example of premillennial thinking from the Worldwide Church of God:

And Christ will rule over and judge nations, UNTIL they beat their swords into plowshares, their weapons of destruction into implements of peaceful PRODUCTION.

When, at last God *takes over*—puts down Satan, and the WAYS of Satan's world . . . then the NEW World—The WORLD TOMORROW shall reap what it then sows—PEACE, HAPPINESS, HEALTH, ABUNDANT, INTERESTING LIVING, OVERFLOWING JOY! It will be a Utopia beyond man's fondest or wildest dreams. Herbert W. Armstrong, *1975 in Prophecy* (Pasadena, CA: Ambassador College Press, 1952), p. 31. Quoted in Paul N. Benware, *Ambassadors of Armstrongism: An Analysis of the History and Teachings of the Worldwide Church of God* (Nutley, NJ: Presbyterian and Reformed, 1975), p. 72.

in an inerrant and infallible Bible. Liberalism is based on the belief that the Bible is riddled with error. Therefore, liberalism by its very nature denies predictive prophecy. The "postmillennialism" of liberalism or modernism is not at all Christ-centered. Their idea of a millennium is evolutionary. Jesus Christ is not a part of their millennium.

Conclusion

Dispensationalism is an interwoven system. To disturb a single element of dispensationalism is to destroy the system. Once the literal hermeneutic begins to break down, the Israel/Church dichotomy gradually disappears. Then the pre-tribulational rapture is no longer needed. The pre-trib rapture doctrine had its beginning in the 1830s. There is no support for it in Scripture.

For a long time, dispensationalists have tried to use historical evidence to bolster their weak exegetical position. As has been shown, the historical argument is weak. Even dispensationalists are calling for it to be abandoned.

14

TOMMY ICE: A RESPONSE
Part II

Tommy Ice continued his critique of Christian Reconstruction with a brief exposition of Matthew 24:1-34. For Ice, this seemed to be the central issue in the debate. He maintained that Matthew 24:1-34 describes the great tribulation, the rapture, and the return of Christ—all future events. Ice does believe that some of Matthew 24:1-34 has already been fulfilled. This is a convenient way to look at the Olivet Discourse, but it leads to interpretive subjectivity. How can we distinguish between those verses that pertain to an A.D. 70 fulfillment and those verses that address a yet future fulfillment? With this approach, the interpreter is left with the pick and choose method. But if the interpreter allows the time texts of Matthew 23:36 and 24:34 to be his guide and the Bible to define terms and phrases, there is no problem fitting the entire section within an A.D. 70 fulfillment.

So What?

But there is a more basic issue to consider. Why was a single interpretation of Matthew 24:1-34 made the keystone in a debate over Christian Reconstruction? There is nothing novel about a preterist interpretation of this passage. As was noted in the previous chapter, the fourth-century historian Eusebius interpreted the Olivet Discourse as having its fulfillment in A.D. 70.[1] So then,

---

1. Eusebius, in recounting the writings of Josephus and his description of the destruction of Jerusalem by the Romans in A.D. 70, writes that

it is fitting to add to these accounts [of the secular historian Josephus] the true prediction of our Saviour in which he foretold these very events. His

while a debate over how Matthew 24:1-34 should be interpreted is an interesting one, a preterist interpretation is not unique to Christian Reconstruction. Christian Reconstruction does not stand or fall on any single interpretation of this controversial passage. We do believe, however, that the preterist interpretation is the correct one.

Does Tommy Ice know when these events will be fulfilled? Will it be tomorrow or a thousand years from now? Let's assume it's tomorrow. Does this mean that Christians should abandon reforming their own lives and the world in which they live? I don't think so. What if the fulfillment is a thousand years off?[2] Keep in mind that it's been nearly two thousand years since Jesus predicted His "imminent" appearing.[3] If Tommy Ice's views had been prevalent in the church for the last two millennia, the church would be much worse off than it is today. Such a view of history only cripples the body of Christ (1 Thessalonians 5:1-11; 2 Thessalonians 3:6-15).

As has been mentioned numerous times in previous chapters, a postmillennial eschatology is only one pillar of support for

---

words are as follows: "Woe unto them that are with child, and to them that give suck in those days! But pray ye that your flight be not in the winter, neither on the Sabbath day. For there shall be great tribulation, such as was not since the beginning of the world to this time, no, nor ever shall be." Eusebius, *History of the Church*, "Predictions of Christ," Book III, Chapter VII. Many editions.

The verses that Eusebius quotes are found in Matthew 24:19-21, the very section of Scripture that Tommy Ice relegates to a future fulfillment. Eusebius writes that "these things took place in this manner in the second year of the reign of Vespasian [A.D. 70], in accordance with the prophecies of our Lord and Saviour Jesus Christ, who by divine power saw them beforehand as if they were already present, and wept and mourned according to the statement of the holy evangelists. . . ." Eusebius had Luke's description of the destruction of Jerusalem in mind: Luke 19:42-44; 21:20, 23-24. The passages in Luke 21 parallel those in Matthew 24:1-34.

2. Traditional premillennialism has taught that "Christ may return tomorrow or a thousand years from now." Garry Friesen, "A Return Visit," *Moody* (May 1988), p. 31.

3. This makes perfect sense with a preterist interpretation. It makes no sense with dispensationalism.

Christian Reconstruction. Postmillennialism is an orthodox millennial position held by some of the finest Christian thinkers the church has produced.[4] Many non-Reconstructionists are postmillennialists, and numerous Reconstructionists are non-postmillennial. Ice and Hunt, with their emphasis on eschatology, have left the impression that only Reconstructionists believe in postmillennialism and that postmillennialism is a recent theological innovation. There is much more to Christian Reconstruction than postmillennialism.

The most controversial distinctive of Christian Reconstruction is how God's law should be applied to society. But the application of God's law to this world is the weakest area for the dispensationalist. For the most part, this issue was ignored in the debate. Eschatology was made the sole debate topic for Ice and Hunt because dispensationalism stands or falls on the millennial issue. They had to make eschatology the point of contention in order to discredit Christian Reconstruction and salvage their own system.

Since the issue of eschatology played such a prominent role in the debate, it's necessary that we look at what Tommy Ice had to

---

4. J. A. Alexander (1809-1860), professor of oriental languages at Princeton Theological seminary, wrote four commentaries that can be described as "postmillennial": *The Prophecies of Isaiah*, *A Commentary on Matthew* (complete through chapter 16), *A Commentary on Mark*, and *A Commentary on Acts*. Charles Hodge (1797-1878) set forth his postmillennial position in his three-volume *Systematic Theology* and his *Commentary on Romans*. His son, A. A. Hodge (1823-1886), described his postmillennial position in his *Outlines of Theology*. John Owen (1616-1683) and John Brown of Edinburgh (1784-1858) have already been mentioned as being postmillennial. Owen's *Works*, including his seven volume exposition on Hebrews, add up to twenty-three volumes. John Brown wrote commentaries on *The Discourses and Sayings of Our Lord* and commentaries on Romans, Hebrews, and 1 Peter. John Brown of Haddington (1722-1787) is best known for his *Self-Interpreting Bible*. It too is postmillennial, taking a preterist view of Matthew 24. David Brown (1803-1897) is widely recognized (along with R. Jamieson and A. R. Faussett) through the six-volume *Commentary, Critical, Experimental, and Practical on the Old and New Testaments*. His work on *The Four Gospels* is postmillennial as is his *Christ's Second Coming: Will it be Premillennial?* The Baptist theologian A. H. Strong (1836-1921) outlined his postmillennial views in his multi-volume *Systematic Theology*. Another Baptist, B. H. Carroll (1843-1914), presented his postmillennialism in his extensive commentary on Revelation. Iain Murray's *The Puritan Hope: Revival and the Interpretation of Prophecy* is a virtual gold mine of Christian authors, preachers, and missionaries who were postmillennial. The list could go on.

say about Matthew 24:1-34. It is the key to Tommy Ice's presentation and one of the most difficult chapters in the Bible to interpret.

Matthew 24: Setting the Scene

Matthew 24:1-34, like all Scripture, cannot be understood without surveying its context. The context for Chapter 24 is found in Chapter 23. Keep in mind that in the original manuscripts, there were no chapter and verse divisions. In the Greek text, Chapter 24 follows immediately after Chapter 23. The disciples had just heard Jesus pronounce His seven "woes" on the Pharisees. Jesus ends with this bombshell: "Behold, your house is being left to you desolate!" (Matthew 23:38). Chapter 24 begins with, "And Jesus came out from the temple and was going away when His disciples came up to point out the temple buildings to Him" (24:1). So then, the "house" that is being left "desolate" is the "temple." The disciples were obviously curious. So they asked the following question: "Tell us, when will these things be, and what will be the sign of Your coming, and of the end of the age" (v. 3).

Jesus told the Pharisees, "Truly I say to you, all these things shall come upon *this generation*" (23:36). Jesus answers the disciples' questions relating to the time and signs of Jerusalem's destruction. The Old Covenant order would end with the destruction of Jerusalem. This would be the "sign" of the "end of the age" of the Old Covenant and the consummation of the New Covenant.

The Time Text: "This Generation"

The time texts are found in Matthew 23:36 and 24:34. They form eschatological bookends for this study:

> Truly I say to you, all these things shall come upon this generation (23:36).

> Truly I say to you, this generation will not pass away until all these things take place (24:34).

Sandwiched between these two time texts are the "sign" texts. Ice asserts that "this generation" does not mean the generation to whom Jesus was speaking. Rather, it refers to the generation alive at the time when these events will take place. There are a number of difficulties with this position.

First, Jesus says that "this generation will not pass away until *all these things take place.*" "All these things" take place within the "this generation" time frame. There cannot be a partial fulfillment in A.D. 70 and a partial but final fulfillment at the end of the twentieth century. Nor can there be a gap between some of the A.D. 70 events and the events that lead up to the last days, nearly 2000 years from the time when Jesus first made the prophecy. This would make nonsense of the passage. "This generation" and "all these things" are tied together. The "this generation" of Matthew 24:34 is either the generation to whom Jesus was speaking or it's a future generation that experiences the prophetic fulfillment. It cannot be some of both. Neither is there anything in the passage to lead us to believe in some type of "double fulfillment," where these events repeat themselves in a future tribulational period with a rebuilt temple.

Second, "this generation" means the generation to whom Jesus was speaking. It is the *contemporary generation*. How do we know this? Scripture is our interpreting guide. We do not have to speculate as to its meaning. Those who deny that "this generation" refers to the generation to whom Jesus was speaking in the Matthew 24 context must maintain that "this generation" means something different from the way it's used in other places in Matthew and the rest of the New Testament! Matthew 23:36 clearly has reference to the Pharisees and their contemporary generation. Why should we interpret "this generation" in Matthew 24:34 different from 23:36, since Jesus is answering His disciples' questions regarding His statement to the Pharisees about their house — the temple — being left to them desolate in Matthew 23:36? The usual rejoinder is, "Well, some of these events *could not* have been fulfilled during the life of the apostles. There *must be* a future fulfillment even though 'this generation' *seems* to refer to those who heard Jesus' words." This is not the way we should interpret Scripture. If Jesus said that all the events prior to Matthew 24:34

would occur within the contemporary generation (within a forty year period), then we must take Him at His word. Dispensationalists insist on literalism. Why not in this instance?

Third, the use of "this generation" throughout the Gospels makes it clear that it means the generation to whom Jesus was speaking. It never means "race," as many dispensationalists and non-dispensationalists assert, or some future generation. The adjective "this" points to the contemporary nature of the generation. If some future generation were in view, Jesus could have chosen the adjective "that": "*That* [future] generation which begins with the budding of the fig tree [Israel regathered to the land of their fathers] will not pass away until all these things take place."

Here is a list of every occurrence of "generation" or "**this generation**" in the Gospels: Matthew 1:17; **11:16**; 12:39, **41, 42, 45**; 16:4; 17:17; **23:36**; **24:34**; Mark **8:12, 38**; 9:19; **13:30**; Luke 1:48, 50; **7:31**; 9:41; **11:29, 30, 31, 32, 50, 51**; 16:8; **17:25**; **21:32**. In each and every case, these verses describe events occurring within a current time frame. David Chilton summarizes the argument succinctly:

> *Not one* of these references is speaking of the entire Jewish race over thousands of years; *all* use the word in its normal sense of *the sum total of those living at the same time*. It always refers to *contemporaries*. (In fact, those who say it means "race" tend to acknowledge this fact, but explain that the word suddenly *changes* its meaning when Jesus uses it in Matthew 24! We can smile at such a transparent error, but we should also remember that this is very serious. We are dealing with the Word of the living God.)[5]

Fourth, notice how many times Jesus uses the word "you" in the parallel passage in Luke 21: "They will lay their hands on *you* and will persecute *you*, delivering *you* to the synagogues and prisons, bringing *you* before kings and governors for My name's sake" (v. 12; see verses 13, 14, 15, 16, 17, 18, 19, 20, 28, 30). Matthew 24 and Mark 13 use the same contemporary address. Now, if you heard

---

5. David Chilton, *The Great Tribulation* (Ft. Worth, TX: Dominion Press, 1987), p. 3.

Jesus say that all these things would happen to "this generation," and you also heard Him say that when "you" see these things, what would you conclude? The most natural (literal) interpretation is that it would happen to *your generation* and maybe even to *you* personally (cf. Matthew 16:27-28). Again, if it were a future generation, we would expect Jesus to have said, "when *they* see . . . they will bring *them* . . . they will persecute *them*."

Fifth, Jesus warned His followers that they should flee *Judea* (Matthew 24:16) when they saw the events described by Him. Jesus assured them that these judgmental events would be cut short for the sake of the "elect" (24:22). Those who endured to the end would be saved, that is, they would not die in the conflagration if they heeded Jesus' words and left the city before the descent of the Roman army (24:13). These events make up "the great tribulation" (24:21) — the same tribulation in which John had a part as he wrote about what was shortly to come to pass (Revelation 1:1, 3, 9; compare 6:10-11; 7:14).

Early Warning Signs

The earliest chapters of the Gospels — especially Matthew's Gospel — point forward to the impending destruction of Jerusalem later prophesied by Jesus and the apostles. John the Baptist leads the way with his indictment of the self-righteous religious leaders, the very ones who engineered the crucifixion of the Lord of glory. In Matthew 3:7-12 we read:

> But when he saw many of the Pharisees and Sadducees coming for baptism, he said to them, "You brood of vipers, *who warned you to flee from the wrath to come?* Therefore bring forth fruit in keeping with your repentance; and do not suppose that you can say to yourselves, 'We have Abraham for our father'; for I say to you, that God is able from these stones to raise up children to Abraham. "And the axe is already laid at the root of the trees. . . . And His winnowing fork is in His hand, and He will thoroughly clean His threshing floor; and He will gather His wheat into the barn, but He will burn up the chaff with unquenchable fire."

There are numerous prophetic statements in the Gospels regarding Jerusalem's demise (e.g., Matthew 21:33-46; 22:1-14; 23:31-38; 24:1-34).

Later, in Acts 2:16-24, the Pentecostal manifestation of tongues in Jerusalem was an indicator of the approaching "day of the Lord." Tongues-speaking was a warning sign to the present audience of the necessity of their being "saved from *this perverse generation*" (Acts 2:40).[6]

Acts 2:43-47 and 4:32-37 present corroborating evidence that the destruction of Jerusalem was imminent. There would be little use for property that was located in a nation dominated by invading Roman armies. Practically speaking, the revenue from such sales would be better spent on gospel outreach. This is quite a different scenario from Jeremiah's day, when the Lord instructed him to *buy* land in Israel for an eventual return (Jeremiah 32:25).

The selling of property is mentioned as occurring only in Jerusalem. This action did not become part of early church doctrine, contrary to contemporary Christian socialists.[7] The sale of property and distribution of the profits can be related to the imminent destruction of the city prophesied by Jesus in Matthew 24:34 and elsewhere, and heeded by the disciples. Jerusalem's destruction was coming in that generation. The land would be worthless to the escaping Christians who were warned by Jesus to "flee."

The Jewish leaders continued to reject Jesus during this forty year period of extended mercy. Stephen called them "stiff-necked and uncircumcised in heart and ears and always resisting the Holy Spirit" (Acts 7:51). Paul speaks of these Jews as those who "always

---

6. See O. Palmer Robertson, "Tongues: Sign of Covenantal Curse and Blessing" in *Westminster Theological Journal* (1977), pp. 43ff.; Richard Gaffin, *Perspectives on Pentecost* (Phillipsburg, NJ: Presbyterian and Reformed, 1979), pp. 102ff.; Kenneth L. Gentry, Jr., *Crucial Issues Regarding Tongues* (Mauldin, SC: Good-Birth, 1982), pp. 14-20.

7. For a critique of a socialistic interpretation of this passage, see David Chilton, *Productive Christians in an Age of Guilt-Manipulators* (3rd rev. ed; Tyler, TX: Institute for Christian Economics, 1985), pp. 169-170; and Gary DeMar, *God and Government: Issues in Biblical Perspective* (Atlanta, GA: American Vision, 1984), pp. 203-206.

fill up the measure of their sins" and upon whom "the wrath has come . . . to the utmost" (1 Thessalonians 2:16). In Hebrews 12:28-29, Judaism (the old order) is contrasted with its fulfillment, Christianity (the new order). There is a looming "shaking" of the old order. John Owen, in his masterful commentary on Hebrews, describes the nature of this "shaking":

> It is the dealing of God with *the church*, and the alterations which he would make in the state thereof, concerning which the apostle treats. It is therefore the *heavens of Mosaical worship*, and the Judaical church-state, with the *earth of their political state* belonging thereunto, that are here intended. These were they that were shaken at the coming of Christ, and so shaken, as shortly after to be removed and taken away, for the introduction of the more heavenly worship of the gospel, and the immovable evangelical church-state. This was the greatest commotion and alteration that God ever made in the heavens and earth of the church, and which was to be made once only.[8]

There are additional verses which point to a dramatic and earth-shaking series of events that the first-century world would soon experience (Romans 13:11-12; 1 Corinthians 7:26, 29-31; Colossians 3:6; Hebrews 10:25, 37; James 5:8-9; 1 Peter 4:5,7; 1 John 2:17-18).

Matthew 24: A Brief Exposition

After all this evidence, what compels some interpreters to make "this generation" mean either some distant, non-contemporary generation alive at the time the fig tree buds, that is, the Jewish race is one again regathered in Israel? We're told that some of the events described in Matthew 24:1-34 could not have been fulfilled prior to A.D. 70. The language is too "eschatological," too future, for an A.D. 70 fulfillment. Properly understood, in the light of the *Bible's* use of prophetic language, all the events prior to

---

8. John Owen, *An Exposition of the Epistle to the Hebrews*, 7 vols. (Grand Rapids, MI: Baker Book House, [1855] 1980), vol. 7, p. 366. See Owen's comments on the passing of "heaven and earth" in *The Works of John Owen*, 16 vols. (London: Banner of Truth Trust, [1850-53] 1965-68), vol. 9, pp. 134-35.

Matthew 24:34 were fulfilled within a period of 40 years after Jesus gave the prophecy.

In the section that follows, we will look at and address some of the *most difficult* passages. A cursory reading of the Book of Acts and early church history will show how verses 4-12 were fulfilled prior to A.D. 70. There were false messiahs (Acts 8:9-10),[9] "wars and rumors of wars,"[10] earthquakes in various places,[11] famines (Acts 11:28), false prophets who misled many, and general lawlessness and apostasy (Acts 20:29; 2 Timothy 1:15; 4:10, 16; 2 Peter 2:1; 1 John 4:1). For a comprehensive study of Matthew 24:1-34, and the verses that we will not discuss, see the following books and tapes:

1. J. Marcellus Kik, *An Eschatology of Victory* (Nutley, NJ: Presbyterian and Reformed, 1971), pp. 59-173.

2. David Chilton, *The Great Tribulation* (Ft. Worth, TX: Dominion Press, 1987).

3. William R. Kimball, *What the Bible Says About the Great Tribulation* (Phillipsburg, NJ: Presbyterian and Reformed, [1983] 1984).

4. Rousas J. Rushdoony, *Thy Kingdom Come: Studies in Daniel and Revelation* (Nutley, NJ: Presbyterian and Reformed, 1971), pp. 235-243.

5. Roderick Campbell, *Israel and the New Covenant* (Phillipsburg, NJ: Presbyterian and Reformed, [1954] 1982).

---

9. "Jerome quotes Simon Magus as saying, 'I am the Word of God, I am the Comforter, I am Almighty, I am all there is of God' (Mansel, *The Gnostic Heresies*, p. 82). And Irenaeus tells us how Simon claimed to be the Son of God and the creator of angels." J. Marcellus Kik, *An Eschatology of Victory* (Phillipsburg, NJ: Presbyterian and Reformed, 1975), p. 92.

10. See the *Works of Josephus*, 4 vols. (Grand Rapids, MI: Baker Book House, 1974).

11. "And as to earthquakes, many are mentioned by writers during a period just previous to 70 A.D. There were earthquakes in Crete, Smyrna, Miletus, Chios, Samos, Samos, Laodicea, Hierapolis, Colosse, Campania, Rome, and Judea. It is interesting to note that the city of Pompeii was much damaged by an earthquake occurring on February 5, 63, A.D." Kik, *Eschatology of Victory*, p. 93.

6. Ralph Woodrow, *Great Prophecies of the Bible* (Riverside, CA: Ralph Woodrow Evangelistic Association, 1971).

7. James B. Jordan, "Matthew 24," eleven taped lectures (Geneva Ministries, Box 131300, Tyler, Texas 75713).

8. Philip Mauro, *Seventy Weeks and the Great Tribulation* (Swengel, PA: Reiner Publications, n.d.).

9. R. T. France, *Jesus and the Old Testament: His Application of Old Testament Passages to Himself and His Mission* (Grand Rapids, MI: Baker Book House, [1971] 1982), pp. 227-239.

10. James W. Lee, ed., *The Self-Interpreting Bible*, 4 vols. (Philadelphia, PA: Keeler & Kirkpatrick, 1895), vol. 4, pp. 98-101.

11. Cornelis Vanderwaal, *Hal Lindsey and Biblical Prophecy* (St. Catherines, Ontario: Paideia Press, 1978).

12. T. Boersma, *Is the Bible a Jigsaw Puzzle: An Evaluation of Hal Lindsey's Writings* (St. Catherines, Ontario: Paideia Press, 1978).

13. Thomas Newton, *Dissertations on the Prophecies Which Have Remarkably Been Fulfilled, and at This Time are Fulfilling in the World* (London: J. F. Dove, 1754).

14. Philip Schaff, *History of the Christian Church*, 8 vols. (Grand Rapids, MI: Eerdmans, 1910), sections 37-38, 101.

1. "The one who endures to the end will be saved" (v. 13).

The end of what? Jesus is answering questions about the destruction of the Temple and the "end of the age," the end of the Jewish dispensation, the Old Covenant order. Remember, the disciples had just heard Jesus predict that the temple was going to be left to the Pharisees "desolate" (Matthew 23:38), that these things would happen to "this generation," that is, to the generation that Jesus was addressing (v. 36). This is the end Jesus had in mind. The Apostle Paul tells us that the "end of the age" is not in the distant future: "Now these things happened to them [the Israelites in the wilderness] as an example, and they were written for our instruction, *upon whom the end of the ages have come*" (1 Corinthians 10:11).

The New Testament describes the nearness of the Lord's coming and the "end of all things," that is, the end of the distinctly Jewish era with the shadows of the Old Covenant. These events were to happen "soon." There's no getting around this language. Forcing these verses to describe a period nearly 2000 years in the future twists the Scriptures. Jesus made it clear to the religious leaders of His day that the kingdom of God would be taken away from them to be "given to a nation producing the fruit of it" (Matthew 21:43). When would this happen? "And when the chief priests and the Pharisees heard His parables, *they understood that He was speaking about them*" (v. 45). They would experience the kingdom transfer. Here are a number of verses that describe the near end of the Old Covenant order:

1. "*The night is almost gone and the day is at hand.* Let us therefore lay aside the deeds of darkness and put on the armor of light" (Romans 13:12).

2. "For the form of this world *is passing away*" (1 Corinthians 7:31).

3. "Now these things happened to them as an example, and they were written for our instruction, *upon whom the end of the ages have come*" (1 Corinthians 10:11).

4. "Let your forbearing spirit be known to all men. *The Lord is near*" (James 4:5).

5. "*The end of all things is at hand*; therefore, be of sound judgment and sober of spirit for the purpose of prayer" (1 Peter 4:7).

6. "You too be patient; strengthen your hearts, *for the coming of the Lord is at hand.* Do not complain, brethren, against one another, that you yourselves may not be judged; behold, *the Judge is standing right at the door*" (James 5:8-9).

7. "Children, *it is the last hour*; and just as you heard that antichrist is coming, even now many antichrists have arisen; from this *we know that it is the last hour*" (1 John 2:18).

8. "The Revelation of Jesus Christ, which God gave Him to show to His bond-servants, *the things which must shortly take place*" (Revelation 1:1).

John Brown, in his exceptional three-volume commentary on Peter's first epistle, gives the following interpretation of "the end of all things is at hand" (1 Peter 4:7):

> After some deliberation, I have been led to adopt the opinion of those who hold that "the end of all things" here is the entire and final end of the Jewish economy in the destruction of the temple and city of Jerusalem, and the dispersion of the holy people. That was at hand; for this epistle seems to have been written a very short while before these events took place, not improbably after the commencement of "the wars and rumours of war" of which our Lord spake. This view will not appear strange to any one who has carefully weighed the terms in which our Lord had predicted these events, and the close connection which the fulfillment of these predictions had with the interests and duties of Christians, whether in Judea or in Gentile countries.
>
> It is quite plain, that in our Lord's predictions, the expressions "the end," and probably "the end of the world," are used in reference to the entire dissolution of the Jewish economy [Matt xxiv. 3, 6, 14, 34; Mark xiii. 30; Luke xxi. 32].[12]

The Old Testament uses similar "end times" language to describe a localized and specific judgment of sin. Ezekiel writes:

> Moreover, the word of the LORD came to me saying, "And you, son of man, thus says the Lord GOD to the land of Israel, 'An end! The end is coming on the four corners of the land. Now the end is upon you, and I shall send My anger against you, I shall judge you according to your ways, and I shall bring all your abominations upon you'" (Ezekiel 7:1-4; also vv. 5-19).

The "end" here is not the end of the world but the end of the apostasy exhibited by the nation. God was judging the world of that

---

12. John Brown, *Expository Discourses on the First Epistle of the Apostle Peter*, 3 vols. (Marshallton, DE: The National Foundation for Christian Education, n.d.), vol. 3, pp. 84-85. See his equally fine comments on the passing of "heaven and earth" in *The Discourses and Sayings of our Lord*, 3 vols. (London: Banner of Truth Trust, [1852] 1967), vol. 1, pp. 171-74.

time. It would be the end. The people had trusted in the "temple of the LORD, the temple of the LORD, the temple of the LORD" (Jeremiah 7:4). God called this "deception." A life-style of theft, murder, idolatry, and adultery would nullify anything the temple could do. The end would come upon them "for the LORD has rejected and forsaken the generation of His wrath" (v. 29).

The themes in Ezekiel are almost identical with those set forth by Jeremiah. Apostasy brings God's judgment—it is "the end." "Ezekiel was not the first to use the refrain *the end has come*. Amos had used it in 8:2 when he made his famous pun on the basket of summer fruit. From there it became part of the common language of eschatology and was associated with the day of the Lord's judgment on all men. For Ezekiel, the destruction of Jerusalem was an act of almost apocalyptic intensity; it was a tragic, but necessary, culmination of centuries of human sin and divine long-suffering."[13] For those who see Ezekiel's description as the end of the world, notice that these judgments are to happen "shortly" (v. 8).

2. "This gospel of the kingdom shall be preached in the whole world for a witness to all the nations, and then the end shall come" (v. 14).

This verse can find its fulfillment in a number of ways. First, at Pentecost there were in Jerusalem Jews from "every nation under heaven" (Acts 2:5-11). They took the gospel with them as they left Jerusalem after the feast of Pentecost.

Second, Colossians 1:23 tells us that the gospel "was proclaimed in all creation under heaven" (see v. 6; Romans 1:8; 10:18). This statement by Paul is a fulfillment of what Jesus told His disciples would be a prelude to the destruction of Jerusalem.

Third, Paul was making plans to go "to Spain" (Romans 15:24, 28). Prior to A.D. 70 the inhabited earth had heard the gospel—"all creation under heaven." This section of Matthew 24 was

---

13. John B. Taylor, *Ezekiel* (Downers Grove, IL: InterVarsity Press, [1969] 1978), pp. 92-93.

fulfilled within a generation. Matthew 24:14 is different from the Great Commission in 28:19-20. Here we're told to "make disciples of all the nations." This is yet to be fulfilled.

Fourth, the word translated "world," is the Greek word *oikoumene*, "the inhabited earth." The prophecy clearly shows that the gospel will be preached throughout the Roman empire before Jesus comes. The same word is used in Luke 2:1: "Now it came about in those days that a decree went out from Caesar Augustus, that a census be taken of all *the inhabited earth*." In the New American Standard Version, the marginal reading is "the Roman empire."

3. "Therefore when you see the ABOMINATION OF DESOLATION which was spoken of through Daniel the prophet, standing in the holy place (let the reader understand)" (v. 15).

Tommy Ice gives the following description of the "abomination of desolation": (a) It happens in the Jewish temple in Jerusalem; (b) it involves a person setting up a statue in the place of the regular sacrifice in the holy of holies; (c) it results in the cessation of the regular sacrifice; (d) there will be a time of about three and a half years between this event and another event which is the second coming; (e) it involves a person setting up a statue or image of himself so that he may be worshipped in place of God; (f) the image is made to come to life (Revelation 13:15); (g) a worship system of this false god is thus inaugurated.

First, the key to Ice's interpretation is the 70th week[14] of Daniel. He, like all dispensationalists, disconnects the 70th week from the 69th week. The 70th week, according to dispensationalists, is still future. Ice has not proved this, nor has any dispensationalist. Ice and all dispensationalists assume that a "gap" exists between the 69th week and 70th week of Daniel 9:24-27. There is no warrant for stopping Daniel's prophecy of the 70 weeks after the 69th week. The separation is one of the most unnatural and non-literal

---

14. Nearly all commentators, dispensational and non-dispensational, are agreed that a "week" represents a "week of years," that is, seven years.

interpretations of Scripture found anywhere within the dispensational system. In order for Ice's future fulfillment of Matthew 24 to work, the 70th week of Daniel *must* still be future. It is not.[15] Daniel tells us that "seventy weeks are decreed" (v. 24), not 69 weeks, a gap, and a yet future week. The weeks form a unit without separation.

Dispensationalists should be challenged to produce a single Bible verse that considers such a gap. Why is this so important? The dispensational system stands or falls on this doctrine. It's a point of orthodoxy among dispensationalists. Why is there no mention of this "great parenthesis" in the Bible and nearly 1900 years of church history?!

Second, Ice has not proven that Matthew 24, Luke 21, and Mark 13 address two separate events: the destruction of Jerusalem in A.D. 70 and some future fulfillment. He understands Matthew and Luke as describing two separate events. No, they are describing the same event with a different language. Luke's description is historical, while Matthew's is more theological.

Third, Ice's view mandates that a future temple must be rebuilt. There is not one verse in the New Testament that mentions

---

15. The separation of the 70th week from the 69th week is unique to dispensationalism. Any non-dispensational commentary on Daniel will give the orthodox view. Here's a list of readily available books on the subject: R. Bradley Jones, *The Great Tribulation* (Grand Rapids, MI: Baker Book House, 1980), pp. 43-61; E. J. Young, *The Prophecy of Daniel* (Grand Rapids, MI: Eerdmans, 1949); pp. 191-221; Owen, *Exposition of the Epistle to the Hebrews*, vol. 1, pp. 305-31; Philip Mauro, *The Seventy Weeks* (Swengel, PA: Reiner Publications, [1923] n.d.). Mauro, as a former Dispensationalist, wrote:

That system of interpretation I had accepted whole-heartedly and without the least misgivings, for the reason that it was commended by teachers deservedly honored and trusted because of their unswerving loyalty to the Word of God. But I had eventually to learn with sorrow, and to acknowledge with deep mortification, that the modern system of "dispensationalism". . . to which I had thoroughly committed myself, not only was without scriptural foundation, but involved doctrinal errors of a serious character. Philip Mauro, *How Long to the End?* (Boston MA: Hamilton Brothers, 1927), pp. 4, 15. Quoted in William R. Kimball, *The Rapture: A Question of Timing* (Grand Rapids, MI: Baker Book House, 1985), p. 178.

a rebuilt temple. The temple of God in the New Testament writings is quite obviously the Church of Christ or Jesus Himself (John 2:19-21). The Old Testament passages that mention a rebuilt temple were fulfilled in the post-exilic period and in the first coming of Christ. Those verses that mention a future temple, specifically Ezekiel 40-48, have reference to the church.[16] We, the church, are living stones (1 Peter 2:5) being joined together in a living temple (Ephesians 2:19-21; 1 Corinthians 3:16; 6:19; 2 Corinthians 6:16).

Fourth, a variety of interpretations has been given on the correct meaning of what or who the abomination of desolation/the man of sin is. Tommy Ice prejudices his audience against Christian Reconstruction by implying that those who have written on the subject, and assert that the abomination of desolation is the invading Roman armies or an Edomite rebellion,[17] are somehow out of accord with the history of interpretation of this passage. Yet, Desmond Ford in *The Abomination of Desolation in Biblical Eschatology* lists six possible interpretations, all held by Bible-believing Christians throughout church history: The statue of Titus erected on the side of the desolated temple; statues erected by Pilate and Hadrian; the atrocities of the Zealots; Caligula's attempted profanation; the Antichrist as the abomination of desolation; the abomination of desolation as the invading Roman armies.[18]

---

16. William Hendriksen, *Israel in Prophecy* (Grand Rapids, MI: Baker Book House, 1968). Many expositors believe, however, that Ezekiel's temple was a visionary expression of the post-exilic community and its temple, first of all, and only by extension a picture of the New Covenant. This position is maintained by James B. Jordan, *Through New Eyes* (Nashville: Wolgemuth and Hyatt, 1988), chapter 17. In defense of this Jordan cites Matthew Henry, and especially E. W. Hengstenberg, *The Prophecies of Ezekiel* (Minneapolis: James Reprints, [1869]). "With the exception of the Messianic section in ch. 47:1-12, the fulfillment of all the rest of the prophecy belongs to the times immediately after the return from the Chaldean exile. So must every one of its first hearers and readers have understood it." Hengstenberg, p. 348.

17. Chilton, *The Great Tribulation*, pp. 11-13.

18. (Washington, D.C: University Press of America, 1979), pp. 158-168. Ford, who is not a Reconstructionist, believes the abomination of desolation is the invading Roman armies: "This viewpoint gives weight to both profanation and devastation, and certainly the Roman invasion brought both. This understanding, *and this understanding alone*, rings true to the demands of the literary, philological, and historical evidence of Mk. 13." (p. 169).

What then is the abomination that makes desolate? Let's put all the references together, reconciling Matthew 24:15, Mark 13:14, Luke 21:20, Daniel 9:24-27, 11:31, 12:11, 2 Thessalonians 2:1-12, and Revelation 13:11-18 and see how these fit an A.D. 70 fulfillment.

We can dismiss Revelation 13:11-18 as having nothing to do with the abomination of desolation. Therefore, we should not be looking for the fulfillment of an image being set up in the temple that comes to life for the people to worship. Remember Ice's first point: "It happens in the Jewish temple in Jerusalem." There is no mention of the "temple in Jerusalem" in Revelation 13, the only place where an image is said to come to life. In fact, the temple is last mentioned in Revelation 11:19, and it's "in heaven." The temple is mentioned again in 14:14. It too is in heaven. None of the other passages, including 2 Thessalonians 2:1-12, refer to an image coming to life. We can conclude, therefore, that Revelation 13 has nothing to do with the abomination of desolation.

What about Daniel 9:27? Again, the dispensationalist, in order to make this a future event, must separate the 70th week from the 69th week. Whatever the interpretation is, it comes on the heels of the 69th week. It's a past event from our perspective. We do not need to look for a future fulfillment.[19]

---

19. Dispensational premillennialism, in order to salvage their eschatological system, must construct a revived Roman Empire. Leon J. Wood, a noted dispensational commentator writes:

> At some point in this symbolism [of Nebuchadnezzar's statue] an extended gap in time *must be fixed*, because by verse 44 the interpretation describes the future day of Christ's millennial reign, as will be seen. *Daniel: A Study Guide Commentary* (Grand Rapids, MI: Zondervan, 1975), pp. 39, 40. Emphasis added.

The gap "must be fixed" because a 70th week that immediately follows the 69th week doesn't fit the dispensationalist's eschatological system. Since no gap is mentioned or even inferred, the interpreter should not speculate and create an unnatural gap of nearly 2000 years!

For a rather humorous "picture" of this interpretation, see "Daniel and Revelation Compared," a chart designed and drawn by Clarence Larkin and reproduced in George M. Marsden, *Fundamentalism and American Culture: The Shaping of Twentieth Century Evangelicalism: 1870-1925* (New York: Oxford, 1980), pp. 58-59. The "ten toes" are stretched like "Silly-Putty" over more than two thousand years of history.

Luke's Gospel describes the approaching "abomination of desolation" in this way: "When you see Jerusalem surrounded by armies, then recognize that her desolation is at hand" (Luke 21:20). Whatever the "abomination of desolation" is, we do know that it came on the heels of Israel's being surrounded by armies. This has already occurred. Jesus said "when *you* see Jerusalem surrounded by armies." In a futuristic interpretation we would expect "when *they* see Jerusalem surrounded by armies." Israel was surrounded by armies (a reference to the Idumean-Zealot conspiracy that let the Edomites into the Temple) prior to A.D. 70. Soon after that, the desolation came.

The abomination that makes desolate is the high priest continuing to offer sacrifices in the Temple. This action is a flagrant rejection of the finished work of Christ, and thus, an abomination.

> False worship is idolatrous worship. When the Jews rejected Jesus and kept offering sacrifices, they were engaged in idolatry. This was the "wing of abominations" that took place in the Temple. It is why the Temple was destroyed.
>
> A full picture of this is provided in Ezekiel 8-11. . . . There you will see that when the apostate Jews of Ezekiel's day performed the sacrifices, God viewed it as an abomination. He called the holy shrine an "idol of jealousy, that provokes to jealousy" (8:3). The Jews had treated the Temple and the ark as idols, and so God would destroy them, as He did the golden calf. Ezekiel sees God pack up and move out of the Temple, leaving it empty or desolate. Once God had left, the armies of Nebuchadnezzar swept in and destroyed the empty Temple. (When we recognize that Ezekiel and Daniel prophesied at the same time, the correlation becomes even more credible.)[20]

John Calvin put forth a similar interpretation of Daniel 12:11: "First of all, we must hold this point; the time now treated by the angel begins at the last destruction of the Temple. That devastation happened as soon as the gospel began to be promulgated.

---

20. James B. Jordan, "The Abomination of Desolation: An Alternative Hypothesis." See Appendix A, p. 240, below.

God then deserted his Temple, because it was only founded for a time, and was but a shadow, until the Jews so completely violated the whole covenant that no sanctity remained in either the Temple, the nation, or the land itself."[21]

As in all fulfilled prophecy, there are still future applications. Jesus died for our sins two centuries ago, but His finished work is just as applicable to the lost today as it was to those who witnessed the events. "The destruction of the Temple and of its Jerusalem-culture, as portrayed in the remainder of revelation, was thus a warning to the Seven Churches: If you do the same, God will do this to you. Thus, the principles are still in force, and serve to warn us: If our churches depart from Christ, he will destroy both them and our society, which grew up around them."[22]

> **4. "There will be a great tribulation, such as has not occurred since the beginning of the world until now, nor ever shall" (v. 21).**

This verse follows the verses that present a localized judgment. The people are from Judea. They are still living in houses with flat roofs. It's mainly an agricultural economy. The Sabbath is still in force. The tribulation has reference to the Jews, the people of Judea (Luke 21:20-24); it is not a world-wide tribulation. The evaluation of the tribulation, however, is universal. In comparison to all the tribulations the world has experienced or ever will experience, this one is the most dreadful and horrifying.

Why? Matthew 24:21 must be seen in the light of a number of verses that show why the language used by Jesus is so incomparable:

> *The blood of all the prophets, shed since the foundation of the world, may be charged against this generation*, from the blood of Abel to the blood of Zechariah, who perished between the altar and the house of God; yes, I tell you, *it shall be charged against this generation* (Luke 11:50-52).

---

21. John Calvin, *Commentaries on the Book of the Prophet Daniel*, 2 vols. (Grand Rapids, MI: Baker Book House, 1979), vol. 2, p. 390.

22. Jordan, "Abomination of Desolation." Appendix A, p. 243.

They therefore cried out, "Away with Him, away with Him, crucify Him!" Pilate said to them, "Shall I crucify your King?" The chief priests answered, *"We have no king but Caesar"* (John 18:15).

And when Pilate saw that he was accomplishing nothing, but rather that a riot was starting, he took water and washed his hands in front of the multitude, saying, "I am innocent of this Man's blood; see to that yourselves!" And all the people answered and said, *"His blood be on us and on our children!"* Then he released Barabbas for them; but Jesus he scourged and delivered over to be crucified (Matthew 27:24-26).

And He was casting out a demon. . . . and the multitudes marveled. But some of them said, *"He casts out demons by Beelzebul, the ruler of the demons"* (Luke 11:14-15).

Therefore I say to you, any sin and blasphemy shall be forgiven men, but *blasphemy against the Spirit shall not be forgiven*. And whoever shall speak a word against the Son of Man, it shall be forgiven him; but *whoever shall speak against the Holy Spirit, it shall not be forgiven him, either in this age, or in the age to come* (Matthew 12:31-32).

For you, brethren, became imitators of the churches of God in Christ Jesus that are in Judea, for you also endured the same suffering at the hands of your own countrymen, even as they did from the Jews, who both killed the Lord Jesus and the prophets, and drove us out. They are not pleasing to God, but hostile to all men, hindering us from speaking to the Gentiles that they might be saved; *with the result that they always fill up the measure of their sins. But wrath has come upon them to the utmost* (1 Thessalonians 2:14-16).

The severity of the punishment and the hyperbolic language used by Jesus is evidence of the severity of the crime. George Murray writes that "it was the nature, rather than the magnitude of the tribulation that our Lord had in mind and which he said was to be without equal in all of history."[23] No other crime was as heinous as killing the "Lord of glory" (1 Corinthians 2:8). No group of people will ever experience a punishment as severe as this. There have been wars and rumors of wars, but a tribulation

23. George Murray, *Millennial Studies* (Grand Rapids, MI: Baker Book House, 1948), p. 107.

of this magnitude has never and will never come on the world again. God's judgment upon Jerusalem was prompted by a "covenant lawsuit." Hosea describes it as the Lord having a "case against the inhabitants of the land" (Hosea 4:1). In another place, Hosea writes:

> The LORD also has a dispute with Judah, and will punish Jacob according to his ways; He will repay him according to his deeds (12:2).

Jeremiah says it this way:

> "Therefore will I bring charges against you," says the LORD, "and against your children's children will I bring charges" (Jeremiah 2:9, NKJV).

God calls on the mountains as a witness against Israel.

> Listen, you mountains, to the indictment of the LORD, and you enduring foundations of the earth, because the LORD has a case against His people; even with Israel He will dispute (Micah 6:2).

Israel had broken the demands of the covenant. The demands of the covenant are simple: faith-filled obedience brings life, while faith-less disobedience brings death (Deuteronomy 28). The rejection of Jesus as God's promised Anointed Savior brings down God's covenant wrath upon all those who reject Him. "He who believes in the Son has eternal life; but he who does not obey the Son shall not see life, *but the wrath of God abides on him*" (John 3:36). To Israel was given "the adoption as sons and the glory of the covenants and the giving of the Law and the temple service and the promises" (Romans 9:4). Jesus was rejected as the promised Messiah early in His ministry (Luke 4:14-30). The chief priests and the elders of the people were always looking for ways to murder Him. They were hindered because of His popularity with the people (Matthew 21:46; 26:5). These were His parting words as He left the Temple:

> Behold, your house is being left to you desolate! For I say to
> you, from now on you shall not see Me until you say, "Blessed is
> He who comes in the name of the Lord" (Matthew 23:38-39).

When Jesus left the Temple for the last time, He was leaving it
empty and desolate. Just as when the shekinah glory departed
from the Temple in Ezekiel 8-11, the Temple was left desolate. The
desolate Temple was shortly filled with demons (Luke 11:20-26).
What was spiritually true in A.D. 30 became visibly true in A.D.
70: The Temple and the city were made a desolation. The Bible
teaches this in no uncertain terms. Jesus told His disciples that all
these things would come upon "this generation."

Can we really maintain that this happened in A.D. 70 when
Jesus says that this tribulation is greater than anything before it,
and it will be greater than anything after it? We know that not
even the predicted future "Great Tribulation" of dispensationalism
will be greater than the flood that left only eight people alive (cf.
Revelation 8:8-12). Jesus is using a figure of speech, proverbial
language, common to the Jewish ear to make His point of certain
destruction.

> And the locusts came up over all the land of Egypt and settled
> in all the territory of Egypt; they were very numerous. There had
> never been so many locusts, nor would there be so many again
> (Exodus 10:14).
>
> And I will give you [Solomon] riches and wealth and honor,
> such as none of the kings who were before you possessed, nor
> those who will come after you (2 Chronicles 1:12; cf. 1 Kings 3:12).
>
> A day of darkness and gloom, a day of clouds and thick dark-
> ness. As the dawn is spread over the mountains, so there is a
> great and mighty people; there has never been anything like it,
> nor will there be again after it to the years of many generations
> (Joel 2:2).

In terms of this single generation's great sin of crucifying their
Savior, the judgment that was poured out upon the once-holy city
was quite appropriate. The language that Jesus used to describe

those "days of vengeance" (Luke 21:22) fits the magnitude of the offense. The translator of Josephus's works makes the following comment in a footnote to Josephus's eyewitness account of what Jesus predicts in Matthew 24:1-34:

> That these calamities of the Jews, who were our Saviour's murderers, were to be the greatest that had ever been since the beginning of the world, our Saviour had directly foretold, (Matt. xxiv. 21; Mark xiii. 19; Luke xxi. 23, 24:) and that they proved to be such accordingly, Josephus is here a most authentic witness.[24]

5. "But immediately after the tribulation of those days THE SUN WILL BE DARKENED, AND THE MOON WILL NOT GIVE ITS LIGHT, AND THE STARS WILL FALL from the sky, and the powers of the heavens will be shaken" (v. 29).

The tribulation described above took place just prior to the destruction of Jerusalem in A.D. 70 upon the city that had rejected the Messiah, the same city that Jesus wept over. It was this Jerusalem, "who kills the prophets and stones those who are sent to her" (Matthew 23:37), that experienced this "great tribulation." With this in mind, it's important to notice that verse 29 begins with, "But *immediately after* the tribulation of those days. . . ." Whatever verse 29 means, it follows "immediately after" the tribulation described in verses 15-28. " 'Immediately' does not usually make room for much of a time gap—certainly not a gap of over 2000 years."[25]

Should we expect the sun literally to be darkened and the moon to cease reflecting the light from the sun? Will literal stars

---

24. William Whiston, "Preface" to "The Wars of the Jews" in *Josephus: Complete Works* (Grand Rapids, MI: Kregel, [1867] 1982), p. 428. The works of Josephus describe the events predicted by Jesus in Matthew 24. For a shortened version of the account, see David Chilton, *Paradise Restored: A Biblical Theology of Dominion* (Tyler, TX: Dominion Press, [1985] 1987), pp. 237-90.

25. Paul T. Butler, *The Gospel of Luke* (Joplin, MO: College Press, 1981), p. 485. Quoted in William R. Kimball, *What the Bible Says About the Great Tribulation* (Grand Rapids, MI: Baker Book House, 1985), p. 155.

fall from heaven? Now, with God all things are possible. There is the possibility of a solar eclipse, but I do not believe that text mandates such an interpretation. The dispute over what this passage means does not center on God's ability to cause these things to happen. Rather, the issue is, What does Jesus mean by the use of this type of language? Again, the Bible is our guide. Keep in mind that all these events, including those in verse 29, are to happen in the generation prior to A.D. 70: "This generation will not pass away until *all these things* take place" (v. 34).

The Old Testament is filled with lunar and stellar language depicting great political and social upheavals. In fact, Jesus quotes Isaiah 13:10; 24:23; Ezekiel 32:7; Amos 5:20; 8:9; Zephaniah 1:15, and He has in mind many more verses that use language that describes the darkening of the sun and the moon, the rolling up of the heavens like a scroll, and the falling of heavenly bodies.[26] In each case, these verses describe a judgment upon contemporary nations: Babylon (Isaiah 13:10), Egypt (Ezekiel 32:7), Israel (Amos 5:20; 8:9), Judah (Zephaniah 1:15). The judgment of nations is like the "shaking of the heavens and the earth," since when governments undergo judgment (invasions from other nations), the entire world order is in upheaval (Haggai 2:6, 21; cf. Acts 17:6: "These men who have *upset the world* have come here also."). Haggai says that this shaking will happen in "a little while" (2:6). If this is a prediction of something that's to occur 2500 years in the future, then "a little while" cannot be taken literally. But verse 21 makes it clear that the judgment is to happen during or soon after the reign of "Zerubbabel, governor of Judah," and the shaking of "the heavens and the earth" refers to the judgment of kingdoms and nations.

How do we know that this is the correct interpretation? The text immediately moves to kingdoms: "And I will overthrow the *thrones of kingdoms and destroy the power of the kingdoms of the nations.*" But couldn't this be a description of the "Great Tribulation" pre-

---

26. *Symbolic language and Israel*: Ecclesiastes 12:1-2; Amos 5:18-20; 8:2-9; Zephaniah 1:4, 15; Jeremiah 4:23; Joel 2:28-32; *Symbolic language and the nations*: Ezekiel 30; 32:7-15; Isaiah 34:4-10; 13:9-20.

dicted by the dispensationalists for the distant future? I don't believe so. The text tells us that God "will overthrow the *chariots and their riders, and the horses and their riders will go down, everyone by the sword of another*" (2:22). This is a description of pre-modern armies. Now, unless we say that the writer had no way of describing future events, some might conclude that chariots and swords are nothing more than a description of implements of war for any age.[27] But doesn't this severely damage the "literal hermeneutic" espoused by dispensationalists?

What about stars falling from the sky? In the Bible, leaders and nations are described as stars. Their fall is an indicator of judgment. Hal Lindsey makes this point for us:

> The "star" of Revelation 9:1 has to be a person rather than a literal star, since "he" is given a key with which he opens the bottomless pit. I believe this fallen star is none other than Satan himself, described in Isaiah 14:12 as "Lucifer" or "Star of the Morning."[28]

But some dispensationalists insist that there must be a future fulfillment that includes the falling of stars. Here's one example:

> Rev. 6:12 describes the sixth seal; a great earthquake, the sun darkened, the moon becoming like blood and the stars falling. To relate this symbolically ignores the context; it isn't poetic as some of the OT passages are, and the response of the men is to hide in caves. Rev. 8:12 says a third of the sun and moon and stars will be

---

27. The extremes of a forced literalism are found in a number of dispensational tracts that try to be "consistent" with the literal hermeneutic. In describing the battle of Gog and Magog of Ezekiel 38 and 39, one author tries to force his futuristic interpretation on the chariots that are burned for fuel in a future battle between Israel and Russia (*Rosh*). He asks this question: "Why should nations in the future give up guns, tanks, airplanes, cannon and weapons of steel for a reversion to implements of wood?" (p. 49). Future "warring nations will have to turn to weapons of wood — or rubber!" to nullify the effects of a type of weapon that only reacts to metal. Harry Rimmer, *The Coming War and the Rise of Russia* (Grand Rapids, MI: Eerdmans, 1940), p. 50. Maybe Howard Hughes's "Spruce Goose" is a fulfillment of Bible prophecy!

28. Hal Lindsey, *There's a New World Coming: "A Prophetic Odyssey"* (New York: Bantam Books, [1973] 1984), p. 121.

darkened. How can this be? Physiologically or scientifically it may be difficult to comprehend exactly how this takes place. Does it mean that the light is reduced, that heat is reduced, clouds block the vision of man, or what? I believe that Rev. 8:10, 11 helps clarify part of this. The waters of the earth are polluted by the falling of a great star. This is clearly physiological, but spoken in a language of appearance. Just as we know that it is the earth that revolves around the sun, yet still speak of sunrise and sunset, so we, speaking of comets as "shooting stars," when we know they are not stars. Even though we may not understand exactly how this takes place, that something dramatic will take place in the heavenly bodies cannot be doubted.[29]

This dispensational author tells us that the language "isn't poetic as some of the OT passages." Let's test this assertion: The stars of the sky fell to the earth, "as a fig tree casts its unripe figs" (Revelation 6:13); the "sky was split apart like a scroll when it is rolled up" (v. 14); "*the Lamb* broke one of the seven seals" (v. 1); John "heard one of the *four living creatures* say as with a *voice of thunder*, 'Come.'"

The entire Book of Revelation reads like this. It's absurd to claim that this chapter is not poetic. Dean tells us that hiding in caves proves that the chapter cannot be symbolic or poetic. If the point of the chapter is to describe economic and political upheaval in descriptive terms reminiscent of the plagues on Egypt, then hiding in a cave is a natural thing (Judges 6:1-6). But hiding in a cave seems to indicate a localized judgment as well as a first-century judgment. David Chilton's comments are to the point:

> The *name* of this fallen star is *Wormwood*, a term used in the Law and the Prophets to warn Israel of its destruction as a punishment for apostasy (Deut. 29:18; Jer. 9:15; 23:15; Lam. 3:15, 19; Amos 5:7). Again, by combining these Old Testament allusions, St. John makes his point: Israel is apostate, and has become an Egypt; Jerusalem has become a Babylon; and the covenant breakers will be destroyed, as surely as Egypt and Babylon were destroyed.[30]

---

29. Robert L. Dean, "Essentials of Dispensational Theology," *Biblical Perspectives* (Jan/Feb, 1988), p. 4. This newsletter is published by Tommy Ice.

30. David Chilton, *The Days of Vengeance: An Exposition of the Book of Revelation* (Ft. Worth, TX: Dominion Press, 1987), p. 240.

With this background, we can conclude that immediately after the destruction of Jerusalem there would be a great shake-up of the world powers. The church would be freed from the womb of Judaism, and would go forth to "turn the world upside down."

> **6. "And then the sign of the Son of Man will appear in the sky, and then all the tribes of the earth will mourn, and they will see the SON OF MAN COMING ON THE CLOUDS OF THE SKY with power and great glory" (v. 30).**

This single verse is one of the most difficult to interpret in light of an A.D. 70 fulfillment, especially as translated in the New American Standard Version. Is Jesus "coming down" to earth to set up His thousand year millennial reign? Or, does His "coming" refer to something else? Let's begin by seeing what the Bible means by God "coming on the clouds." "Behold, the LORD is riding on a swift cloud, and is about to come to Egypt" (Isaiah 19:1). God riding on a swift cloud is an expression of His sovereignty over the nations as their judge.[31]

> He makes His clouds His chariots; He walks upon the wings of the wind; He makes the winds His messengers; flaming fire His ministers (Psalm 104:3).

God didn't literally appear on a cloud, using them as a "chariot" as He is depicted in Psalm 104:3. This is the language of judgment and retribution. No one takes this literally.

This same language is used by Isaiah to describe God's coming in judgment upon Egypt. Who judged Egypt? God did. Did the Egyptians "see" Him? Yes and no. They saw Him in the judgment that He meted out. They *understood* and *realized* that He was the true God by what they *saw* coming upon them. John Calvin writes that Isaiah "speaks of the defeat of the Egyptians by the Assyrians, and shews that it ought to be ascribed to God, and not,

---

31. Edward J. Young, *The Book of Isaiah*, 3 vols. (Grand Rapids, MI: Eerdmans, 1969), vol. 2, p. 14.

as irreligious men commonly do, to fortune. He shows it to be a judgment of God, by whose hand all things are governed."[32]

At first reading, Matthew 24:30 seems to indicate that we should expect to see Jesus "appear in the sky . . . coming on clouds." But this is not what it says, and as we've seen, coming on the clouds of heaven is a general description of judgment. Unfortunately, we're working with a poor translation. The older *American Standard Version* (1901) reads, "And then shall appear the sign of the Son of Man in heaven." But let's go further and translate from the Greek:

> Then the sign of the Son of Man will appear *in heaven*, and then all the tribes of the *land*[33] will mourn, and they will see[34] the Son of Man coming on the clouds *of heaven* with power and great glory.

This is a word-for-word translation from the Greek. The "sign" is that the Son of Man is *in heaven* at His Father's right hand. Isn't this what Peter preached at Pentecost?: "Therefore *having been exalted to the right hand of God*, and having received from the Father the promise of the Holy Spirit, He has poured forth this which you both see and hear" (Acts 2:33). How were the gathered Jews to know that Jesus had been "exalted to the right hand of God"? According to Peter, it was the outpouring of the Holy Spirit at Pentecost. By "seeing" and "hearing" they knew that Jesus was in heaven. This was God's *sign to Israel*. Isn't this also what Stephen saw? "Behold, I see the heavens opened up and the Son of Man *standing at the right hand of God*" (Acts 7:56).

The Book of Daniel is the reference point for Jesus' words in Matthew 24:30, not our twentieth-century imaginations. When

---

32. John Calvin, *Commentary on the Book of the Prophet Isaiah*, 4 vols. (Grand Rapids, MI: Baker Book House, 1979), vol. 1, p. 49. Dave Hunt has a problem with this concept of coming. According to Hunt, Jesus just could not have "come" in A.D. 70 to destroy Jerusalem through the agency of the Roman armies. See his May 1988 *CIB Bulletin*, p. 2. But the Bible expresses God's coming in just this way.

33. Compare with Luke 21:23.

34. Compare with Matthew 26:64.

you look at Daniel 7:13-14, you will notice something very interesting. The coming of the Son of Man is not *down* but *up*! Jesus
comes *up* "with the clouds of heaven" *to* "the Ancient of Days and
was presented before Him." There is nothing unusual about this
interpretation. The following quotation from R. T. France expresses the view above:

> Our discussion of the meaning of Daniel 7:13 in its Old Testa-
> ment context led us to the conclusion that its keynote is one of
> vindication and exaltation to an everlasting dominion, and that
> the 'coming' of verse 13 was a coming *to* God [the Ancient of
> Days] to receive power, *not* a 'descent' to earth. When we studied
> Jesus' use of the these verses, we found that in every case this
> same theme was the point of the allusion, and, in particular, that
> nowhere (unless here) was verse 13 [in Daniel 7] interpreted of his
> coming to earth at the Parousia. In particular, the reference to
> Mark 14:62, where the wording is clearly parallel to that in the
> present verse [Mark 13:26], was to Jesus' imminent vindication
> and power, with a secondary reference to a manifestation of that
> power in the near future. Thus, the expectation that Jesus would
> in fact use Daniel 7:13 in the sense in which it was written is amply
> confirmed by his actual allusions. He saw in that verse a predic-
> tion of his imminent exaltation to an authority which supersedes
> that of the earthly powers which have set themselves against God.[35]
> Jesus is using Daniel 7:13 as a prediction of that authority which
> he exercised when in A.D. 70 the Jewish nation and its leaders,
> who had condemned him, were overthrown, and Jesus was vindi-
> cated as the recipient of all power from the Ancient of Days.[36]

This description fits very well with Matthew 16:28 and Matthew
26:64.

So, then, what does verse 30 mean? After the destruction of
Jerusalem, God begins to shake down the nations with the gospel.
All the tribes of the land (localized judgment) will see, that is, will
recognize and acknowledge that the Son of Man has gone to heaven

---

35. R. T. France, *Jesus and the Old Testament* (Grand Rapids, MI: Baker Book
House, [1971] 1982), p. 235. Emphasis added.

36. *Ibid.*, p. 236.

and is enthroned at the Father's right hand. They will "see the sign of the heavenly enthronement of the Son of Man" in the destruction of Jerusalem. The Old Covenant order with its types and shadows has passed away. The heavenly Jerusalem remains. After all, the destruction of Jerusalem was to serve as a sign to Jesus' tormentors in Matthew 26:64 that He was the predicted Son of Man who was to receive "dominion, glory, and a kingdom, that all the peoples, nations, and men of every language might serve Him" — a kingdom "which will not pass away" or "be destroyed" (Daniel 7:13-14).

But what is the "sign"? Jesus said that the only sign that would be given to that generation, which is the generation upon which all these things was going to come, was the sign of Jonah (Matthew 12:38-45; 16:1-4). These verses show that the "sign of Jonah" involved three things. First, the death, resurrection, and glorification of Jesus Christ. Second, judgment upon demonized (apostate) Israel, as God told Jonah to leave Israel. And third, salvation to the Gentiles, as Jonah preached to Nineveh and Nineveh was converted, or as the Queen of Sheba came to Solomon.

The sign of the Kingdom, then, is the whole complex of events in the first century, as pictured in type by Jonah. *After* the destruction of Jerusalem, the Gentiles would perceive this sign as well. They would perceive the redemptive work of Jesus Christ, and they would perceive that the gospel had been sent to them.

7. And He will send forth His angels WITH A GREAT TRUMPET and THEY WILL GATHER TOGETHER His elect FROM THE FOUR WINDS, FROM ONE END OF THE SKY [HEAVEN] TO THE OTHER" (v. 31).

Here again we find symbols that we should let the Bible interpret for us. Immediately after the destruction of Jerusalem, God begins to shake down the world (Matthew 24:29). The nations begin to recognize Christ as King (v. 30). What else? In context, verse 31 is not jumping to the end of the world. Rather, it is speaking of the sending out of the gospel to the nations of the world.

"Angels," in Greek, is simply "messengers" (cf. Matthew 11:10; Mark 1:2; Luke 7:24; 9:52; James 2:25; cf. Isaiah 52:7-10). These messengers call together God's people "from the four winds," a reference to the four corners of the earth (Luke 13:29), and from one end of the sky to the other, again a reference to the entire horizon of the world (Psalm 22:27; Deuteronomy 4:32; cf. Matthew 28:18-20).

The trumpet here is the call of the gospel. It refers back to Numbers 10:1-10, where silver trumpets were made to call the people together for worship, and to set them on their march. It also alludes to the Year of Jubilee, the year when the world reverts to its original owners, the year when Satan is dispossessed and Christ reclaims the world (Acts 3:19-21). "Now is the acceptable time" (2 Corinthians 6:2). This year was also announced by trumpets, and portrayed the coming of Christ's kingdom (Leviticus 25:8-17; Luke 4:16-21; Isaiah 61:1-3).

Of course, the gospel began to go to the world at Pentecost, but throughout Acts we always see the gospel going "to the Jew first" (Romans 1:16). With the destruction of Jerusalem, however, the gospel went out to the Gentiles with a new fullness.

This verse is highly symbolic: trumpet, four winds, from one end of the sky to another. The trumpet is symbolic of a great work about to commence, the great gathering of God's people into a new nation. The word for "gather" is the Greek word *sunagoge*. A gathering of Jews met in a synagogue. Judaism, in its rejection of Christ, had become a "synagogue of Satan" (Revelation 2:9; 3:9). The true synagogue of God—the church—is made up of believing Jews and Gentiles. The elect are scattered around the world, "from the four winds, from one end of the sky to the other" (cf. Matthew 28:18-20). God heralds the great ingathering of His elect from every tribe, tongue, and nation by sending His angels, ministers of the gospel.

8. "Now learn the parable from the fig tree: when its branch has already become tender, and puts forth its leaves, you know that summer is near; even so you too, when you see all these things, recognize that He is near, right at the door" (vv. 32-33).

Some interpreters have taken these verses to be speaking of Israel returning to their land in fulfillment of a number of Old Testament prophecies.[37] For them, the "fig tree" would be identified with Israel becoming a nation again. But where is the biblical evidence for this? There is no biblical evidence. Even Hal Lindsey admits this when he writes: "The figure of speech 'fig tree' has been a *historic* symbol of national Israel."[38] It may be an *historic* symbol, but it's not a *biblical* symbol. Lindsey doesn't even prove how it's an historic symbol.

Some commentators tell us that Jesus is undoing the curse that He placed on the fig tree — Israel — in Matthew 21:19. Jesus saw a "lone fig tree by the road" and He "found nothing on it except leaves only; and He said to it, 'No longer shall there ever be any fruit from you.' And at once the fig tree withered." This passage is quite clear. If the withered fig tree is Israel, Jesus tells us that "*no longer shall there ever be* any fruit from you." Would Jesus undo in Matthew 24:32 what He just did in such an emphatic way in Matthew 21:19?

The parallel passage in Luke 21:29 shows that it's not just the fig tree; it's "all the trees."

> And He told them a parable: "Behold the fig tree, *and all the trees*; as soon as *they* put forth, you see it and know for yourselves that the summer is now near. Even so you too, when you see these things happening, know that the kingdom of God is near (vv. 29-30).

Thus, it is not the fig tree in isolation, but all the trees whose budding heralds summer. The parable of the fig tree is used as an analogy. When you see leaves on a fig tree, and for that matter, all the trees, you know that summer is near. In a similar way, when you see all these signs, then know that Jesus is near, "right at the door" (Matthew 24:33).

---

37. For an evaluation of this interpretation, see Hendriksen, *Israel in Prophecy.*
38. Hal Lindsey, *The Late Great Planet Earth* (Grand Rapids, MI: Zondervan, [1970] 1971), p. 53. Emphasis added.

Jesus used a similar analogy in Matthew 16:1-4. The Pharisees and Sadducees were asking Jesus to produce a sign from heaven to prove who He was. The Pharisees and Sadducees were able to discern the signs regarding approaching weather, but they could not discern the signs that Jesus had already produced proving His Messiahship. Jesus often used natural phenomena to make His points with the stiff-necked religious leaders of His day.

One final point should be made about the fig tree representing Israel. The New Testament is very clear that the preferred symbols for Israel are the vine (John 15:1-11), the olive tree (Romans 11:16-24), the lump of dough (Romans 11:16), and the flock (Isaiah 40:11; Jeremiah 23:2; Matthew 26:31; Luke 12:32; John 10:16; 1 Peter 5:2). In the case of the flock and the olive tree, both Jews and Gentiles make up these representative groups of God's people. Jesus said that He has "other sheep, which are not of this fold; *I must bring them also*, and they shall hear My voice; *and they shall become one flock with one shepherd*" (John 10:16). There is one olive tree with Gentiles grafted in to make one tree, consisting of believing Jews and Gentiles.

All these events are a prelude to Jesus' coming in judgment upon apostate Judaism. This destruction will be the manifestation of Jesus' enthronement in heaven, the passing away of the old covenant order, and the inauguration of the age to come. Jesus will consummate His work in a yet future day:

> Then comes the end, when He delivers up the kingdom to the God and Father, when He has abolished all rule and all authority and power. For He must reign until He has put all His enemies under His feet. The last enemy that will be abolished is death. For He has put all things in subjection under His feet. But when He says, "All things are put in subjection," it is evident that He is excepted who put all things in subjection to Him. And when all things are subjected to Him, then the Son Himself also will be subjected to the One who subjected all things to Him, that God may be all in all (1 Corinthians 15:24-28).

Conclusion

A preterist interpretation is not essential to the basic tenets of Christian Reconstruction. But as has been shown in this chapter, the preterist interpretation is a biblical one. It is not an interpretation invented by Reconstructionists to prop up their system. The preterist interpretation has been used by many fine biblical scholars. It is an ancient view. The following remarks summarize the points made in this chapter.

> If, as is more probable [than "this generation" referring to the Jewish race], the Saviour uttered these words in connection with the prophesied distress of the Jewish people and the destruction of Jerusalem, His words mean that, before the generation then living should have died out, these things would occur. And this is what actually happened. Towards the end of A.D. 70 (i.e. some forty years after Jesus uttered these words) everything predicted by Him in verses 10-24 [of Luke 21] in connection with the events before and during the destruction of Jerusalem was already fulfilled—the temple was destroyed to the last stone, all Jerusalem was a ruin, the Jewish people were slain by hundreds of thousands . . . and carried off into captivity.[39]

Few Christians are even aware that another interpretation of the Olivet Discourse has been a part of the church for centuries. In fact, it goes back at least to Eusebius in the early part of the fourth century. No matter what your view, search the Scriptures daily to see whether these things are so (Acts 17:11).

---

39. Norval Geldenhuys, *Commentary on the Gospel of Luke* (Grand Rapids, MI: Eerdmans, 1951), pp. 538-39.

15

DAVE HUNT: A RESPONSE

Dave Hunt began his presentation by telling the audience that he found very little that he would disagree with in my opening remarks. Of course, I was heartened by such an endorsement. But as he continued with his presentation, I began to realize that the debate was going to revolve around fairly minor points of theology that have become major points in a questionable theological system, dispensational premillennialism. If a Christian does not believe Hunt's interpretation of the millennium or the rapture, his theology is suspect. If a Christian does not understand dominion Hunt's way, he may be judged to be "deviant." Centuries of theological thought are thrown out the window to support a novel and narrow interpretation of Scripture. This, unfortunately, seems to be the way the church is moving. Theological popularizers maintain that only they are carrying the banner of orthodoxy.

In Dave Hunt's sequel to the *Seduction of Christianity*, entitled *Beyond Seduction*, he states in the subtitle that he's dealing with *A Return to Biblical Christianity*. This is misleading. Dave Hunt does not take his readers through the history of theological debate. For him, orthodoxy was fashioned in the nineteenth century.

Dave Hunt admitted in the question and answer period of the debate that he isn't a scholar. Of course, one does not have to be a scholar to discuss theology. But one ought to know at least something of the history of theology to participate constructively in any debate over theology. Keep in mind that Hunt's *The Seduction of Christianity* has sold nearly 700,000 copies since 1985.[1]

---

1. Peter Steinfels, "Idolatries of the 1980's," *The New York Times Book Review*, April 17, 1988.

Christians view Dave Hunt as an authority. Yet by his own admission, he isn't an authority, at least on the history of doctrine. He even admits that he doesn't understand what Christian Reconstructionists mean by dominion! There are certainly enough books that could inform even the most casual reader what Reconstructionists mean by dominion. *The Reduction of Christianity* has a long and detailed definition.[2] Hunt gives the impression to his audience that the Reconstructionists' views on dominion are confusing since even he is not able to figure out what we mean.

I've chosen Dave Hunt's main points of disagreement with Christian Reconstruction and have answered them in terms of the Bible, the history of doctrine, their relationship with "orthodox" dispensational theology, and logical consistency.

Natural Law and Norman L. Geisler

"I would agree," Dave Hunt said, "that it is a blessing to those who obey God and that all of Scripture applies to all of life." Hunt's next series of comments create a great rift within the dispensational camp.

> And I certainly, regardless of what Norm Geisler believes, do not believe in natural law. There are no laws in nature. There are no moral amoebas or anything like that. Laws come only from God.

It's important to stop here and discuss why this is such a staggering admission. Dr. Geisler, who was at the time Professor of Systematic Theology at Dallas Theological Seminary, is a spokesman for dispensational premillennialism, and a vocal critic of Christian Reconstruction. Hunt was responding to the following statement made by Dr. Geisler and quoted by me in the debate.

> Government is not based on special revelation, such as the Bible. It is based on God's general revelation to all men. . . .

---

2. Gary DeMar and Peter Leithart, *The Reduction of Christianity: A Biblical Response to Dave Hunt* (Ft. Worth, TX: Dominion Press/Atlanta, GA: American Vision, 1988), pp. 24-29.

Thus, civil law, based as it is in natural moral law, lays no specifically religious obligation on man.[3]

Of course, the question of what "natural law" means is complex. Often, I suspect, it is just a smokescreen for fuzzy thinking. I imagine that Geisler believes that "natural law" comes from God, and is not "in" nature in any pantheistic sense, so that he would agree with Hunt's statement. It is refreshing, however, to find that Dave Hunt does not want to waste time with the vagaries of "natural law," whatever that is, and wants to stick with the Bible. In that regard, he is much closer to Christian Reconstruction than he is to Dr. Geisler.

The Old Testament Law

Dave Hunt says that he would not "throw out the Old Testament law." This single statement keeps him in the orthodox and confessional faith. Keep in mind that dispensationalist writers frequently "attack" the Old Testament law as if it had no usefulness in the New Covenant at all. For many, law in the Old Testament is "Jewish law."[4] In Dallas Theological Seminary's scholarly journal, *Bibliotheca Sacra*, S. Lewis Johnson, a former professor at the seminary, argued that the Ten Commandments should not *as such* be a part of the Christian's ethical life. He quotes Donald Grey Barnhouse for his support:

> Donald Grey Barnhouse, a giant of a man in free grace, wrote: "It was a tragic hour when the Reformation churches wrote the Ten Commandments into their creeds and catechisms and sought to bring Gentile believers into bondage to Jewish law, which was never intended either for the Gentile nations or for the church." He was right, too.[5]

---

3. "A Premillennial View of Law and Government," *The Best in Theology*, gen. ed. J. I. Packer (Carol Stream, IL: Christianity Today/Word, 1986), vol. 1, p. 259.

4. "To be sure, dispensational premillenarians insist that the Old Testament Law was given only to the Jews and not to Gentiles." *Idem.* See the multi-volume dispensational work, Lewis Sperry Chafer, *Systematic Theology*, 8 vols. (Dallas, TX: Dallas Seminary Press, 1947), vol. 4, pp. 234-43.

5. S. Lewis Johnson, "The Paralysis of Legalism," *Bibliotheca Sacra*, Vol. 120 (April/June, 1963), p. 109.

I believe these statements from Barnhouse and Johnson are extreme[6] and certainly "on the edge" of what the Bible teaches and historic Christianity has taught. Consider the Bible. God's standard of justice is the same for all His creatures, whether Jew or Gentile. This even includes nations which consider themselves to be non-Christian. Some believe that because they do not acknowledge God as Lord and King they somehow are exempt from following the law of God. Sodom and Gomorrah enjoyed no such exemption: "Now the men of Sodom were wicked exceedingly and sinners against God" (Genesis 13:13). This wicked city was destroyed for breaking God's law: in particular, the sin of homosexuality (Genesis 19:4-5; Leviticus 18:22; 20:13).[7] Jonah went to preach to the non-Israelite city of Nineveh because of its national sins. If the Ninevites were not obligated to keep the law of God, then how could they be expected to repent, and why was God about to judge them (Jonah 3)?

The stranger, an individual *outside* the covenant community of Israel, was obligated to obey the law of God: "There shall be one standard for you; it shall be for the stranger as well as the native, for I am the LORD your God" (Leviticus 24:22; cf. Numbers 15:16; Deuteronomy 1:16-17).

The law as given to Israel was a standard for the nations surrounding Israel also. When these nations heard of the righteous judgments within Israel, they would remark with wonder: "Surely this great nation is a wise and understanding people" (Deuteronomy 4:6). The psalmist proclaims to the kings and judges of the earth "to take warning . . . and worship the LORD with reverence . . ." and to do "homage to the Son" (Psalm 2:10-11).

> It is striking how frequently the other nations are called upon in the Psalms to recognize and to honor God, and how complete is the witness of the prophets against the nations surrounding Israel. God does not exempt other nations from the claim of his

---

6. In talking with a number of dispensationalists and former students of Dallas Theological Seminary, I've been told that this statement by Barnhouse is mild in comparison with some other dispensational writers.

7. See Gary DeMar, "Homosexuality: An Illegitimate Alternative Deathstyle," *The Biblical Worldview* (January 1987), Vol. 3, No. 1.

righteousness; he requires their obedience and holds them responsible for their apostasy and degeneration [e.g., Amos 1:3-15 - 2:1-5].[8]

The New Testament and the Law

The New Testament presupposes the validity of the law of the Old Testament. John the Baptist used the law of God to confront Herod—an Idumean—in his adulterous affair: "Herod . . . had John arrested and bound in prison on account of Herodias, the wife of his brother Philip, because he had married her. For John had been saying to Herod, '*It is not lawful for you to have your brother's wife*' " (Mark 6:17-18; Leviticus 20:10; Deuteronomy 22:22).[9] This was not mere advice. John lost his own head in the exchange.

The psalmist declares he "will speak of Thy testimonies before kings, and shall not be ashamed" (Psalm 119:46). These testimonies are the "commandments" which he loves (v. 47). Similarly, Jesus tells His disciples that persecution will give them an opportunity to speak "before governors and kings . . . as a testimony to them and to the Gentiles" (Matthew 10:18).

Notice what John the Baptist told some civil servants who approached him regarding their obligations to the law of God: "Some tax-gatherers also came to be baptized, and they said to him, 'Teacher, what shall we do?' And he said to them, 'Collect no

---

8. J. H. Bavinck, *An Introduction to the Science of Missions* (Nutley, NJ: Presbyterian and Reformed, 1960), pp. 12-13.

9. Norman Geisler writes that "Nowhere in the Bible are Gentiles ever condemned for not keeping the law of Moses. God always measured them by the truths of the general revelation (see Jonah 1; Nah. 2)." "Should We Legislate Morality?," *Fundamentalist Journal* (July/August 1988), p. 17. Dr. Geisler is mistaken. The inhabitants of Sodom and Gomorrah were destroyed for breaking a specific law that would eventually be codified in the Mosaic legislation—sodomy (Genesis 13:13; 19:4-5; cf. Leviticus 18:22; 20:13). There were always special revelational laws prior to Moses: "Abraham obeyed Me, and kept My charge, My commandments, My statutes, and My laws" (Genesis 26:5; cf. Job 22:22; 23:12). A sacrificial system was introduced by God through special revelation before the Mosaic legislation (e.g., Genesis 8:20; 22:13; Job 1:5; 42:7-9). The *stranger*, an individual *outside* the covenant community of Israel, was required to obey the Mosaic legislation: "There shall be *one standard* for you; *it shall be for the stranger as well as the native*, for I am the LORD your God" (Leviticus 24:22; cf. Numbers 15:16; Deuteronomy 1:16-17). Belshazzar, a Gentile, broke specific laws from the Mosaic legislation relating to idolatry (Daniel 5).

more than what you have been ordered to.' And some soldiers were questioning him, saying, 'And what about us, what shall we do?' And he said to them, 'Do not take money from anyone by force, or accuse anyone falsely, and be content with your wages'" (Luke 3:13-14). John was not appealing to them on the basis of some "neutral" law; instead, he referred them to the sixth, ninth, and tenth commandments of the Decalogue (Exodus 20).

Zaccheus, an unscrupulous tax collector, followed the laws of restitution by promising to pay back those he defrauded: "If I have defrauded anyone of anything, I will give back four times as much" (Luke 19:8; cf. Exodus 22:1; Leviticus 6:5).

Christians are obligated to inform those who rule in the civil sphere of the demands of the law and the consequences of disobedience. There is no area of life where man is exempt from the demands of the law of God. In Romans 13 the civil magistrate is said to be a "minister of God" who has the responsibility and authority to punish evildoers. As God's servants they are obligated to rule God's way. Just as a minister in the church is obligated to implement the law of God as it touches on ecclesiastical matters, a civil servant must implement the law of God as it relates to civil affairs. The determination of good and evil must derive from some objective standard.

Paul ends the section dealing with the civil magistrate by quoting from the Ten Commandments, and proceeds to tell us that they are summed up in the single commandment, "You shall love your neighbor as yourself" (Romans 13:9). But this isn't something unique to the New Testament. Paul quotes from Leviticus 19:18 for this summary of the law. Now, some might want to maintain that love *supplants* the law since it's a summary of all the law is. But a summary does not nullify what it summarizes. Does a summary at the end of a chapter in a book nullify and supplant what it summarizes? Of course not. In the same way, love as the summary of the law does not nullify the details of what it summarizes.

Others might want to maintain that love is our sole guide when it comes to ethical behavior since Paul says that "he who loves his neighbor has fulfilled the law" (v. 10). But the question remains: How do you know when you are loving your neighbor?

Again, love without specifics becomes license. Love must always be defined in some way. The law gives definition to love. Besides, did not Paul "confirm" the law (Romans 3:31), which was "holy, just, and good" (7:12, 14)?

The redemptive work of Jesus does not free us from an obligation to keep the moral law—including the social ones—laid down in the Bible. Scripture shows no instance of an individual, Christian or pagan, who is no longer required to keep the laws outlined in Scripture. Christians are freed from the "curse of the law" (Galatians 3:13), but not from the demands of the law: "Do we then nullify the Law through faith? May it never be! On the contrary, we establish the Law" (Romans 3:31). Of course, the non-Christian is free neither from the curse of the law nor from the demands of the law: "He who believes in Him is not judged [because he is free from the law's curse]; he who does not believe has been judged already, because he has not believed in the name of the only begotten Son of God" (John 3:18).

Now, I recognize that Geisler, Johnson, Barnhouse, and other dispensationalists might want to say that the "fundamental morality" of the Old Testament law is binding on all peoples and binding in the New Testament. They would go to New Testament passages to show this. Also, I recognize that *some* orthodox dispensationalists may teach that the New Testament "church" is the "mystery form" of the "Millennial Kingdom," and thus that the laws of the Kingdom have some "shadowy" relevance to us. It is also true that ignoring the Old Testament law is hardly a problem unique to dispensationalism. No branch of Christianity has done much with the Mosaic law in the last two centuries. It remains a fact, however, that the Mosaic law is absolutely fundamental to the wisdom of Proverbs, the praise of the Psalms, the preaching of the Prophets, and the glories of the New Covenant. We are not "bound" under the Mosaic law in the sense that we live under the Old Covenant, but at the same time we dare not despise its wisdom. After all, God wrote it for our good. Some dispensationalists say that "All the Bible is *for* us, though not all the Bible is addressed *to* us." Very well, then, let us assiduously study the Mosaic law to see what it has to say *for* us, and for our good. And let us stop *attacking* biblical law as if it were an enemy!

Dave Hunt assures us that he "would not throw out the Old Testament law." For this we are thankful. This single statement should place him nearer to the Reconstructionists than to the dispensationalists. Later in the debate, however, during the question and answer session, Dave Hunt seemed to contradict his belief in the abiding validity of the Old Testament law. We'll approach this subject again at that point in the debate.

Reconstruction, Suffering, and Victory

Now, Dave Hunt moves to what he believes Reconstructionists do not teach. He states:

> I certainly also agree on the authority of all Scripture, but I think that you [i.e., Reconstructionists] tend to ignore certain Scriptures. Those that speak of suffering. You emphasize the victory, and the positive side of it. I think you have a lot of affinity with those we call the "positive confession" movement.

So then, where is the "deviance"? Is it because we do not *emphasize* suffering? As I state later in the debate, Christian Reconstruction is a theology of emphasis. Our writings are directed to Christians to show them how the Bible applies to our world in the midst of suffering, persecution, and evil. Why didn't Dave Hunt respond to the sections in *The Reduction of Christianity* where we discuss suffering?[10] Dave Hunt and Tommy Ice continued to misrepresent Christian Reconstruction in spite of the detailed definitions and explanations set forth in *The Reduction of Christianity*. The topic of suffering is no different.

R. J. Rushdoony, a noted Reconstructionist, writes: "St. Paul, after the shattering experience of his conversion, did not eat or drink for three days (Acts 9:9); he knew what it meant to be a Christian, and it was not a 'fun thing' with him but an experience

---

10. DeMar and Leithart, *Reduction of Christianity*, pp. 136-38, 193-94.

which brought him persecution and trouble as well as the glory of God's grace."[11]

It's clear, after listening to Dave Hunt compare Christian Reconstructionism with the "Positive Confession" movement, that he does not understand the Reformed theology (Calvinism) that is an essential distinctive of Christian Reconstruction.[12] Let's take a brief look at how each group understands "victory."

The Reconstructionist believes that no matter what happens to the Christian, he is, by God's grace, victorious. Whether he is going through tribulation, persecution, suffering, ill-health, paralysis, poverty, joblessness, or even death, he is victorious because he is *in Christ and Christ is in him*. We always have the victory, no matter what the circumstances. The kingdom still advances even though Christians are suffering and are being persecuted. Outward circumstances might not show the victory, but God is on His throne, and He will turn these circumstances to His glory.[13] Tertullian was right when he said that "the blood of martyrs is the seed of the church." The more the church bleeds, the more quickly she grows. Those outside of Christ "will not make further progress" (2 Timothy 3:9). Consider some of the most encouraging and victorious words in the Bible:

> Who shall separate us from the love of Christ? Shall tribulation, or distress, or persecution, or famine, or nakedness, or peril, or sword? Just as it is written, "For Thy sake we are being put to death all day long; we were considered as sheep to be slaughtered." *But in all these things we overwhelmingly conquer through Him who loved us. For I am convinced that neither death, nor life, nor angels, nor principalities, nor things present, nor things to come, nor powers, nor height,*

---

11. R. J. Rushdoony, *God's Plan for Victory: The Meaning of Postmillennialism* (Fairfax, VA: Thoburn Press, 1977), p. 48.

12. DeMar and Leithart, *Reduction of Christianity*, pp. 31-36. Tommy Ice, Dave Hunt's debating partner, is also a Calvinist.

13. R. J. Rushdoony said, "I hold to postmillennialism not because I look at the world, but because I look at the Bible. And the Bible tells me all things shall be put under Christ's feet before the end." Quoted in Rodney Clapp, "Democracy as Heresy," *Christianity Today* (February 20, 1987), p. 19.

nor depth, nor any other created thing, shall be able to separate us from the love of God, which is in Christ Jesus our Lord (Romans 8:35-39).

Reformed theology has always taught that suffering is in God's hands, that He administers and oversees it. Because it is God's doing, we can rejoice even in suffering. The book of Job is a testimony of one man's experience in the midst of suffering. God was in control throughout the ordeal. Satan was on God's leash (Job 1:6-12; 2:1-6). In the end, God gets the glory for Job's suffering. R. J. Rushdoony writes that it was the book of Job that made him a Calvinist.[14] The book of Job forces the Christian to give up any lingering autonomy to the uncompromised sovereignty of God. Rushdoony shows the significance of suffering in terms of God's sovereignty:

> Many a godly man has been afflicted as Job was afflicted, has seen his life's work dissolved by catastrophe, has seen the wicked prosper while he has been brought low, humbled, and destroyed, has cried out with Job in agony of spirit and bitterness and wondered at the ways of God that permitted such things to come to pass. The conclusion that Job reached therefore, whereby he understood the standard of God in dealing with himself and with all men, becomes especially relevant to our generation. When Job was first laid low, found himself stripped of all his possessions, his family destroyed, and he himself sick both in body and soul, his immediate reaction was one of faith, "Naked I came out of my mother's womb, and naked shall I return thither: The Lord gave, and the Lord hath taken away: blessed be the name of the Lord. In all this Job sinned not, nor charged God foolishly" (Job 1:21, 22).[15]

Job didn't deny suffering, confess wellness, give a "positive confession," think positively, or blame God. He responded in faith in the midst of his distress, knowing that in the end, either in life or in

---

14. R. J. Rushdoony, *By What Standard: An Analysis of the Philosophy of Cornelius Van Til* (Tyler, TX: Thoburn Press, [1958] 1983), p. 189.

15. *Ibid.*, pp. 189-90.

death, God would vindicate him. In Job's case, God vindicated him both in life and in death (Job 42:10-17). Even death is "swallowed up in victory" for the Christian (1 Corinthians 15:54).

Illness and even death can be the direct result of sin (1 Corinthians 11:27-30). But this is not usually the case. Consider the words of Jesus: "And as He passed by, He saw a man blind from birth. And His disciples asked Him, saying, 'Rabbi, who sinned, this man or his parents, that he should be born blind?' Jesus answered, *'It was neither that this man sinned, nor his parents; but it was in order that the works of God might be displayed in him'* " (John 9:1-3; compare Exodus 4:11). The Reconstructionists see glory in suffering and affliction. We do not deny suffering or think positively to ward it off. Joni Eareckson-Tada describes people, the afflicted included, as "God's showcase."[16] She writes: "Today as I look back, I am convinced that the whole ordeal of my paralysis was inspired by God's love. I wasn't the brunt of some cruel joke. God had *reasons* behind my suffering, and learning some of them made all the difference in the world."[17]

The Positive Confession movement views the issues of victory and suffering in a radically different way from Reformed theology. The practice of "positive confession" has nothing to do with confession of sin. "Rather, it is a statement, spoken in faith, of what one desires or is requesting from God. God will honor that expression of faith, Hagin and Copeland teach, by fulfilling our desires. To receive healing from physical illness, for example, we should 'claim' our healing by praying for it and promptly concluding that we *are* (not *will be*) healed."[18]

---

16. Joni Eareckson and Steve Estes, *A Step Further* (Grand Rapids, MI: Zondervan, 1978), p. 50. *A Step Further* is a popularly written book on suffering, healing, and the sovereignty of God from a *Reformed* perspective. Steve Estes was a student at Westminster Theological Seminary when he wrote this book with Joni. Westminster is considered to be the leading Reformed seminary in the English-speaking world. Many in the Christian Reconstruction movement are graduates of Westminster Seminary and Reformed Theological Seminary.

17. Back cover copy of *A Step Further.*

18. Bruce Barron, *The Health and Wealth Gospel: What's Going on Today in a Movement That has Shaped the Faith of Millions?* (Downers Grove, IL: InterVarsity Press,

It would be helpful for Dave Hunt to read a Reformed analysis of pain and suffering, like Joni Eareckson-Tada's *A Step Further*, William Bridge's *A Lifting Up of the Downcast*,[19] or Edith Schaeffer's *Affliction*,[20] and compare them with Don Hughes's *God's Not Guilty*,[21] Kenneth E. Hagin's *Must Christians Suffer?*,[22] or Charles Capps's *Why Tragedy Happens to Christians*.[23]

So then, Dave Hunt is wrong in even considering that Reconstructionists' views on victory are similar to those in the Positive Confession Movement. The two groups look at suffering in radically different ways.[24]

And how does Dave Hunt define victory? As we'll see, it's the *imminent* rapture and martyrdom. With his narrow definition of victory, we could then conclude that millions upon millions of Christians who have died to "be with the Lord," and did not experience the rapture, or were not martyred did not experience vic-

---

1987), pp. 9-10. The author makes a very important point when dealing with areas of theological controversy:

> In an area as fluid and controversial as the teaching of contemporary evangelists, caution is even more essential. Regrettably, many who are critical of the faith teachers do not reflect an accurate grasp of their teachings. Misrepresentations and partial information abound, leading only to further confusion and dissention between Christians. Some critics have singled out extreme examples which do not represent the movement as a whole (pp. 64-65).

The same could be said about Christian Reconstruction. Identifying the Positive Confession Movement with Christian Reconstruction is an indication of a serious lapse in study and understanding of both movements.

19. William Bridge, *A Lifting Up of the Downcast* (London: Banner of Truth Trust, [1648] 1961), especially pages 192-212.

20. Edith Schaeffer, *Affliction* (Old Tappan, NJ: Revell, 1978).

21. Don Hughes, *God's Not Guilty* (Broken Arrow, OK: Don Hughes Ministries, 1982).

22. Kenneth Hagin, *Must Christians Suffer?* (Tulsa, OK: Faith Library Publications, 1983).

23. Charles Capps, *Why Tragedy Happens to Christians* (Tulsa, OK: Harrison House, 1980).

24. For a striking comparison of how theology shapes a Christian's response to suffering, see the stories of Joni Eareckson-Tada and Brian Sternberg, two Christians who will spend the rest of their earthly lives in wheelchairs. Philip Yancey, *Where is God When it Hurts?* (Grand Rapids, MI: Zondervan, 1977), pp. 99-123.

tory. He also maintains that victory is "the martyrs going to their death, singing of their love for the Lord, and trusting in Him."[25] Is this the only way to be victorious? I don't think so. If we are in Christ, we are always victorious, no matter what the circumstances. But what if we're not suffering? Are we to conclude that we're out of God's will? If we are doing something God calls us to do, should we expect failure or success? Should the Apostle Paul have chosen to drown rather than be rescued as he was shipwrecked off the coast of Malta? (Acts 28:1). Who gave Paul "victory" over the "viper" that came out of the fire? (vv. 2-6).

To support his claim that suffering is normative for the Christian, Dave Hunt quotes a few verses out of Hebrews 11: "By faith Moses, when he had grown up, refused to be called the son of Pharaoh's daughter; choosing rather to endure ill-treatment with the people of God, than to enjoy the passing pleasures of sin; considering the reproach of Christ greater riches than the treasures of Egypt" (Hebrews 11:24-26). He then goes on to quote how some of God's people were victorious. It was not Moses and the Israelites who were drowned in the Red Sea (v. 29); it was not Rahab and her family who were destroyed as the walls of Jericho came tumbling down (vv. 30-31).

Dave Hunt continues by telling us how some of these men, "by faith conquered kingdoms, performed acts of righteousness, obtained promises, shut the mouth of lions, quenched the power of fire, escaped the edge of the sword, from weakness were made strong, became mighty in war, put foreign armies to flight" (vv. 33-34). Isn't this victory? Why, of course it is!

Reconstructionists do not deny that the people of God are imprisoned, stoned, tempted, and put to death with the sword (vv. 36-37). But this too is victory! Christian Reconstructionists do not teach that a positive confession will dismiss these persecutions.

---

25. *Dominion: A Dangerous New Theology*, Tape #1 of *Dominion: The Word and New World Order*, distributed by the *Omega-Letter*, Ontario, Canada, 1987. Quoted in DeMar and Leithart, *Reduction of Christianity*, p. 138. See pages 136-143 for a full refutation of Dave Hunt's views on "victory."

This is an unfair and inaccurate depiction of Christian Reconstruction. Christian Reconstruction teaches that true faith perseveres through suffering and trials, which God uses to perfect us.

Chuck Colson, in relating some of his experiences with stomach cancer, gives us some insight into the biblical view of suffering. A Hindu man, when he discovered that Colson was a Christian, wanted to know if God would heal his son if he became a Christian. The Hindu man had heard this type of theology on television. Upon reflection, Colson wrote:

> I often thought in the hospital of the words of Florida pastor Steve Brown. Steve says that every time a non-Christian gets cancer, God allows a Christian to get cancer as well — so the world can see the difference. I prayed I might be so filled with God's grace that the world might see the difference.
>
> Steve's words represent a powerful truth. God does not witness to the world by taking his people out of suffering, but rather by demonstrating his grace through them in the midst of pain.[26]

But why is Dave Hunt willing to take the suffering that comes to Christians (Hebrews 10:24-31, 36-40), but he is not willing to acknowledge victory (vv. 32-35) through suffering? Christian Reconstructionists acknowledge both as being a part of God's plan for His glory.

We affirm with Joseph:

> And as for you, you meant evil against me, but God meant it for good in order to bring this present result, to preserve many people alive (Genesis 50:20).

We affirm with Paul:

> And we know that God causes all things to work together for good to those who love God, to those who are called according to His purpose (Romans 8:28).

---

26. Charles Colson, "My Cancer and the Good Health Gospel," *Christianity Today* (April 3, 1987), p. 56.

We affirm with James:

> Consider it all joy, my brethren, when you encounter various trials, knowing that the testing of your faith produces endurance. And let endurance have its perfect result, that you may be perfect and complete, lacking in nothing (James 1:2-4).

By admitting our weakness, God's strength is revealed in us (2 Corinthians 12:9-10). The Reformed response to pain and suffering is one of wonder, not of denial. We do not often see God's purposes in pain and affliction, but we know they are there. It is only when we die to be with the Lord that our frail and broken bodies will no longer hinder us. The sting of death will be gone.

Reconstruction and Dominion

"Reconstructionists have a very deviant view of dominion." Dave Hunt says that Christian Reconstructionists want to have "dominion over other people." What does he mean by this? Is he implying that we want to create a church-state like Iran? He doesn't say. He leaves definitions up to the audience. A very clever ploy. Reconstructionists are not looking to impose a top-down ecclesiastical or political regime where voting will be outlawed, the two party system done away with, the Constitution abolished, and everyone will take orders from an autocratic band of elite technocrats. The Constitution is a workable and fundamentally sound governing document. There's very little wrong with it. The problem is in the implementation. It sets forth a decentralized *social* order, while the electorate is voting for and getting a centralized *political* order. Our Constitution insists on a Republican form of government, while the electorate lives in terms of a democracy.[27] For nearly three

---

27. For these distinctions, see Gary DeMar, *God and Government: A Biblical and Historical Study* (Atlanta, GA: American Vision, 1982), pp. 80-83. In a May 1988 speech to the General Assembly of the Church of Scotland, British Prime Minister Margaret Thatcher outlined the spiritual beliefs that underpin her political philosophy. Mrs. Thatcher, who said she was "speaking personally as a Christian as well as a politician," stressed self-reliance and personal responsibility. She also spoke on the subject of "democracy": "When Abraham Lincoln spoke in his famous

decades, the writings of Reconstructionists have been noted for espousing a decentralized social order where *more* freedom will operate in the world if biblical law were chosen over autonomous law. The State has usurped control from individuals, families, schools, businesses, and local governments. What's even more tragic, we've sat back and let it happen.[28]

Dave Hunt does not give us an example of what he means by what Reconstructionists mean by "dominion over other people." His fabricated "dominion over people" definition was dealt with at length in *The Reduction of Christianity*.[29]

But evil men must be restrained. In this sense, there must be dominion over *some* people because of their actions to harm others. God ordained civil government for this very purpose (Romans 13:1-7). Is it wrong to "dominate" other men through the God-ordained channels of civil government to remove law-makers from public office (e.g., voting, swaying public opinion, etc.) when they continue to enact and enforce laws that allow women, for example, to abort their unborn babies? Should Christians remain silent when laws are passed that restrict parents from sending their children to Christian schools or from educating their children at home? Education is a tool to exercise dominion over a culture, for good or evil. Is Dave Hunt telling us that sodomites

---

Gettysburg speech of 1863 of 'government of the people,' he gave the world a neat definition of democracy which has sinced been widely and enthusiastically adopted. But what he enunciated as a form of government was not in itself especially Christian, for nowhere in the Bible is the word democracy mentioned. Ideally, when Christians meet, as Christians, to take counsel together, their purpose is not (or should not be) to ascertain what is the mind of the majority but what is the mind of the Holy Spirit — something which may be quite different." "Thatcher: Sow, and ye Shall Reap for All," *World* (June 20, 1988), p. 5.

28. "Only 50 percent of Christians eligible to vote are registered. Of those registered, only 25 percent actually vote on election day. This means just 12.5 percent of eligible Christians actually take part in the political process." *California Voter's Guide.* Quoted in *Intercessors For America* (July/August 1988), p. 4.

29. See pages 24-29 of *Reduction of Christianity.* Throughout the debate, I got the distinct feeling that Dave Hunt had not read *The Reduction of Christianity.* Why was he raising issues that were already dealt with in the book? A more helpful approach would have been to interact with the definitions and explanations outlined in *Reduction.*

should not be stopped from recruiting young boys for the "homosexual lifestyle"?[30] Should Christians ignore dominion in these areas? Hopefully Dave Hunt would say no. I'm sure he would say no. This is dominion.

Hunt continues by stating that Christian Reconstructionists want to "set up kingdoms and governments." Again, Hunt offers no proof for this charge. What does it mean? First, Reconstructions (and a lot of other Christians) believe that we are already living in God's kingdom. Jesus tells us that God's kingdom has come upon us (Luke 11:20). Scripture informs us that God "delivered us from the domain of darkness, and transferred us to the kingdom of His beloved Son" (Colossians 1:13). So then, we are not working to "set up kingdoms." Second, civil governments are presently in existence. Reconstructionists, as well as all Christians, should be working—"ministering as priests the gospel of God" (Romans 15:16; cf. 1 Peter 2:9; Revelation 1:6)—to help "ministers of God" in the area of civil government (Romans 13:4; cf. Deuteronomy 17:18-20), rule in terms of God's law so they can promote "good behavior" (Romans 13:3), bring "wrath upon the one who practices evil" (v. 5), and make conditions favorable for the preaching of the gospel (1 Timothy 2:2-4).

Dave Hunt also has a problem with "taking dominion over cultures." Would he rather leave dominion to the humanists? Hitler had "dominion" in Germany and terminated the lives of millions of people. The same is true of Mao Tse-tung in Red China and Josef Stalin in Russia.

Dominion in the sense of exercising authority is inevitable and inescapable. As was noted above, there must be *some* domination of other men to restrain their evil. Paul tells individuals to "leave room for the wrath of God" (Romans 12:19). As individuals, we are not to "dominate other men" (Matthew 5:38-42; cf. Exodus 21:22-24), nor are we to use the State as a means to push a social agenda. But God has not left evil without some checks in this world. The civil magistrate is ordained by God to exercise *His*

---

30. Frank York, "Does Your Public School Promote Homosexuality?," *Focus on the Family: Citizen* (June 1988), pp. 6-8.

wrath in this world before Jesus returns in judgment. This is spelled out very clearly in Romans 13:

> For *rulers* are not a cause of fear for good behavior, but for evil. Do you want to have no fear of authority? Do what is good, and you will have praise from the same; for it is a *minister of God* to you for good. But if you do what is evil, be afraid; *for it does not bear the sword for nothing; for it is a minister of God, an avenger who brings wrath upon the one who practices evil* (vv. 3-4).

You see, dominion isn't an option. When Christians fail to exercise dominion, humanists take up the banner, and a nation, Christians included, must live in terms of their dominion. The kind of dominion that Dave Hunt fears is a dominion that dominates unrighteously, whether by Christians or by humanists. We certainly agree. But this question still remains: What standard will be used to determine whether righteous dominion is taking place? The Christian Reconstructionist says it's the Bible. Dave Hunt denies that there is a mandate to take dominion over cultures. We disagree, and we believe that we have the Bible and history on our side.

The "Cultural Mandate"

Again, we find that Hunt fails to give any definitions. It seems that Hunt wants to reduce "culture" to "environment." Culture is broader than the environment. Henry Van Til states that the term "culture" is "that activity of man, the image-bearer of God, by which he fulfills the creation mandate to cultivate the earth, to have dominion over it and to subdue it." He goes on to explain:

> The term is also applied to the result of such activity, namely, the secondary environment which has been superimposed upon nature by man's creative effort. Culture, then, is not a peripheral concern, but of the very essence of life. It is an expression of man's essential being as created in the image of God, and since man is essentially a religious being, it is expressive of his relationship to God, that is, of his religion.

That man as a covenantal creature is called to culture cannot be stressed too much. For the Lord God, who called him into being, also gave him the cultural mandate to replenish the earth and to have dominion over it. David was so filled with ecstasy at this glory-filled vocation that he exclaimed in awe and wonder: "What is man, that thou art mindful of him? . . . For thou hast made him a little lower than God, And crownest him with glory and honor. . . . Thou hath put all things under his feet."

To say that culture is man's calling in the covenant is only another way of saying that culture is religiously determined.

My thesis, then, is that Calvinism furnishes us with the only theology of culture that is truly relevant for the world in which we live, because it is the true theology of the Word.[31]

Hunt tells us that everything flows from this "false view of dominion," a view of dominion that he never defines for the audience. The above definition of "dominion" was not written by a Christian Reconstructionist. Notice that it grows out of a Calvinistic world view that millions of Christians hold.[32] A Reconstructionist's view of dominion flows, as Van Til writes, from the belief that "Calvinism furnishes us with the only theology of culture that is truly relevant for the world in which we live, because it is the true theology of the Word." It is also interesting that Henry Morris, a dispensational premillennialist, teaches a very similar view of dominion in his book, *The Biblical Basis for Modern Science.*

---

31. Henry Van Til, *The Calvinistic Concept of Culture* (Grand Rapids, MI: Baker Book House, [1959] 1971), pp. 7-8.

    Culture is often conceived too narrowly. The resulting definition lacks both scope and insight, breadth and depth. There are people, for instance, who identify culture with refinement of manners, social courtesy and urbanity, with the veneer of polite society. For others it is synonymous with good taste in interior decorating, paintings, music and literature.

    However, the idea that development of the artistic, scientific or social aspect of man's nature constitutes culture is altogether too narrow. The whole man must be involved, and all the aspects of human life have a bearing on the issue (p. 25).

32. Again, this is shown in *Reduction of Christianity*, pp. 30-37.

According to Morris, the "dominion mandate" (his usage) includes science, technology, the humanities, commerce, law, civil government, and education, in short, every facet of human culture. Morris notes:

. . . long before [the Great Commission] another great commission was given to all men, whether saved or unsaved, merely by virtue of being men created by God in His image. It also had worldwide scope, and has never been rescinded. It had to do with implementing God's purpose in His work of creation, just as Christ's commission was for implementing His work of salvation and reconciliation.[33]

Morris says that the command to subdue the earth means "bringing all earth's systems and processes into a state of optimum productivity and utility, offering the greatest glory to God and benefit to mankind."[34] So then, there is nothing unusual about advocating dominion. Even some dispensationalists support it.

Our Dominion Task

Dave Hunt says that He "doesn't see a task being given" in Genesis 1:26-28. But there are several listed: (1) "Be fruitful and multiply and fill the earth"; (2) "subdue" the earth; and (3) "rule over" the animal creation (Genesis 1:28). Even the dispensational author Herman Hoyt acknowledges man's dominion task:

The issue of dominion is introduced in the opening chapter of the Bible. Immediately after creating man in the image of God the

---

33. Henry M. Morris, *The Biblical Basis for Modern Science* (Grand Rapids, MI: Baker Book House, 1984), p. 41. "The responsibility of administering capital punishment is the greatest responsibility of human government. It implicitly entails the obligation also to control those human actions which, if unchecked, could easily (and often do) lead to murder (e.g., robbery, adultery, slander, greed). The dual role of government is that of both protection and punishment — protection of the lives, property, and freedoms of its citizens, and just retribution on those citizens who deprive other citizens of life, possessions, or liberty." *Ibid.*, pp. 45-46.

34. *Ibid.*, p. 41.

first command given to him concerns the exercise of sovereign control over creation (Gen. 1:26, 28). This theme unfolds in progressive wonder through the Bible until at last the throne of God is established on the earth (Rev. 22:1, 3) and the redeemed saints reign with Christ forever (Rev. 22:5).[35]

Psalm 8 reiterates the dominion mandate of Genesis by telling us that "Thou dost make him to rule over the works of Thy hands" (v. 6). Included in the works of God's hands, but not limited to this, is the animal creation. In his commentary on the Psalms, Leupold writes of Psalm 8:6: "How much ['the works of Thy hands'] involves neither this statement nor Gen. 1 specifies, *but it certainly cannot indicate a mere nominal control*, for the parallel statement of v. 6 . . . *extends man's authority to 'everything'* and . . . claims that these things may be said to have been 'put under his feet.'"[36]

There were commands for man to perform. Keeping and cultivating the garden, a microcosm of the world, was a significant task (Genesis 2:15). Prior to the fall these tasks were pleasurable and easy. After the fall, however, the work became more difficult. There would be pain in childbirth (3:16), difficulty in cultivating the earth (3:17-19), and a man-killing animal creation with which to contend (9:5). And man himself would shed other men's blood (4:8).

How does Dave Hunt answer the Reconstructionist view of dominion? He reverts to ridicule rather than to careful analysis, research of Reconstruction literature, and sound biblical exegesis. "Does this mean," he says, "depleting the earth of it's natural resources or spoiling the environment? Is this what dominion is all about?" He is correct in telling us that we are to be "stewards of God's creation." But stewardship is an integral aspect of the dominion mandate. Man rules in God's name according to His law. This is exactly what Reconstructionists have been saying. Dominion is ethical. It means acting in terms of God's law as it applies to

---

35. Herman A. Hoyt, "Dispensational Premillennialism," *The Meaning of the Millennium: Four Views*, Robert G. Clouse, ed. (Downers Grove, IL: InterVarsity Press, 1977), p. 64.

36. H. C. Leupold, *Exposition on Psalms* (Grand Rapids, MI: Baker Book House, [1959] 1977), pp. 104-105.

the world. Having dominion over the earth does not in itself lead to abuse. Gary North writes that "Our polluted regions of the earth are rebelling against man's rebellious, lawless rulership, not against rulership as such."[37]

Dominion and the Great Commission

Hunt's next point is that "Reconstructionists link the Dominion Mandate with the Great Commission in Matthew 28." He wants to have his audience believe that Reconstructionists see these as the *same* tasks. Again, he never quotes a source for his contention. They can be linked, but they cannot be made to mean the same thing. No Reconstructionist says they are. David Chilton writes:

> The Great Commission to the Church does not end with simply *witnessing* to the nations. Christ's command is that we *disciple* the nations — *all* the nations. The kingdoms of the world are to become the kingdoms of Christ. They are to be discipled, made obedient to the faith. This means that every aspect of life throughout the world is to be brought under the lordship of Jesus Christ: families, individuals, business, science, agriculture, the arts, law, education, economics, psychology, philosophy, and every other sphere of human activity. Nothing may be left out. Christ "must reign, until He has put all enemies under His feet" (1 Cor. 15:25). We have been given the responsibility of converting the entire world.[38]

Tommy Ice, in an article on Christian Reconstruction, asserts that Chilton is telling us that Matthew 28:19-20 is "not talking about soteriological evangelism, as most understand it."[39] But

---

37. Gary North, *The Dominion Covenant: Genesis* (Tyler, TX: Institute for Christian Economics, [1982] 1987), p. 33. See chapter three of *The Dominion Covenant* for a definition of the cultural or dominion mandate. If Dave Hunt had read this chapter, he would know what Reconstructionists mean by dominion.

38. David Chilton, *Paradise Restored: A Biblical Theology of Dominion* (Ft. Worth, TX: Dominion Press, [1985] 1987), p. 213.

39. Tommy Ice, "An Evaluation of Theonomic Neopostmillennialism, *Bibliotheca Sacra*, Vol. 145 (July, 1988).

what does Chilton really say? He says that "the Great Commission to the Church does not *end* with simply *witnessing*." The implication is that the Great Commission *begins* with witnessing and *ends* with discipleship. Ice continues his evaluation of Chilton's quotation by maintaining that "Chilton is reading into the passage his theology, and then citing it as proof for his theology."[40] Of course, this is the essence of the debate between Christian Reconstruction and the brand of dispensational premillennialism espoused by Hunt and Ice.

Chilton tells us that the Great Commission's emphasis on discipleship means that every "sphere of human activity" is part of this discipleship process. Didn't Jesus tell us to teach the nations "to observe *all* that I commanded you"? (Matthew 28:20). The Gospels themselves are filled with instruction beyond evangelism. Reconstructionists are only importing what Jesus tells us to import: *all* that He commanded.

The dominion mandate of Genesis 1 was given prior to the fall. Evangelism was not part of it. The Great Commission of Matthew 28 deals primarily with evangelism. Nothing can be changed until man is changed. Evangelism sets fallen man back on track. But the Great Commission does not end with evangelism; it moves on to teaching the nations *all* that Jesus taught. Our task is not accomplished until the *nations* are *discipled*. Evangelism is the church's *primary* mission.[41] But a priority does not exclude the second, third, and fourth steps in the process. What are we to do with all the spiritual babies that we bring into the world through the preaching of the gospel? What if Jesus does not return for a thousand years? We'll have millions of baby Christians walking around in a world dominated by humanists. What are they to do if Jesus does not return for another thousand years?

---

40. *Idem.*

41. See DeMar and Leithart, *Reduction of Christianity*, pp. 178-83. The relationship between the dominion mandate of Genesis 1 and the Great Commission of Matthew 28 has been discussed in DeMar, *God and Government: Issues in Biblical Perspective*, pp. 67-69. Again, it makes me wonder if Dave Hunt has really read the material that has been produced on these topics. Also, see R. J. Rushdoony, *The Philosophy of the Christian School Curriculum* (Vallecito, CA: Ross House Books, 1981), p. 148.

Defeatism

Dave Hunt objects to Reconstructionists describing his view of the millennium as "defeatism." Well, it is defeatism for the church *prior to Jesus' coming to set up His millennial kingdom.* And because victory can only occur in the rapture or in martyrdom, the church has been defeated for the last 2000 years! And, again, if Jesus does not return for another thousand years, then the church is saddled with defeat for another thousand years before the rapture occurs. But even the upcoming millennium is a failure for Dave Hunt:

> In fact, dominion—taking dominion and setting up the kingdom of Christ—is an *impossibility*, even for God. The millennial reign of Christ, far from being the kingdom, is actually the final proof of the incorrigible nature of the human heart, because Christ Himself can't do what these people say they are going to do.[42]

This isn't defeatism?! Even God can't take dominion and set up a kingdom! This is the ultimate defeat! Based on the above quotation and others in Hunt's *Beyond Seduction*,[43] the question remains: Whose theology is deviant?

But let's allow Dave Hunt's own words from the debate to tell us why he does not consider his view of eschatology as defeatist:

> I believe that Jesus Christ is going to return very soon, to rapture His bride out of here, to meet Him in the air, to be married to Him in that marriage supper of the Lamb. He's going to return with the armies of heaven. He's going to rescue His people Israel. He's going to stop destruction on planet earth. He's going to destroy his enemies. He's going to set up His kingdom. . . . Jesus will rule on the throne of His father David. And He's going to rule on this earth and reign. That's defeatism?!

---

42. See DeMar and Leithart, *Reduction of Christianity*, p. 157.

43. "How could the church be expected to establish the kingdom by taking over the world when even God cannot accomplish that without violating man's freedom of choice?" This is the essence of humanism. God's will is determined by man's will. Dave Hunt, *Beyond Seduction: A Return to Biblical Christianity* (Eugene, OR: Harvest House, 1987), p. 250.

Dave Hunt's evaluation of Christian Reconstruction rests on the "any-moment rapture" doctrine.[44] He believes that Jesus is going to return "soon": First, to rapture the church; second, to rescue Israel during the tribulation period; and third, to set up an earthly kingdom. But what is the "any-moment rapture" doctrine based on? The Bible does not give us *any* signs to indicate when Jesus will return. A staunch dispensationalist like J. Dwight Pentecost states emphatically that there are no signs leading up to Jesus' second coming![45] So how does Dave Hunt know when Jesus will return? He doesn't.

Those not familiar with "orthodox" dispensational theology have been teaching an "imminent," that is, a soon coming, for decades. Most of this speculation is based on "signs." But the Bible does not give us any signs that will signal Jesus' return. Of course, many will point to Matthew 24. But as we've seen, Matthew 24 predicts what will happen in the forty year period between the crucifixion and the destruction of Jerusalem in A.D. 70.

When "Soon" Means "Late"

But the heart of the problem is much more fundamental. How can the Bible state that Jesus is coming "soon" and then postpone it for nearly 2000 years (Matthew 10:23; 16:28; Mark 9:1; John 21:18-23; etc.)? "Soon" does not mean "soon" for the dispensationalist, and yet they insist on interpreting the Bible literally. Those passages that talk about Jesus returning soon are describing Jesus coming to pour out His wrath in the destruction of Jerusalem. For this "coming" Jesus set forth certain signs (Matthew 24; Mark 13; Luke 21). But for His coming at the end of history, there are no signs. Anyone who states that Jesus is returning "very soon" at this stage in history is going beyond what Scripture says.[46]

---

44. "Any-moment" does not necessarily mean "soon." This distinction is inherent in dispensational rhetoric. Dave Hunt fails to recognize the difference.

45. J. Dwight Pentecost, *Things to Come: A Study in Biblical Eschatology* (Grand Rapids, MI: Zondervan/Academie Books, [1958] 1987), pp. 202-203.

46. For a full treatment of the various meanings of "coming," see Loraine Boettner, *The Millennium* (Philadelphia, PA: Presbyterian and Reformed, 1972), pp 252-262. He demonstrates eight ways in which Jesus is said to "come."

This was Hal Lindsey's mistake when he wrote *The Late Great Planet Earth* in 1970. He stated that the budding of the fig tree in Matthew 24:32 was Israel becoming a nation in 1948. This was the beginning of the "this generation" of Matthew 24:34. A generation, forty years, would not pass away until all the events predicted in Matthew 24:1-33 were fulfilled. This means that Jesus should have returned around 1981 to rapture His church because Lindsey believes in a seven year tribulation period that *precedes* the return of Christ. The rapture takes place *before* the beginning of the tribulation.[47] Consider Hunt's and Lindsey's views in light of this recent critique of *The Late Great Planet Earth*:

> Despite *Late Great's* success, the book is now standing on the cracking limb of Lindsey's interpretation of the fig tree in Matthew 24:32-34. Only a few pages after warning readers against "unscriptural attempts at calculating dates," Lindsey indulged in some date setting of his own, identifying the fig tree as Israel, and the fig's first leaves as Israel's national rebirth in 1948. The Tribulation, according to Lindsey, will begin before that generation.[48]

The article continues by telling us that Lindsey no longer holds this view. "He believes 'all the signs' are present today, however,

---

47. This scenario is outlined by Lindsey in *The Late Great Planet Earth* (Grand Rapids, MI: Zondervan, 1970), pp. 53-54. Since this false prediction, Lindsey changed his views by claiming that Israel never "secured" the land in 1948. It wasn't until the "six-day war" in 1967 that Israel actually had repossessed Old Jerusalem. This added nineteen years to the calculation. The forty years now should be calculated from 1967. This means that the year 2000 is the date for the rapture. But things are not that simple. While in 1970 Lindsey stated in *The Late Great Planet Earth* (p. 54) that "a generation in the Bible is something like forty years," in 1977 he said that he didn't "know how long a Biblical generation is. Perhaps somewhere between sixty and eighty years." W. Ward Gasque, "Future Fact? Future Fiction?," *Christianity Today* (April 15, 1977), p. 40.

So we move from Hunt's view that Jesus is returning "very soon" to Hal Lindsey whose outside prediction moves the coming of Christ to rapture His church to 2040, with Jesus' return to set up His millennial kingdom to be in 2047. But at this date, can we say that Israel has possession of the land? The Palestinians could make a good case that Israel is not fully in possession. This means that the generation that sees all these signs has not been born yet.

48. Garry Friesen, "A Return Visit," *Moody* (May 1988), p. 31.

and still believes that the rapture and Tribulation are near."[49] But this next point is important to Hunt's belief that "Jesus is going to return very soon." Lindsey's and Hunt's opinion about the nearness of Jesus' return is "at odds with most premillennial teachers, who say that Christ may return tomorrow or a thousand years from now."[50] Dave Hunt's theology is defeatism if the church has another 1000 years to go before Jesus returns, and the church is still putting its hope in the rapture with no task of dominion or any hope that the world can be made better in Christ. Christians can only achieve victory in martyrdom.

Dave Hunt has put his hope in the soon-rapture of the church, a doctrine that the church never held until it was manufactured by Darbyites in the nineteenth century. Hunt then implies that anyone who does not believe in the soon-rapture doctrine subscribes to a "deviant theology." Apparently this includes historical premillennialists, since for them, the rapture could be a thousand years away! The Reconstructionists, on the other hand, put their hope in the reality of Jesus' return and not in its nearness.[51]

But what of those passages that tell us to "watch" for Jesus' return? Don't they teach an imminent, any-moment return? They do not. Rather, they teach us always to be ready to be held accountable because we do not know when Jesus will return.

> It should be stressed that none of the exhortations to watchfulness are undermined because of the factor of delay. If they did not threaten or dilute the early church's resolve to remain watchful, then they will not weaken ours either. Delay does not lessen our anticipation or expectancy. In spite of pretribulational arguments that the church cannot be genuinely motivated to watchfulness unless they believe the Lord's coming could happen any moment, reality does not support this premise. The true motivation for watching is not based on imminency, but on our ultimate

---

49. *Idem.*
50. *Idem.*
51. Herbert Bowsher, "Will Christ Return 'At Any Moment'?," *The Journal of Christian Reconstruction*, Symposium on Evangelism, ed. Gary North, Vol. VII, No. 2 (Winter, 1981), p. 51. The entire article is worthy of study.

accountability to Christ for the sum total of our personal conduct, heart devotion, and life style; and because of our earnest desire to be found unblamable in holiness before Him at His coming (I Thess. 3:13; see also Titus 2:12, 13 and II Peter 3:11), we endeavor to remain such.[52]

Watching and waiting relate to the Christian's moral or ethical behavior, not to watching *for* Christ's return. The Bible does not tell us to watch *for* our Lord's second advent. The emphasis is on being ready because we do not know when He will return, contrary to what Dave Hunt espouses (Matthew 24:42, 44; 25:13). Dispensationalists remind me of the early disciples:

> And as they were gazing intently into the sky while He was departing, behold, two men in white clothing stood beside them; and they also said, "Men of Galilee, why do you stand looking into the sky? This Jesus, who has been taken up from you into heaven, will come in just the same way as you have watched Him go into heaven" (Acts 1:10-11).

Who Occupies David's Throne?

One last item in Dave Hunt's view of the end times needs to be discussed: Jesus occupying David's throne. Hunt sees this as still ahead. The Bible describes it as already fulfilled. As a prophet, David knew "that God had sworn to him with an oath to seat one of his descendants upon his throne" (Acts 2:30). How long did David have to wait? Scripture says that David saw in "the resurrection of the Christ" (v. 31) and in His exaltation (ascension and session) "to the right hand of God" (v. 33) the fulfillment of the promise that one of his descendants would occupy his throne. All of David's descendants died and underwent decay. But Jesus "was neither abandoned to Hades, nor did his flesh suffer decay" (v. 31). So then, is Jesus now sitting on David's throne? Yes!

---

52. William R. Kimball, *The Rapture: A Question of Timing* (Grand Rapids, MI: Baker Book House, 1985), p. 167.

And so, because he [David] was a prophet, and knew that God had sworn to him with an oath to seat one of his descendants upon his *throne*. . . . Therefore having been *exalted* to the right hand of God, and having received from the Father the promise of the Holy Spirit, He has poured forth this which you both see and hear. For it was not David who ascended into heaven, but he himself says: "The Lord said to my Lord, 'Sit at My right hand, until I make Thine enemies a footstool for Thy feet.' " Therefore let all the house of Israel know for certain that God has made Him both Lord and Christ—this Jesus whom you crucified (Acts 2:33-36).

David's throne was temporary, earthly, and susceptible to decay as was David himself. But the throne that endures forever is in heaven, and the One who sits upon it is an everlasting King. Just as there is a true heavenly tabernacle of which the earthly tabernacle was a copy, so there is a true heavenly throne of which David and Solomon's throne was a dim shadow.

Is it necessary that Jesus, as a descendant of David, sit on a material throne? John F. Walvoord, who tells us that David's throne was occupied during the Babylonian captivity when no descendant of David actually sat on his throne, says no. He writes:

By the term "throne" it is clear that no reference is made to a material throne, but rather to the dignity and power which was sovereign and supreme in David as king. The right to rule always belonged to David's seed.[53]

Why would a dispensationalist admit this with respect to David's throne in the Old Testament but will not recognize this same principle for Jesus in the New Testament? It's baffling.

The earth is not the place for Jesus to sit as King, the One who is "both Lord and Christ." The earth is his "footstool." Heaven is God's throne. There are not two thrones as some dispensational-

---

53. John F. Walvoord, *The Millennial Kingdom* (Grand Rapids, MI: Zondervan, 1959), p. 196; see p. 201.

ists teach.[54] The promises made to David have been fulfilled in Christ at His resurrection and exaltation (Romans 8:34; Hebrews 1:3, 13; 10:12-13). Interestingly, the most quoted Old Testament passage appearing in the New Testament is Psalm 110:1—which speaks of Jesus *present* rule!

Similarly, there is no need for a rebuilt tabernacle or temple, since Jesus has entered into the true tabernacle and cleansed the heavenly things. In order to protect dispensationalism's futuristic interpretation of prophecy, however, such writers as Hal Lindsey predict a future rebuilding of the tabernacle. In a discussion of Acts 15:12-21, Lindsey places a gap of (at least) 2000 years between verses 14 and 15. Lindsey admits that verse 14, which describes the admission of the Gentiles into God's favor, was being fulfilled in the first century. But when verses 15-21. talk about a rebuilt "tabernacle of David," Lindsey arbitrarily assumes that this prophecy is still to be fulfilled. James's words, however, cannot bear this misinterpretation. The whole point of the quotation about David's tabernacle is that God is gathering together a new Israel, in which the distinction of Jew and Greek is erased.

The Manifest Sons of God

How many of you know who the Manifest Sons of God are? Do you know what they believe? No? Well, you're not alone. I looked in a number of books on the cults, and I couldn't find one that dealt with this theological movement. (Of course, this doesn't mean that there are no books that deal with the movement. They don't seem, however, to be readily available for research purposes.)

Dave Hunt accuses Christian Reconstructionists of having a theology similar to the Manifest Sons of God. But he never tells us

---

54. According to dispensationalism, Jesus "must reign on David's throne on the earth over David's people forever." J. Dwight Pentecost, *Things to Come* (Grand Rapids, MI: Zondervan, "[1958] 1987), p. 112. But the Bible talks about a heavenly throne (Revelation 12:5). The dispensationalist has an answer for this. "This heavenly city will be brought into a relation to the earth at the beginning of the millennium, and perhaps will be made visible above the earth" (*Ibid.*, p. 546).

who they are or what they believe. Neither Gary North nor I have so much as *seen* such a creature. Still, Hunt garbles a few sentences from an article by Kenneth Gentry, entitled "The Greatness of the Great Commission,"[55] and plays the guilt-by-association game. It goes like this: The Manifest Sons of God are a heretical sect. You all know that this is true. Let me read to you something from a Reconstructionist that sounds *something* like the Manifest Sons of God (their heresy is never defined). Reconstructionists hold doctrines similar to that of the Manifest Sons of God (not shown to be true). Therefore, Reconstructionists are heretics, too. Clever, but not true.

I challenge anyone to go through Gentry's article and come away with any evidence that he is espousing anything remotely identifiable with the teachings of the Manifest Sons of God. Dave Hunt does not even give a clear reading of the section he lifted from Gentry's article.

Let me try the same thing with Mormonism and premillennialism: Mormonism is a cult. You all know that this is true. Mormons are premillennial. Premillennialists hold a millennial position similar to that of Mormonism. Therefore, premillennialism is a cult. The same can be said about Jehovah's Witnesses, the Worldwide Church of God (Armstrongism), and the Children of God and premillennialism.[56] This is nonsense, of course, and certainly not scholarship. It is also highly unfair.

Who and what are the Manifest Sons of God? The teachings that are usually associated with the Manifest Sons of God are closely tied to the Latter Rain Movement that had its beginnings in 1948. Dissension broke out early within this movement.

---

55. Kenneth L. Gentry, Jr., "The Greatness of the Great Commission," *The Journal of Christian Reconstruction*, Symposium on Evangelism, ed. Gary North, Vol. VII, No. 2 (Winter, 1981), pp. 19-47. There is nothing in this article that hints at being analogous to the theology of the Manifest Sons of God. Dave Hunt just doesn't like any talk about dominion, no matter who advocates it. Nearly any article can be made to say almost anything by quoting a small portion of it out of context.

56. Guilt by association has been dealt with in DeMar and Leithart, *Reduction of Christianity*, chapter 7.

> Spiritualistic trends were evident in the doctrine of the "manifestation of the Sons of God." The doctrine originated from the predictive prophecyings [sic] of Rev. E. Crane of the Northwest Bible Institute in Edmonton [Alberta, Canada]. He believed that he had seen a vision of the victorious saints as a mighty army. . . . His entire class was affected by his belief and soon there grew the doctrine that the "elect" would receive "redemptive bodies" here and now and that any person who died had not been able to "appropriate the redemption body" and was therefore not one of the "overcomers."[57]

The doctrines of the Manifest Sons of God are a mixed bag. You can find some very orthodox statements in their theology and some heretical ones as well. In my research on them, however, I learned that there is no real systematic theology articulated by the leaders in the group. In fact, it's hard to find out who the leaders are.

The most unorthodox doctrines are:

1. Some teach that an elite group in the church, namely themselves, have been perfected prior to glorification. These are the manifested sons of God. "They believe that they have fully attained the state of spiritual and moral perfection that the redeemed will possess in heaven. Thus, they see themselves in a class above the average Christian."[58] Do Reconstructionists believe this? No! Does Gentry's article even suggest this idea? No!

2. "A few even go to the extreme of saying that Christ and the Church are meant to become one in essence or nature. Thus, some of them teach that ultimately there will be no distinction between Christ and His Church."[59] Do Reconstructionists believe this? No! Does Gentry's article even suggest this idea? No!

---

57. Cornelius J. Jaenen, "The Pentecostal Movement" (M.A. Thesis, University of Manitoba, 1950), p. 89. Quoted in Richard Michael Riss, "The Latter Rain Movement of 1948 and the Mid-Twentieth Century Evangelical Awakening" (B.A. Thesis, University of Rochester, 1974), p. 134.

58. Elliot Miller, *The Manifestation of the Sons of God*, Christian Research Fact Sheet, 1979, Christian Research Institute, Box 500, San Juan Capistrano, California 92693.

59. *Idem.*

3. Manifest Sons of God, based on the teachings of Franklin Hall's teachings concerning immortalization, taught that the "manifestation of the sons of God" spoken of in Romans 8:19 was to occur as a result of the final shower of the Latter Rain just prior to Christ's return. These "sons of God" would be drawn from a remnant of the church, and would be individual extensions of the Incarnation or replicas of Christ, who was regarded as the "Pattern Son." Do Reconstructionist believe this? No! Does Gentry's article even suggest this outrageous teaching? No!

Dave Hunt probably objects to strains of dominion in their theology. But there are strains of premillennialism in numerous cults, including the Manifest Sons of God.[60] Should we then conclude that premillennialism is deviant? As has been shown repeatedly, dominion has been a part of the church for centuries. This has been pointed out in *The Reduction of Christianity*. Even some dispensationalists support the dominion mandate, defining it in terms similar to that of Reconstructionists.

Conclusion

Dave Hunt has majored on the minors of theology. He has then taken these minor doctrinal differences and has made them tests of the orthodox faith. Further, he leads his audiences astray by rarely defining terms or quoting Reconstructionists in context or even interacting with the detailed analysis of Christian Reconstructionist beliefs set forth in *The Reduction of Christianity*. Dave Hunt, therefore, is unreliable as a critic of Christian Reconstruction.

---

60. One critic of the excesses of the Manifest Sons of God theology laments the fact that some were teaching that they would "call the shots" in the tribulation, a distinctive of premillennialism. George Hawtin, "Mystery Babylon," *The Page* (Battleford, Sask.: n.d.), twelfth printing, p. 10. Quoted in Richard Michael Riss, "Latter Rain Movement of 1948," p. 135.

16

QUESTIONS AND ANSWERS

During the second and final hour of the debate, the audience was given an opportunity to ask questions of the speakers. Questions were written out and handed to Kerby Anderson, the moderator. Each side was given three minutes to respond. In this chapter, I will address the answers given by Tommy Ice and Dave Hunt.

Question 1: What is the origin of the pretribulational rapture doctrine?

Tommy Ice began by telling the audience that the word "rapture is from the Latin translation of the Bible . . . and was carried into the English" from Jerome's Latin Vulgate. Ice continued with this statement:

> The rapture originated in the Scriptures, and it was the development of theology, the application of a literal interpretation of Scripture, which was absent from the church for a good 1400 years. The early church was premillennial for the first 250 years to a man, as far as early church records show. They were clearly futuristic in their interpretation and premillennial. It was about 150-300 A.D. that you began to have a shift due to Greek philosophy into an amillennialism of Augustine around 425 A.D. and [it] swept the church for a number of years. [In] the 1800s especially you had a return to a more consistent literal hermeneutic, especially in the British Isles, and you had the issue of what do we do with Israel. I believe that it was this theological climate which enabled the church for the first time, in the early 1800s, to understand the rapture. A number of people apparently came up with

179

it almost simultaneously within a three to four year period. J. N. Darby is the most famous. The big question is why did the whole interpretative system of [the] preterist interpretation not arise until the 1600s within the reconstructionist camp, and the whole postmillennial system did not really develop until the 1600s to the 1700s. The rapture is a sub-point within premillennialism.

The question was over the origin of a *pretribulational* rapture. Tommy Ice admits that a pretribulational rapture wasn't articulated until 1830. The early church knows *nothing* of a pretribulational rapture. George Eldon Ladd, a highly respected authority in the area of premillennial studies, made an extensive survey of the eschatological writings in the history of the church. This included the early church fathers. This was his conclusion:

> We can find no trace of pretribulationism in the early church: and no modern pretribulationist has successfully proved that this particular doctrine was held by any of the church fathers or students of the Word before the nineteenth century.[1]

Ladd is not alone in his assessment.[2]

Ice calls the nineteenth-century pretribulational rapture doctrine a "development of theology." You can't call something a development when it was absent from the records of church history

---

1. George Eldon Ladd, *The Blessed Hope* (Grand Rapids, MI: Eerdmans, 1956), p. 31.

2. Clarence B. Bass, *Backgrounds to Dispensationalism: Its Historical Genesis and Ecclesiastical Implications* (Grand Rapids, MI: Baker Book House, [1960] 1977), pp. 13-16. Even dispensationalists would deny Ice's assertion. One dispensational student came to this conclusion:

> Indeed, this thesis would conclude that the eschatological beliefs of the period studied would be generally inimical [contrary] to those of the modern system (perhaps, seminal amillennialism, and not nascent [emerging] dispensational premillennialism ought to be seen in the eschatology of the period).

Alan Patrick Boyd, "A Dispensational Premillennial Analysis of the Eschatology of the Post-Apostolic Fathers (Until the Death of Justin Martyr)" (Th.M. thesis, Dallas Theological Seminary, 1977), pp. 90-91.

for 1800 years. There's not a trace of it anywhere in church history before 1830. This is not development. On the other hand, postmillennialism and amillennialism are truly developmental. There are traces and a development of these positions throughout church history: From Athanasius (c. 296-373) and Augustine (354-430), from Calvin (1509-1564) and the Puritans, and from Charles Hodge, B. B. Warfield, and J. A. Alexander to present-day Reconstructionists.

Ice wants us to believe that premillennialism was held by everyone — he says, "to a man" — in the early church. But then he modifies this assertion by stating, "as far as early church records show." We really don't know if premillennialism was *the one and only view*. Justin Martyr (c. 100-165) certainly recognized other orthodox positions, and the creeds do not outline a specific millennial position.[3] He also says that the early church's views on eschatology were "futuristic." But all millennial positions are futuristic to some degree.

Ice then makes an unsubstantiated accusation regarding the influence of "Greek philosophy" and the development of "amillennialism." This is almost impossible to prove. A postmillennialist could just as easily say that premillennialism was influenced by Judaism and its emphasis on an earthly millennial kingdom. Arnold Ehlert traces dispensationalism back to "Jewish and pre-Jewish thought."[4] But we know that Jesus rejected the apostate Jews' understanding of the kingdom, and Paul had his greatest battles with these Jews. We also know that Greek influence had an early impact on the church during the apostolic age (1 Corinthians 1:18-25; Colossians 2:8) as well as the compromised worldview of the Nicolaitans (Revelation 2:6, 15). Using Tommy Ice's logic, couldn't we just as easily assert that premillennialism grew out of apostate Judaism or Greek philosophy since these are closer to the time of Justin Martyr than they are to Athanasius and Augustine? This would be just as impossible to prove as is Ice's inference about Greek philosophy and Augustine.

---

3. See the discussion of this in chapter 12.
4. Bass, *Backgrounds to Dispensationalism*, pp. 15-16. See also Leon Morris, *The Revelation of St. John* (Grand Rapids, MI: Eerdmans, 1969), p. 234.

Tommy Ice wants us to believe that a literal hermeneutic was absent from the church for 1400 years. This means from Augustine to J. N. Darby the church was without a biblically based hermeneutic. This would mean that John Wycliffe (c. 1329-1384), John Calvin, and the great Puritan commentators did not interpret Scripture literally. Of course, if you mean the strained and inconsistent literalism outlined by Darby, Scofield, and dispensationalism in general, then Ice is correct. But it's a dangerous thing to wipe out some of the greatest Bible expositors and commentators the church has had from 400 to 1830. Even today there are innumerable non-dispensational scholars who would take issue with the hermeneutical methodology of dispensationalism.

Moreover, there is the hint of cultism when someone maintains that the biblical position was lost for nearly 1500 years and was only recently rediscovered. Nearly all modern cults take this approach to gain converts: "Only we have rediscovered the lost truths of the Bible." This is not to accuse dispensationalism of being a cult, but the argumentation by Ice is nearly identical to the reasoning given by numerous modern cults. Dispensationalism will have to be supported from another line of reasoning before it can be considered to be biblical.

Supposedly, this literal hermeneutic enabled the church for the first time to answer the question, "What do we do with Israel?" The Westminster Assembly (1643-48), written nearly 200 years before Darby, considered the place of Israel in biblical prophecy. The answer to question 191 from the Larger Catechism reads:

> In the second petition, (which is, *Thy kingdom come*,) acknowledging ourselves and all mankind to be by nature under the dominion of sin and Satan, we pray, that the kingdom of sin and Satan may be destroyed, the gospel propagated throughout the world, *the Jews called*, the fullness of the Gentiles brought in; the church furnished with all gospel-officers and ordinances, purged from corruption, countenanced and maintained by the civil magistrate: that the ordinances of Christ may be purely dispensed, and made effectual to the converting of those that are yet in their sins, and are already converted: that Christ would rule in our

hearts here, and hasten the time of his second coming, and our reigning with him for ever: and that he would be pleased so to exercise the kingdom of his power in all the world, as may best conduce to these ends.

The calling of the Jews was a prominent theme in Puritan theology. The *Savoy Declaration of Faith* (1658), which John Owen, a congregational minister, helped to write, is very similar to the Westminster Larger Catechism. It reads in part: "So, according to His promise, we expect that in the latter days, Antichrist [the Papacy] being destroyed, *the Jews called,* and the adversaries of His Son broken, the churches of Christ being enlarged and edified through a free and plentiful communication of light and grace, shall enjoy in this world a more quiet, peaceable, and glorious condition than they have enjoyed."[5] For a fuller discussion of the place of the Jews in biblical prophecy, see Appendix B.

Tommy Ice ends his answer to the question by stating that "the rapture is a sub-point within premillennialism." Now, if it's a sub-point in premillennialism, then why is it being made by some to be a test of orthodoxy in the debate over Christian Reconstruction? Why does Dave Hunt consider the rapture the key to his eschatological system? Why does Ice minimize a doctrine that is essential to dispensationalism? Without a pretribulational rapture, Israel and the church cannot remain separate peoples. This is essential to dispensationalism.[6] It is a *major* and *essential* doctrine

---

5. Quoted in Peter Toon, *God's Statesman: The Life and Work of John Owen* (Grand Rapids, MI: Zondervan, 1973), p. 81. John Owen "had a very strong belief in the doctrine of the restoration of the Jewish nation to Palestine and published a widely read book, *Israel Redux* (1677), which was reprinted several times" (p. 152).

John Owen did not interpret the Bible literally, that is, according to the narrowly defined parameters of Dispensationalism. Owen maintained that the "passing of heaven and earth" in 2 Peter 3:5-7 had reference, "not to the last and final judgment of the world, but to that utter desolation and destruction that was to be made of the Judaical church and state" in A.D. 70. Owen *Works*, 16 vols. (London: The Banner of Truth Trust, 1965-68), vol. 9, p. 134.

6. See, however, the dispensational *post*-tribulational approach of Robert H. Gundry, *The Church and the Tribulation* (Grand Rapids, MI: Zondervan, 1973). Hal Lindsey critiques Gundry's views in *The Rapture* (New York: Bantam Books, 1983), pp. 147-53.

of dispensationalism. Without it, the entire system falls to pieces. J. Dwight Pentecost states that a *post*-tribulational rapture is inconsistent with dispensationalism. He writes:

> (1) Posttribulationism must be based on a denial of dispensationalism and all dispensational distinctions. It is only thus that they can place the church in that period which is particularly called "the time of Jacob's trouble" (Jer. 30:7). (2) Consequently, the position rests on the denial of the distinction between Israel and the church.[7]

The debate over the rapture is a disagreement over timing and meaning. There is little consensus in the church today over the timing of the rapture, even among premillennialists.[8] Premillennialists of all types subscribe to pre-, mid-, and post-tribulational theories of the rapture. Amillennialists and postmillennialists see the rapture simply as the ascension of the saints on the last day before the general judgment of the living and the dead. For them, the rapture is not separated from the resurrection by a seven year tribulation period or a thousand year millennium.

Dave Hunt states that the rapture comes from the Bible. There is no disagreement about this. For Hunt, the "rapture simply means 'an ecstatic catching away.'" But when does this hap-

---

7. J. Dwight Pentecost, *Things to Come: A Study in Biblical Eschatology* (Grand Rapids, MI: Zondervan, [1958] 1964), p. 164.

8. Robert H. Gundry, *The Church and the Tribulation* (Grand Rapids, MI: Zondervan, 1973); Gleason L. Archer, Jr., et al., *The Rapture: Pre-, Mid-, or Post-Tribulational?* (Grand Rapids, MI: Zondervan, 1984); John F. Walvoord, *The Rapture Question* (rev. and enl.; Grand Rapids, MI: Zondervan, 1979); William R. Kimball, *The Rapture: A Question of Timing* (Grand Rapids, MI: Baker Book House, 1985); Dave MacPherson, *The Great Rapture Hoax* (Fletcher, NC: New Puritan Library, 1983), and *The Incredible Cover-Up* (Medford, OR: Omega Publications, [1975] 1980).

John Walvoord states that "four different views of the rapture have been advanced." He asserts that "among premillenarians a wide variety of views can be found, varying from the extreme of date-setting on the one hand to discounting any imminent hope of the Lord's return on the other." *The Blessed Hope and the Tribulation: A Historical and Biblical Study of Posttribulationism* (Grand Rapids, MI: Zondervan, 1976), p. 7.

pen? The clearest text on the rapture, 1 Thessalonians 4:13-18, doesn't say anything about a rapture prior to the Tribulation, nor does it say anything about a rapture prior to the millennium. Nor does it speak of a "secret" rapture. As a matter of fact, 1 Thessalonians 4:13-18 is one of the noisiest in Scripture—with the voice of the archangel, the trumpet of God, and a shout! It simply states that "we shall always be with the Lord" (v. 17). There is no hint of coming back to the earth after a seven year period of tribulation.

Question 2: What is the relationship between postmillennialism and Christian Reconstruction, and is Christian Reconstruction solely dependent on any millennial position?

At this juncture in the debate, the real differences between Christian Reconstruction and dispensational premillennialism become evident. Tommy Ice states that he and David Schnittger, author of *Christian Reconstruction from a Pretribulational Perspective*,

> tried to put together a premillennial Reconstructionist ethic. *I don't believe you can do it.* The issue of eschatology is: How are you involved in the present world, not whether or not you are involved in the present world. Premillennialists have always been involved in the present world. And basically, they have picked up on the ethical positions of their contemporaries. Gary North keeps telling us that ethics is the issue and not theology [eschatology]. The issue is that your theology tells you what your ethics are. . . . We are motivated ethically by the Second Coming of Jesus Christ. Scripture constantly talks about that, like in 1 John 3:2: "Beloved, now we are children of God, and it has not appeared as yet what we shall be. We know that when He appears, we shall be like Him, because we shall see Him just as He is. And every one who has this hope fixed on Him purifies himself, just as **He is pure.**"

Tommy Ice admits that a Reconstructionist ethic, that is, an ethical system that can be applied, for example, to economics, law, politics, and education, cannot be developed within dispensationalism. Ice tells us that dispensationalists must "pick up on the ethical positions of their contemporaries." What does this mean? For Tommy Ice, dispensationalists must go elsewhere to formulate their "ethical positions" as they relate to social issues. This is quite an admission. What "contemporaries" is he talking about? Are these Christian contemporaries or non-Christian contemporaries? If they are Christian contemporaries, then what theological system are they using to develop their social ethic? According to Tommy Ice, it can't be dispensationalism. Reconstructionists insist that the Bible gives a comprehensive system of ethics for all aspects of society. Christians do not have to "pick up" on any system other than the one the Bible outlines.

Tommy Ice tells us that "premillennialists have always been involved in the present world." There is no doubt that this is true. But the dispensationalist, according to Ice, must look to his contemporaries for assistance. So then, the basis of involvement for the dispensationalist is borrowed from systems that Ice criticizes. Why doesn't Ice say that Christians should not be involved in the present world? Since he believes that his position is the biblical position, and a theory of social involvement cannot be developed within dispensationalism, then why is he still for involvement in the present world?

He then goes on to insist that the *motivation* for ethical living is the imminent return of Jesus Christ. The issue in this debate, however, is not *motivation*. There are a number of things that can motivate Christians to live holy lives: fear, love, the kindness of God, gratitude, and the final judgment. Rather, the issue is what *standard* has God outlined for us to follow once we are motivated to live a holy life? Motivation is not enough. Many evil things have been done in the name of "good motivation." What standard will Jesus use to judge us when He does return? This is the substance of the debate.

Reconstructionists insist that God has given us His law as a guide for proper behavior. There will then be no surprises on judgment day. In fact, God has saved us so that we can walk in terms of God's law.

When Paul says that we are saved by grace through faith, he immediately adds that as God's workmanship *we are expected to walk in good works* (Eph. 2:10). Although it is popular today to look upon the law as an intolerable burden for modern man, the beloved apostle wrote that for the believer God's law is not burdensome (1 John 5:3). When the Psalmist reflected upon the lovingkindness of the Lord, he longed to be taught His statutes and rose at midnight to render thanks for His righteous ordinances (Ps. 119:62-64). Moses viewed the giving of God's law as a sure sign of His love for the people (Deut. 33:2-4).[9]

It's one thing to be motivated to be involved in the present world, but it's another thing to know what to do in the world. On this point, Tommy Ice does not give an answer. Reconstructionists believe that the Bible gives the answers the world needs for ethical direction for all of life. And Who is the motivation for this? Jesus Christ. What is the standard for motivation? God's Word.

Dave Hunt, with his response to the question, articulates a more biblical approach to suffering and prosperity than we've seen before. He no longer commits the either/or fallacy. He states that

> We don't deny, as I said earlier, that God blesses those who obey Him. But, that's not all the Bible says, and there are different ways of blessing. It can be a blessing to be crucified for the sake of Christ. Jesus said, "Happy are you when they persecute you and speak all manner of evil against you for my sake. Rejoice and be exceeding glad." A blessing is not just economic blessing and so forth, and there are countries like Japan that are quite blessed as Buddhist or Shintoist.

How can the Bible tell us to be happy when we are persecuted and "all manner of evil" is spoken against us? Mainly because we have a great reward in heaven. We can rejoice also because there is progress in history. The ungodly do not dominate culture longterm. They "will not make further progress; for their folly will be obvious to all" (2 Timothy 3:9). Dave Hunt is correct, "blessing is not just economic blessing." But blessing does include economics,

---

9. Greg L. Bahnsen, *By This Standard* (Tyler, TX: Institute for Christian Economics, 1985), p. 73.

law, politics, education and every other good thing created by God. These blessings are realized through faithfulness to God. If a person is faithful in carrying out God's commandments, he will prosper (Joshua 1:8). Failure to acknowledge that God is the one who gives these good gifts will mean judgment (Deuteronomy 8). Does this mean that God's people will not encounter tribulation? Not at all. But even in tribulation God's people eventually prosper.

> And not only this, but we also exult in our tribulations, knowing that tribulation brings about perseverance; and perseverance, proven character; and proven character, hope; and hope does not disappoint, because the love of God has been poured out within our hearts through the Holy Spirit who was given to us (Romans 5:3-5).

God uses all things, even tribulation, to make us what He wants us to be. So then, it's wrong to pit tribulation over against prosperity of whatever kind. In terms of the sovereignty of God, we always prosper. Even in death there is victory. Every attempt to thwart the advance of God's kingdom is overthrown by God. Tertullian (c. 160-240) captures the spirit of this truth with these words: "The more ye mow us down, the more quickly we grow; the blood of Christians is seed."

Finally, Dave Hunt seems to say that Christianity as a worldview really has nothing over Shintoism and Buddhism when it comes to economic development. He tells us that Japan has done very well economically without an operating Christian worldview. This is not the place to rehearse Japan's post-World War II progress, but nearly all historians agree that Japan's development is based on the infusion of western capital, education, and technology, which, in turn, is largely based on the western world's historic commitment to Christianity. Thomas Sowell writes:

> Meiji Japan introduced the study of English in its secondary schools in 1876, permitted the establishment of Christian churches and schools, and its leaders and intellectuals publicly expressed strong admiration for the United States and the Amer-

ican way of life. The United States was described as "an earthly paradise," a "benefactor" to Japan by ending its isolation, and American freedom was extolled as something to be both envied and emulated. Government-issued textbooks in the schools held up Benjamin Franklin and Abraham Lincoln as models to be followed by Japanese children, even more so than Japanese heroes. Perhaps never before has a foreign people been so indoctrinated with the American way of life as those of Meiji Japan.[10]

Japan's prosperity was not the result of either Shintoism or Buddhism. It was Japan's isolationism, that is, its inherent pagan worldview that kept it a minor world power prior to both world wars. Japan became "the first Asian country to copy the West,"[11] and this included the worldview that prospered the West.

Douglas MacArthur (1880-1964) claims that the Japanese "world crumbled" upon hearing of the nation's military defeats near the end of World War II. "It was not merely the overthrow of their military might — it was the collapse of a faith, it was the disintegration of everything they had believed in and lived by and fought for. It left a complete vacuum, morally, mentally, and physically." What filled this vacuum? The "democratic way of life" that was Western and vaguely Christian. A spiritual revolution emerged that "almost overnight tore asunder a theory and practice of life built upon 2,000 years of history and tradition and legend." The Japanese people had been told that the "Emperor was divine himself and that the highest purpose of every subject's life was death in his service." Those who led Japan into war "used this religion to further their efforts." The state actually subsidized this belief. MacArthur "ordered state subsidization to cease." On New Year's Day, 1946, the Emperor, echoing Nebuchadnezzar, repudiated "the false conception that the Emperor is divine and that the Japanese people are superior to other races and fated to rule the

---

10. Thomas Sowell, *Ethnic America: A History* (New York: Basic Books, 1981), pp. 156-57.

11. Paul Kennedy, *The Rise and Fall of the Great Powers: Economic Change and Military Conflict from 1500 to 2000* (New York: Random House, 1987), p. 206.

world." He described these beliefs to be based upon "mere legends and myths." Shinto priests were still permitted to practice their religion "so long as church and state were separated." This is how MacArthur sums up Japan's transformation:

> Whenever possible, I told visiting Christian ministers of the need for their work in Japan. "The more missionaries we can bring out here, and the more occupation troops we can send home, the better." The Pocket Testament League, at my request, distributed 10,000,000 Bibles translated into Japanese. Gradually, a spiritual regeneration in Japan began to grow.[12]

So then, it was the *rejection* of Shintoism and Buddhism and the *adoption* of a Western worldview that was at least vaguely Christian that has made Japan what it is today.

Dave Hunt continues by denying that there is any progress in history. This is an astounding admission. Let me quote him in full:

> DeMar says Hunt has no philosophy of historical progress rooted in the sovereign operation of the Spirit of God. No, I don't have a biblical basis for a philosophy of gradual progress. There's not one example in the Bible. There's not one example in history. They give examples like the cessation of slavery in England. But, look at England today. They are not selling literal slaves. They're selling slaves to Satan—the souls of men to Satan. Look at the church today. Look at Holland where Abraham Kuyper was and so forth. But, take a look at it today. He did tremendous things there, but look at it today. We have been going—we have had ups and downs—but we have been going down in history.

Hunt claims that there's not one example of gradual progress in the Bible. What does he think of the advance of God's kingdom as it's depicted in Isaiah 9, 11; Daniel 2, 7 and the "growth parables" in Matthew 13? Isaiah says that at the time when "a child will be born to us" there will be "no end to the increase of His government

---

12. All of these quotations are taken from Douglas MacArthur, *Reminiscences* (New York: McGraw-Hill, 1964), pp. 310-11.

or of peace" (9:7). What is the time frame for this?: "From then on and forever more." This promise is not reserved for some distant earthly millennium. It burst into history at the time of Jesus' birth, and began to be demonstrated in power with Jesus' resurrection and ascension to the right hand of God to sit on "His glorious throne." What is the goal of this? Isaiah continues: "They will not hurt or destroy in all My holy mountain, for the earth will be full of the knowledge of the LORD as the waters cover the sea" (11:9).

In Daniel 2, we're told that God's kingdom "became a great mountain that filled the whole earth" (v. 35). It goes on to say that "in the days of those kings the God of heaven will set up a kingdom which will never be destroyed, and that kingdom will not be left for another people; it will crush and put an end to all these kingdoms, but it will itself endure forever" (v. 44). What is the goal of the kingdom in Daniel?:

> I kept looking in the night visions, and behold, with the clouds of heaven One like a Son of Man was coming, and He came up to the Ancient of Days and was presented before Him. And to Him was given dominion, glory and a kingdom, that all the peoples, nations, and men of every language might serve Him. His dominion is an everlasting dominion which will not pass away; and His kingdom is one which will not be destroyed (Daniel 7:13-14).

The "growth parables" of Matthew 13 are very clear about the progress of God's kingdom in history among the nations. "The kingdom of heaven is like a mustard seed, which a man took and sowed in his field; and this is smaller than all other seeds; but when it is full grown, it is larger than the garden plants, and becomes a tree, so that the birds of the air come and nest in its branches" (v. 32). What does this parable teach? The "birds of the air" represent the Gentile nations who have in the past been excluded from the covenant promises. Under the New Covenant, the Gentiles are brought into the kingdom as they repent and believe in the gospel. We saw this in Daniel 7: "peoples, nations, and men of every language" (v. 13; cf. Revelation 5:9-10; 7:9; 14:6). In the second "growth parable" Jesus states, "The kingdom of heaven is like leaven, which a woman took, and hid in three pecks of meal, until it was all leavened." The parable of the leavened loaf teaches us that the kingdom of God grows among the nations as leaven permeates the dough "until it was *all* leavened" (Matthew 13:33).[13]

The gospel message went as far as Spain in Paul's day (Romans 15:24, 28). Doesn't this constitute progress? From twelve apostles, to seventy disciples, to one hundred and twenty gathered in one place to await the arrival of the Holy Spirit, to five hundred who saw the risen Christ, to nearly three thousand conversions after Peter's first sermon. Aren't these examples of progress? In a span of forty years, the gospel of Jesus Christ had spread throughout the entire inhabited world (Colossians 1:23). Paul preached the gospel to the highest-ranking rulers in the Roman Empire. He may have even preached to Caesar himself. Now, where is the Roman Empire today? It does not exist. Where is God's king-

---

13. Dispensationalists try to get around the growth of the kingdom by maintaining that "leaven is always evil." Ray C. Stedman, a popular dispensational Bible expositor, calls the parable of the woman who places the leaven in the dough, "The Case of the Sneaky Housewife." Ray C. Stedman, *Expository Studies in Matthew 13: Behind History* (Waco, TX: Word, 1976), pp. 79-102. For Stedman, leaven is evil. He contends that Jesus is teaching in this parable that the kingdom is permeated with corruption.

But putting leaven (yeast) in dough is *natural* to the bread-making process. There is nothing sinister about this. Anyway, leaven is not always evil. Leaven is to be included for a "wave offering": "They shall be of fine flour, baked with leaven as first fruits to the LORD" (Leviticus 23:17; also 7:13). Jesus chose leaven because of its expansive quality to illustrate the growth of the kingdom. Like the "wave offering" depicting "first fruits," this parable describes God's kingdom activity among the nations. In other cases leaven is evil: It's called the "leaven of the *Pharisees*" and the "leaven of *Herod*" (Mark 8:15; cf. 1 Corinthians 5:7-8).

If we follow the logic of "leaven is always evil," then we end up with impossible interpretive problems. The "serpent" is generally associated with evil (Genesis 3:13; Psalm 58:4; 140:3; Proverbs 23:32; Isaiah 27:1; Matthew 23:33; 2 Corinthians 11:3; Revelation 12:9, 14-15; 20:2). But God instructs Moses to create a "bronze serpent" so that everyone who looks at it will live (Numbers 21:6-9). In the New Testament, Jesus is to "be lifted up" as "Moses lifted up the serpent" (John 3:14). Jesus instructed His disciples to be "shrewd as serpents, and innocent as doves" (John 10:16). Of course, Satan is described as a "roaring lion" (1 Peter 5:8) and Jesus is the "Lion that is from the tribe of Judah" (Revelation 5:5).

dom? It continues to advance. This is progress! Was history in steady decline after Pentecost?

Dave Hunt goes on to tell us that there is not one example of gradual progress in history. This assertion borders on the unbelievable. The development of Western civilization follows the advance of Christianity. Christopher Dawson writes: "The beginnings of Western Culture are to be found in the new spiritual community which arose from the ruins of the Roman Empire owing to the conversion of the Northern barbarians to the Christian faith."[14]

Dave Hunt is evaluating all of history in terms of his place in history. His perspective in time is used to evaluate all of history. Since moral righteousness is presently at a low ebb in certain quarters, he concludes that there is no gradual progress in history. Are we to believe that technological advances are not progress? Where did technology arise? In the Christian West. Many, if not most, scientists attributed their scientific endeavors to their Christian faith.[15]

Few people would dispute the fact that, in general, life today is better than it was just 200 years ago. Today, for example, we in the "First World" take personal hygiene for granted, but 200 years ago even the aristocracy lived in squalor that we would find intolerable. They had lice in their hair and rotting teeth in their mouths. Even today, millions of people in the "Third World" live without hygienic comforts that we consider necessities. Significantly, the nations that are the envy of the world are nations that were built on a Christian foundation. Obviously there has been progress in the world. The gospel has influenced culture. The history of science parallels the advance of the gospel, as does medicine, publishing, and invention in general. For example, the first book printed on Johann Gutenberg's printing press was the Bible. He wrote:

---

14. Christopher Dawson, *Religion and the Rise of Western Culture* (New York: Sheed & Ward, 1950), p. 23.

15. Henry M. Morris, *The Biblical Basis for Modern Science* (Grand Rapids, MI: Baker Book House, 1984), pp. 29-33.

Religious truth is captive in a small number of little manuscripts, which guard the common treasures instead of expanding them. Let us break the seal which binds these holy things; let us give wings to truth that it may fly with the Word, no longer prepared at vast expense, but multitudes everlastingly by a machine which never wearies—to every soul which enters life.

Is publishing better today than in Gutenberg's day? With the newest computers, the smallest office can turn out near typeset-quality copy that is ready for the printer with very little expense. Even the cost of printing is down so the poorest among us can afford a Bible. Most households have at least one Bible.

The first message sent by Samuel F. B. Morse on a telegraph line was, "What hath God wrought!" Consider how rapidly the communications industry has developed since the simple telegraph was invented. The gospel can be taken to the far reaches of the globe through an inexpensive satellite hook up. An entire college and ministerial course can be put on video tape to be studied at a student's leisure without his ever having to leave his home.

Most people have flown on an airplane invented by two Christians named Wilbur and Orville Wright in 1903. Those who deny progress use the fruits of Christianity to inform large crowds of Christians that there is no evidence of "gradual progress in history."

Dave Hunt uses the abolition of slavery to support his position of an absence of progress in history. Was it better for the slaves before or after abolition? Obviously, we would say after. This is progress. England and the world are better places because of what these Christians did. But Dave Hunt tells us that "they're selling slaves to Satan" today. Who is selling slaves to Satan? Ministers? All ministers? Are there no Christian churches or ministers in England? Were not people being sold as slaves to Satan during Wilberforce's day, at the height of the slave trade? Would the slaves had been better off to be left as slaves? John Newton, author of "Amazing Grace," was a former slave trader who sold his life to Christ and then became a preacher of the gospel.

England is changing. A recent speech by Margaret Thatcher—England's longest-serving British Prime Minister—to the General

Assembly of the Church of Scotland, may give some support that England is returning to the faith of her fathers. Mrs. Thatcher said she was "speaking personally as a Christian as well as a politician." She went on to say: "Ideally, when Christians meet, as Christians, to take counsel together, their purpose is not (or should not be) to ascertain what is the mind of the majority but what is the mind of the Holy Spirit—something which may be quite different."[16]

In fact, for all our nostalgia about the "good old days," the twentieth century has seen vastly more people converted to Christianity than any other century of church history.

Dave Hunt's arguments are very weak on this point. There is progress in history. The church has been advancing. The progress of the gospel can be compared to a boy with a yo-yo going up a flight of stairs. Dave Hunt has his eyes fixed on the yo-yo: up and down, up and down, up and down. Without denying that history appears (from our viewpoint) to be a series of rises and falls, our attention should be fixed on the man ascending the stairs.

> *Question 3:* Eschatological debates tend to sway Christians from their biblical social responsibility whether Jesus returns now or a thousand years from now. Aren't we suppose to occupy till He returns? How can Christians ignore Scripture that specifically calls us to look after our brothers? The dismal state of our country can be traced to a Church that has abdicated its responsibility to mankind.

This question was answered by Dr. North and me at the debate. But for those readers who do not have access to the taped debate, I would like to reiterate some of those same points and also to add a few additional ones. Our good works are designed to draw those without hope to Jesus Christ. Good works are a beacon to the world. "Let your light shine before men in such a way that they may see your good works, and glorify your Father who is in heaven" (Matthew 5:16). These good works do not save people. Our purpose is not to turn the lost into better people through teaching them to do good works.

---

16. "Thatcher: Sow, and Ye Shall Reap," *World* (June 20, 1988), p. 5. See Paul Johnson's article, "Thatcher Pursues Moral Initiative," in the same issue, pp. 4-5.

Dave Hunt says that he has not abdicated his "responsibility to mankind." He goes on to say:

> We have a responsibility not just to feed people, but also to preach the Gospel to them. And there are people out there who put the emphasis in the wrong place. Who, for example, will say that Jesus never preached to any multitude without first of all feeding them. Well, you recall the case where there were 5,000 people and Jesus said to the disciples "give them something to eat." The disciples said, "Well, we don't have anything. Why don't you just send them home and they can buy something on the way." Jesus said, "They have been with me three days and three nights and they haven't had a thing to eat." He preached to them on empty stomachs. He felt there was something more important. He said, "If we send them away without any food now, they will perish in the way." So, I kind of resent being told that we don't have any concern for the social and ethical issues in our world. We certainly do. But, there is something more important and that is their eternal salvation.

Reconstructionists agree with Dave Hunt that the most important thing for the Christian is the salvation of the lost. But, again, this is not the issue in the debate. What does the new creature in Christ do for the next forty or fifty years of his life? Certainly he should lead others to Christ. But what then should *these* new converts do? How does the Christian live *now*? Does the Bible have anything to say about the family, economics, education, law, caring for the poor, politics, journalism, and so forth? This is what Christian Reconstruction is all about.

With the imminent rapture doctrine, preaching the gospel is the only Christian activity because there is no time to pursue long-term reconstruction. But if Jesus does not return for another thousand years, then the world will be worse off than it is today because Christians would have done very little to reconstruct their world. The world will degenerate into hopeless misery. Our salt will have become "tasteless." It will be "thrown out and trampled under foot by men" (Matthew 5:13). If previous generations of Christians had had the same short-term, anti-dominion perspective as Tommy Ice and Dave Hunt, then the freedoms that we now enjoy would not exist. Our Christian forefathers understood the concept of dominion and Christian Reconstruction. They worked hard to ensure that the State would not interfere in the affairs of religion. The United States of America, because of its early Puritan influence, created a decentralized constitutional republic that became the standard of freedom around the world. Christians were not silent in this enterprise.

Dave Hunt uses an incident in Jesus' preaching ministry to try to prove his point that the gospel takes precedence over all other activities (Matthew 15:32-39). Again, Reconstructionists agree that leading people to Christ is the church's primary mission. But the people who came to hear Jesus were not the poor and the disenfranchised. This is hardly an example of "gospel-first" preaching. The people did not come to Jesus for food. They did not expect to stay as long as they did. They had been without food for "three days" (v. 32). But Jesus did eventually feed them. Those who criticize Christian Reconstructionists because we insist that there is duty beyond proclaiming the gospel should heed the words of James:

> If a brother or sister is without clothing and in need of daily food, and one of you says to them, "Go in peace, be warmed and be filled," and yet you do not give them what is necessary for their body, what use is that? Even so faith, if it has no works, is dead, being by itself. But someone may well say, "You have faith, and I have works; show me your faith without the works, and I will show you my faith by my works" (James 2:15-18).

So then, reconstruction and dominion follow necessarily from gospel proclamation and conversion. They cannot be separated. Preaching the gospel must be emphasized along with giving the cup of cold water in Jesus' name. The world is drawn to fruits, whether good or bad. The bad fruit repels, while good fruit attracts.

Tommy Ice, with his comments, points again to the motivation that Christ's return stirs up the Christian for ethical duty (Luke 19:11-27). "The picture is of the good steward who is put in charge of the kingdom because, interestingly enough, the master has gone away to a far country to receive a kingdom, and the motivation, once again there for present operation, is that the master may return at any moment. And, therefore, because he may return at any moment he is supposed to be found doing what God has willed." Again, the debate is not over motivation. Rather, it's over what ethical standard the Christian should follow in anticipation of his Master's return, and should he expect success in his efforts. He must be "found doing what God has willed." Well, what has God willed? How do the slaves know what to do? The one slave who buried his mina in the ground had the best of motives. He also had the master's return in mind (vv. 20-27).[17]

Ice continues by stating that he has not seen "the reconstructionists come up with Scripture from the New Testament or even [to] show where the Old Testament would apply in the New Testament in the way that they teach." I'm not sure what he means by this. He seems to be saying that Reconstructionists must prove that the Christian's task is more than to preach the gospel. His following comments seem to indicate that this is what he means:

> The New Testament teaches that we're supposed to preach the Gospel. The current purpose of this age is for God to call out from among the nations a people for His name. The very word church, *ecclesia* in the Greek, means "called out ones." [The Bible] nowhere says we're to take over the world for Christ. Surely, wherever Christianity goes through history, it produces a much superior culture, but that is not the purpose, according to Scripture, during this particular age. When Christ returns and sets up His kingdom, He will cataclysmically bring in a culture and a society that will conform to the will of God.

Yes, our job is to preach the gospel to those who are in bondage to sin. But Jesus nowhere tells us to leave the world. Jesus

---

17. I'm not sure that Jesus is teaching His Second Coming in this parable. The nobleman returns to the same people to whom He gave the minas. His return seems to occur within a generation, not two thousand years later, in which case the descendants would be required to give an accounting of their ancestors' investments. The citizens are said to hate the nobleman, saying, "We do not want this man to reign over us" (Luke 19:14). This is reminiscent of John 18:15, when the Jewish leaders cried out, "We have no king but Caesar."

prays to His Father, not to take us out of the world, but to keep us from the evil one (John 17:15). Our separation from the world is not geographical, but ethical. By staying in the world we act as salt and light to a decaying and lost humanity. The world has already been taken over by Christ. We do not take over anything. Because we, through adoption, are children of God, "fellow-heirs with Christ" (Romans 8:17). We inherit what He already possesses. As the meek of God, we "inherit the earth" (Matthew 5:5).

In chapter one, I emphasized that the whole Bible is the Christian's standard. The Apostle Paul makes this very clear in 2 Timothy 3:16-17 where he declares that "*all* Scripture is God-breathed." The man of God who follows Scripture will be "equipped for *every* good work" (v. 17). Paul had the Old Testament in mind when he wrote these words. The Old Testament has laws that touch on every facet of life (e.g., Exodus 21-23). These laws are the Christian's guide along with the principles set forth under the New Covenant. Yes, there have been some changes, and modifications have to be made so these laws can be adapted and applied under the New Covenant; but they are there for "our instruction."

Question 4: How would both sides (reconstructionists and dispensationalists) apply Old Covenant or Old Testament teaching to the New Covenant or New Testament teaching?

Numerous books would need to be written before this question could be answered to anyone's satisfaction. There are a number of books that begin to address this very complicated issue.

1. R. J. Rushdoony, *The Institutes of Biblical Law* (Phillipsburg, NJ: Presbyterian and Reformed, 1973).

2. Greg L. Bahnsen, *Theonomy in Christian Ethics* (rev. ed.; Phillipsburg, NJ: Presbyterian and Reformed, [1977] 1984).

3. Greg L. Bahnsen, *By This Standard: The Authority of God's Law Today* (Tyler, TX: Institute for Christian Economics, 1985).

4. James B. Jordan, *The Law of the Covenant: An Exposition of Exodus 21-23* (Tyler, TX: Institute for Christian Economics, 1984).

5. Gary North, *Moses and Pharaoh: Dominion Religion Versus Power Religion* (Tyler, TX: Institute for Christian Economics, 1985).

6. Gary North, *The Sinai Strategy: Economics and the Ten Commandments* (Tyler, TX: Institute for Christian Economics, 1986).

7. Gary North, *Tools of Dominion: The Case Laws of Exodus* (Tyler, TX: Institute for Christian Economics, 1988).

Tommy Ice begins by emphasizing motivation for ethical behavior again. This has already been answered at numerous points in this chapter. Suffice it to say, whatever one's motivation, it does not answer the question of what standard we should live by. Ice continues by stating:

> We [Dave Hunt and Tommy Ice or dispensationalists in general] believe in applying the Old Testament law to today, but we do not believe we are directly under the Old Testament law because of Christ having released us from this.

There's not too much to disagree with here. Still, I do believe that Tommy Ice is confused over one point. While the law no longer condemns the Christian, Christians have not been freed from following the demands of the law. Consequences do follow from disobedience, as even the New Testament shows. Obviously, we have been freed from the sacrificial system and all matters relating to the shedding of blood. But nowhere in the New Testament does it say that we are not to keep the law as summarized in the Ten Commandments. Tommy Ice continues:

> We believe just as Deuteronomy, chapter four, says: The nations even in the Old Testament times would observe Israel's law and realize that it was wise and understanding [for them to follow it].

If the law of God is good—it is, in fact, *God's* law—then why not promote it as the best option for the world to follow? Whether you say it's obligatory for the nations or the best law among all law systems for the nations, Christians should be promoting God's law as a standard for personal, family, ecclesiastical, and civil righteousness. But I'm not sure how many dispensationalists would agree with Tommy Ice on this point.

But if keeping the law is simply a wise thing to do, with no obligation on our part, then how can God hold anyone accountable for breaking the law? Is abortion wrong? Why? Well, we would say the Bible opposes abortion. Are civil governments obligated to follow the laws that apply to the criminalization of abortion? If they are not, then Christians have no real standard by which to influence legislation. We could only go with the wisdom approach: "It would be wise for you to outlaw abortion, but you have no obligation to do so." Ice seems to support this idea with the following:

> The book of Proverbs, in my opinion, is a whole development of meditating on Old Testament law and coming up with wisdom or advice that are general principles. There's not law in Proverbs. It says that a wise person will do this. Therefore, since we are regenerate in the New Testament, we love the law because it reflects God's character, but we're not under the law. Therefore, it was totally done away with as a legal contract and ethical system.

This is an impossible situation. According to Ice, we no longer have law, but only "wisdom or advice." Yes, the Proverbs do rest on the Old Testament law. That's just the point. You can't understand and apply the Proverbs unless you understand the law. Murder is wrong. The Bible says that murder is wrong. A murderer cannot claim to be innocent because he doesn't have enough wisdom to tell him that it's wrong. Certainly, more difficult laws take a great amount of wisdom to interpret and apply. But wisdom is not a substitute for the law. Wisdom is something we pray for: "But if any man lacks wisdom, let him ask of God, who gives to all men generously and without reproach, and it will be given to him" (James 1:5).

This next quotation by Tommy Ice gives us some insight on how this wisdom approach is to be applied:

> We're like Daniel when we're in a foreign country. We look to the law to be our counselor. Daniel was a counselor who whis-

pered in the king's ear. He didn't try to take over Babylon. And
the same is true with the Church. We are called to be wise and to
do this.

Israel was a *captive* nation. Daniel was not simply in a foreign
country; he was one of the few Israelites who had any freedoms,
and these came to him miraculously. The Jews could not vote, influence legislation, or run for political office. Of course, Daniel's
situation does not answer the question of what the Christian does
in the area of civil legislation in his own country where he has access to all the avenues of political reform. Christian Reconstructionists are not "trying to take over" America. Jesus has already
"taken over" (cf. Psalm 2:8; Matthew 28:18-20). Reconstructionists believe that Christians should search the Bible and then live in
terms of its commands in every area of life. Christians have the
freedom in America to pursue all constitutional means to implement their agenda. They can even work to change the Constitution. Every political office is open to the Christian. Daniel had
none of these freedoms. And yet, Daniel still ruled in Babylon,
even with his limited freedoms. What's true in the lesser case of
diminished freedom for Daniel in Babylon, is true in the greater
case of enhanced freedom for Christians in America.

Tommy Ice moves on to inform the audience that "premillennialists have always been involved in ethics and in activity down
through history. It's just that reconstructionists do not like the way
we're involved." No one is denying that premillennialists have
been involved. But Tommy Ice told us in a response to an earlier
question that dispensationalists must "pick up on the ethical positions of their contemporaries." Yes, they are active, but not in
terms of any system from within dispensationalism. Now, if a system is developed, we would expect that it will look something like
what Reconstructionists have been trying to design.

But a question arises: Does the dispensationalist expect any
success in his efforts? The end-time scenario described by Dave
Hunt and Tommy Ice precludes any chance of success. Dave
Hunt has already told us that there is no "gradual progress in history." Working for change under the dispensational system is a

waste of time, money, and effort. Tommy Ice just told us that "the New Testament teaches that we're supposed to preach the Gospel. The current purpose of this age is for God to call out from among the nations a people for His name." It seems to me, that within Tommy Ice's dispensational system, all these other things just get in the way. Which way does Tommy Ice want to have it?

One last point needs to be addressed before we move on to Dave Hunt's response to **Question 4**. Tommy Ice mentions Francis Schaeffer, a premillennialist, who brought the issue of abortion to the attention of Christians. But Francis Schaeffer was a non-dispensational premillennialist! Schaeffer rarely if ever talked about eschatology. And when he set forth his position on Christian activism he quoted from the writings of two *postmillennialists*: John Knox and Samuel Rutherford. Where did Schaeffer get his information on Knox and Rutherford for his book *A Christian Manifesto*? From the *Journal of Christian Reconstruction: Symposium on Puritanism and Law*, Vol. V, No. 2 (Winter, 1978-79). The article on Samuel Rutherford was written by Richard Flinn (pp. 49-74), and the John Knox article was written by David Chilton (pp. 194-206).

In the first edition of *A Christian Manifesto* there is no bibliographical information on the Knox and Rutherford articles that are found in the *Journal of Christian Reconstruction*. But in subsequent editions, you will find that the two articles from the *Journal* are listed, after David Chilton called the error to the attention of Franky Schaeffer, Dr. Schaeffer's son. In the five-volume *Complete Works of Francis Schaeffer* (minus his booklet on baptism), the Rutherford and Knox articles are again absent from the bibliography.

But even in *A Christian Manifesto*, Francis Schaeffer's best-selling book, there is no agenda for long-term action. Schaeffer tells us to "take the steps necessary to break the authoritarian hold which the material-energy, chance concept of final reality has on government and law."[18] But what are those steps? Schaeffer never says.

---

18. Francis A. Schaeffer, *A Christian Manifesto* (rev. ed.; Westchester, IL: Crossway Books, 1982), p. 133. For an analysis of Schaeffer's activist views and his dependence on certain Reconstruction ideas, see Gary North and David Chilton, "Apologetics and Strategy," in Gary North, ed., *Tactics of Christian Resistance*, Christianity and Civiliztion 3 (Tyler, TX: Geneva Ministries, 1983), pp. 116-34.

Dave Hunt begins his answer by stating that he believes that there is a "higher standard than the Old Testament law." For Hunt, being led by the Spirit seems to be this "higher standard." But what does the Spirit use to lead us? Is it something different from God's law? How do we know that it's the Spirit who is leading us? The law is a reflection of God's character. The law is God's eternal standard for righteousness and sanctification. Greg Bahnsen writes:

> The *Holy Spirit* works in the believer to bring about conformity to the inspired *law of God* as the pattern of *holiness*. The "requirement of the law" is "fulfilled in us who do not walk according to the flesh, but according to the Spirit" (Rom. 8:4). When God puts His Spirit within a person it causes that person to walk in the Lord's statutes and keep His ordinances (Ezk. 11:19-20). Therefore, since salvation requires sanctification, and since sanctification calls for obedience to the commandments of God, the New Testament teaches us that Christ "became the author of eternal salvation unto all those who *obey Him*" (Heb. 5:9). This does not contradict salvation by grace; it is its inevitable outworking.[19]

Hunt then tells us why he believes that working to implement biblical law on a society of unbelievers is impossible: "Because nobody could keep the law." Hunt's argument goes something like this: Since godless people cannot obey the law of God, then how can we impose the law of God upon them and expect them to keep it? But the Apostle Paul tells us that the law is for those who are lawless.

> But we know that the Law is good, if one uses it lawfully, realizing the fact that law is not made for a righteous man, but for those who are lawless and rebellious, for the ungodly and sinners, for the unholy and profane, for those who kill their fathers or mothers, for murderers and immoral men and homosexuals and

---

19. Bahnsen, *By This Standard*, p. 66.

kidnappers and liars and perjurers, and whatever else is contrary
to sound teaching (1 Timothy 1:8-10).[20]

This passage teaches the very opposite of what Hunt proposes.
The law does not save. Rather, it keeps law-breakers in check, "if
one uses it lawfully" (v. 8). Notice that these laws pertain to criminal
activity. These are not attitudes of the heart that are reflected in
the fruit of the Spirit. The civil magistrate must have an ethical
code by which he can judge criminal activity. The Bible offers
such a code. Most people, whether regenerate or not, do not commit criminal acts. One of the reasons is the deterrence factor built
into God's law (Deuteronomy 17:12-13; 19:16-21; 21:18-21). So
then, the goodness of the law is manifest because the punishments
enacted will keep potential law-breakers from committing a crime.

Hunt then maintains that promoting the law as a standard for
personal and civil justice will "create some hypocrites who think
they're outwardly acting in conformity to the law, but their hearts
have never been changed by Jesus Christ." Why did Paul state
that the "Law is good"? (1 Timothy 1:8). Why did he apply it to all
sorts of criminal activity? (vv. 9-10). He doesn't seem to have the
same problem with the law that Dave Hunt has. Hypocrisy has
always been present in the church. It's with us today. It's among
those who believe the law should be applied as well as with those
who say that it should not be applied.

Question 5: Dispensationalists separate law and grace using
Romans 6:14, where law is taken out of context. Grace is stressed
to the point that grace is no longer the biblical definition of grace.

Romans 6:14 is one of the most misinterpreted verses in the
Bible. If it's interpreted like some do, it would mean that Paul
contradicts himself in the span of three chapters. In Romans 3:31
Paul writes: "Do we then nullify the Law through faith? May it

---

20. Richard A. Fowler and H. Wayne House tell us that "First Timothy 1:8-11
is a Pauline rendition of the Ten Commandments." *The Christian Confronts His
Culture* (Chicago, IL: Moody Press, 1983), p. 137.

never be! On the contrary, we establish the Law." Paul, therefore, is not saying that Christians are free from the law as a standard of righteousness. Rather, its meaning has to do with the absence of condemnation which the law brings outside of Christ's redeeming work. In the next chapter, the apostle writes that "the Law is holy, and the commandment is holy and righteous and good" (7:12). The Law is said to be "spiritual" (v. 14a). The "requirement of the Law" is equated with walking "according to the Spirit" (8:4). There is even a partial listing of the Ten Commandments in Romans 13:8-10. So then, Paul is not setting the church free from keeping God's righteous commandments in the light of God's redeeming grace.

Tommy Ice begins his answer by stating that he believes that "grace and law are in both the Old and New Testament." He goes on to admit that "some earlier dispensationalists . . . stressed law and grace in a way that" he would not. What is Ice referring to? In the original *Scofield Reference Bible*, footnote 1 on page 1115 gives this description of grace:

> (2) As a dispensation, grace begins with the death and resurrection of Christ (Rom. 3: 24, 26; 4. 24, 25). The point of testing is no longer legal obedience as the condition of salvation, but acceptance or rejection of Christ, with good works as a fruit of salvation (John 1. 12, 13; 3. 36; Mt. 21. 37; 22. 42; John 15. 22, 25; Heb. 1. 2; 1 John 5. 10-12).

Keep in mind Scofield's words: "The point of testing *is no longer legal obedience* as the condition of salvation." Scofield even describes "four *forms* of the Gospel" (p. 1343): "(1) The Gospel of the Kingdom"; "(2) The Gospel of the grace of God"; "(3) The everlasting Gospel"; "(4) That which Paul calls, 'my Gospel' (Rom. 2. 16, *refs.*)."

Lewis Sperry Chafer, in his multi-volume dispensational systematic theology, shows why there has been confusion over the "two ways of salvation" teaching by dispensationalists. Chafer explains that "a distinction must be observed here between just men of the Old Testament and those justified according to the New

Testament. *According to the Old Testament men were just because they were true and faithful in keeping the Mosaic Law.*"[21] He continues with these comments: "Men were therefore just because of their own works for God whereas New Testament justification is God's work for man in answer to faith (Rom. 5:1)."[22] This is not an isolated text in Chafer's *Systematic Theology*.[23]

Tommy Ice admits that some within dispensationalism used language that seemed to have taught two ways of salvation. But Charles C. Ryrie, in his very popular defense of dispensationalism, denies the charge of two types of salvation ever being taught. He maintains that "neither the older nor the newer dispensationalists teach two ways of salvation, and it is not fair to attempt to make them so teach."[24] Now, in order to give dispensationalists the benefit of the doubt, we should only say that some of their writings seem to express two ways of salvation. The fact that the *New Scofield Reference Bible* corrected the notes that seemed to teach two ways of salvation is evidence that there was confusion.

Tommy Ice continues by stating that "in the New Testament there is an emphasis on the graciousness of the gospel because it's going to all the nations. And in that sense, I would say that the New Testament is more gracious than the Old Testament." If he means by this that the gospel message includes the nations beyond the boundaries of Israel, whereas under the Old Covenant it did not, then I will agree that there is an emphasis on the graciousness of the Gospel under the new Covenant. But that grace is not more gracious, while the extent of the grace is. God's demands have not changed. Sin is still sin. Homosexuality, abortion, theft, perjury, and political tyranny are still with us. The law still applies in condemning these acts. The Apostle Paul points this out in 1 Timothy 1:9-10.

---

21. Lewis Sperry Chafer, *Systematic Theology*, 8 vols. (Dallas, TX: Dallas Seminary Press, 1948), vol. 7, p. 219. Quoted in Curtis I. Crenshaw and Grover E. Gunn, III, *Dispensationalism Today, Yesterday, and Tomorrow* (Memphis, TN: Footstool Publications, 1985), p. 345.

22. *Idem.*

23. *Ibid.*, pp. 346-397.

24. Charles C. Ryrie, *Dispensationalism Today* (Chicago, IL: Moody Press, 1965), p. 207.

Grace is still grace. God will save those who turn to Jesus, those who repent of their evil deeds. "Such were some of you," Paul says of the Corinthians (1 Corinthians 6:9). This does not mean, however, that they will necessarily be freed from the temporary punishment that accompanies these crimes. Thieves must still pay restitution (Ephesians 4:28), and those who commit capital crimes may be put to death (Acts 25:11).

Ice also admits that "the law was given to a regenerate . . . people . . . called Israel. It was part of their covenantal agreement after they were delivered from Egypt, and it was given to them to show them how to live." Why can't the law be given to a regenerate people under the *New* Covenant to show them how to live? The Reconstructionists insist that this is one of the main purposes of the law.

Ice discusses the operation of the Spirit as our guide. The mature Christian is "motivated and directed by the Spirit." The "Word of God is his guide." Exactly. The Spirit uses His Word. The fulfilling of the law is not antithetical to keeping the law. They are the same thing. Being led by the Spirit does not free us from keeping the law. The Spirit is not an independent source of law.

What about the issue of the law as a "schoolmaster"? Yes, the law was Israel's "schoolmaster" to lead them to Christ, that they could be justified by faith (Galatians 3:24). In this sense, the law is done away with. This is simply *a* function of the law. As a revelation of God's moral standards, the law cannot change and still binds us, although with significant modification as delineated under the New Covenant.

The law, after we come to Christ, doesn't cease to exist for the Christian. Since sin is lawlessness, we need the law to know when we are sinning (Romans 7:7). While it's no longer a schoolmaster, it remains a standard of righteousness for Christians.

Ice comments: "Let us fulfill the law. If we walk in the Spirit, we will not fulfill the lust of the flesh." As Christians, we are now empowered so we can keep the law. In fact, Scripture tells us that we were created for this very purpose: "For we are His workmanship, created in Christ Jesus for good works, which God prepared beforehand, that we should walk in them" (Ephesians 2:10). How do we know what these good works are? The law of God is our standard.

The real difference, Ice points out, is over "continuity and discontinuity," that is, which laws are still applicable under the New Covenant and which ones are not. If we can agree that there is neither a radical continuity nor a radical discontinuity, then progress can be made in understanding the application of the law of God in our society.

Dave Hunt's answer centers on the issue of justification and the law. This really is not an issue in the debate over Christian Reconstruction. Reconstructionists do not believe in the law as a way to be justified. We do not believe in salvation by law. Salvation by law is the Judaizing heresy described by Paul in the book of Galatians. It is a "different gospel, which is really not another" (Galatians 1:6). Neither do Reconstructionists believe, as Dave Hunt seems to imply, that we can sanctify ourselves "by keeping the law in the future." No, Reconstructionists believe in salvation by grace through faith: "For by grace you have been saved through faith; and that not of yourselves, it is the gift of God; *not as a result of works*, that no one should boast" (Ephesians 2:8-9).

But can a person prosper if he keeps, for example, the many economic laws outlined in the Bible? What if a non-Christian stays out of debt, invests for the future, and commits himself to diligent labor? Will this person prosper? I think most people would agree that he will. Does this save him? Certainly not! But Dave Hunt is correct, however, in pointing out that prosperity based on law-keeping is often a hindrance for some people to come to Christ. The rich young ruler is a perfect example (Luke 18:18-34). But this is different from saying that the law does not work in the economic realm outside of Christ.

Can a non-Christian government act in terms of the law of God without the people or officials being Christian? Of course it can. Laws against murder, abortion, theft, perjury, and homosexuality benefit both the Christian and non-Christian communities. In Romans 13, the Apostle Paul describes the civil magistrate as a "minister of God to you for good" (v. 4). He brings God's "wrath upon the one who practices evil" (v. 4). What kind of civil government does Paul have in mind here? He doesn't say. One can infer that *all* civil governments, whether Christian or non-Christian, are in view here. They are all "ministers of God." What standard is the magistrate to use to determine what is "good behavior" and "evil" behavior? (v. 3). Who benefits by the magistrate's lawful use of the law? All of society, "for rulers are not a cause of fear for good behavior, but for evil" (v. 3).

So then, Dave Hunt does not, at least with this answer, understand Christian Reconstruction. Salvation by law is repudiated by *all* Reconstructionists.

Conclusion

The question and answer portion of the debate showed the differences between the two positions. Again, Tommy Ice and Dave Hunt focussed on a narrow section of theology that—while important for the church—is not the central issue over which a debate on Christian Reconstruction should be argued. Ice and Hunt see the pretribulational rapture as central to their theology, a doctrinal position that developed in the early nineteenth century. Ice maintains that the literal hermeneutic was restored in the nineteenth century and was the key in unlocking the mystery of what will happen to Israel in the future. This just isn't true. The future restoration of Israel was written into the Reformed creeds and confessions nearly two centuries before. Dave Hunt says that he can see no biblical or historical progress of the gospel. This is a denial of all the Bible and of all history.

The fact is, in order to support their claim that Christian Reconstruction is a deviant theology, Dave Hunt and Tommy Ice resorted to overstatements. Any admission that there is progress in history would have been enough to destroy their position.

17

CONCLUDING REMARKS BY
DAVE HUNT AND TOMMY ICE

At this point in the debate, each participant was given an opportunity to offer a summary statement. I pointed out that instead of name-calling, Christians should search out for themselves what the Bible says about the issues raised in the debate. For too long Christians have trusted in Bibles with notes, certain popular Christian teachers, and numerous books that have taken on a status nearly equal with the Bible. It's time that Christians revive the Reformational principle of studying the Bible for themselves, interpreting Scripture with Scripture, before we rise up and yell "heretic."

Gary North gave the following summation.

Our position is not that we take over the world for Christ. Let us get this clear. It is not the Christian Reconstructionist view that you take over anything for Jesus Christ. Because Jesus Christ said in Matthew 28 that "all authority has been given to Me in heaven and on earth."

Sure Moses suffered, but then God delivered all the spoils of Egypt into his hand and delivered Israel out of the land.

We were given the example of Daniel. Yes, Daniel didn't go in to try to take over everything by force. But on the last night of the existence of Babylon, who was senior in command? Who was the one they had to come to, the only one with the answers to what MENE, MENE, TEKEL, UPHARSIN meant? It was Daniel. And when he said what it was, and he prophesied what would happen, he had the chain of authority — as second in command in the nation — put around his neck.

211

That's the basis of the Reconstructionist position. Faithfulness. Preaching the gospel. Understanding in a world of confusion what the principles of righteous action are. Faithful preaching of those righteous rules. And as best we can, to spend our lives and our talent and our money to be good testimonies before the world in the name of Jesus Christ as His representatives. That's all we're calling for. Righteousness in the name of Christ before this fallen world.

This summary statement by Dr. North makes it quite clear that Reconstructionists are in the mainstream of Protestant thought. Ours is the theology of the Reformation. This is the theology of the Bible.

Through continual misrepresentation, Christian Reconstructionists are accused of espousing a "deviant theology." As the summaries of Dave Hunt and Tommy Ice show, the misrepresentations endure.

Dave Hunt: Summary and Response

Dave Hunt began his summary by suddenly resorting to name calling and misrepresentation. His entire tone changed with his final remarks. He called Christian Reconstruction "deviant." Of course, it was his task to prove this during the debate. He did not offer one doctrinal belief that could be described as "deviant." To describe Christian Reconstruction as "deviant" does not make it so. He's still obligated to prove it. As I've shown throughout this book and *The Reduction of Christianity*, Christian Reconstruction is far from deviant.

Who is Ruling Now?

Dave Hunt continued by mentioning what he described as our "false idea of dominion" that "has created some strange theories and many contradictions." Well, let's look at the evidence. What are these "strange theories and contradictions"? He tells us that Christian Reconstructionists "will not allow Jesus Christ to rule over His kingdom on this earth." He tells us that he finds that "incredible." So do I. Notice that he never quotes one Reconstructionist who espouses such an outrageous belief. I challenge anyone to find a single quotation by any Reconstructionist — as defined in *The Reduction of Christianity* — who says that we "*will not allow* Jesus to rule over His kingdom on this earth." Dave Hunt has made a preposterous charge while offering no evidence.

We, along with other postmillennialists and all amillennialists, do not believe that the Bible teaches that Jesus will return to set up an earthly throne in Jerusalem where the temple and its worship are to be restored, including blood sacrifices. Do we believe that Jesus is now ruling "over His kingdom on this earth"? Yes, we do. Jesus now rules from heaven. His physical absence from the earth does not mean that He does not rule over the earth. He is ruling from heaven, now! Heaven is His throne and the earth is His footstool (Isaiah 66:1). "The LORD's throne is in heaven" (Psalm 11:4). Remember, according to dispensationalism, Jesus will rule from a revived Davidic throne in Jerusalem. Does this mean, because His throne is localized in Jerusalem, that He will not be ruling in heaven or in other parts of the universe or in other nations on the earth? They would say that He does not abdicate His heavenly throne just because He has an earthly throne. Jesus would still rule the rest of the universe, heaven included, even if He had a throne on the earth. Well, why would Jesus leave His heavenly throne to sit on a temporal earthly throne that the Bible calls a "footstool"? Why does Jesus have to be physically present to rule anywhere? Jesus said that where two or three are gathered in His name, He is in their midst (Matthew 18:20). Isn't God the Holy Spirit operating in the world? R. C. Sproul explains why the ascension of Christ is a manifestation of His *present* sovereignty and kingship.

> When Jesus left this world He went to the Father. His ascension was to a certain place for a particular reason. To ascend did not mean merely "to go up." He was being elevated to the Right hand of the Father. He was advancing to what the church calls the *Sessio*, the *session* or seating at the Right Hand of God. The

seat He occupies on His departure is the royal throne of cosmic authority. It is the office of the King of the Kings and the Lord of the Lords.

Jesus was not departing in exile. He was leaving for His coronation. He was passing from humiliation to exaltation. The extraordinary benefit in this for every Christian is that he can live in the full assurance that at this very moment the highest political office in the universe is being held by King Jesus. His term of office is forever. No revolution, no rebellion, no bloody coup can wrest Him from the throne.[1]

There's nothing more that Jesus has to do to manifest His kingship. There's no need (or scriptural warrant) for Jesus to set up an earthly kingdom while sitting on a temporal earthly throne in the midst of a sacrificial system that His own shed blood has done away with. Now, whose position is a reduction of *Christ*ianity?

Ruling With Christ

Again, Dave Hunt misrepresents Christian Reconstructionists by implying that we teach that the church *substitutes* for Christ's physical absence on the earth. According to John 14-16, the Holy Spirit substitutes for Christ *in the world*. We are co-rulers or vice-regents *with* Christ, having the Spirit of God within us. The dominion that we have is coextensive with the dominion that Jesus claimed through His perfect life, death, resurrection, ascension, and session (Jude 24-25). We are "fellow-heirs with Christ" (Romans 8:17). God raised Jesus "from the dead, and seated Him at His right hand in the heavenly places, far above all rule and authority and power and dominion, and every name that is named, *not only in this age, but also in the one to come*" (Ephesians 1:20-21). Paul goes on to write that the Father has "put *all things* in subjection under His feet, and gave Him as head *over all things* to the church" (v. 22). And God the Father "raised *us* up with Him, and seated *us* with Him in the heavenly places, in Christ" (2:6). Jesus has made us to "be a kingdom and priests to God" (Revelation 5:10; cf. 1 Peter 2:9-10).

---

1. R. C. Sproul, "Quo Vadis?," *Tabletalk* (June 1983), Vol. 12, No. 3, p. 3.

Dave Hunt says that Reconstructionists teach that "it would be a defeat if Jesus came and intervened in history and took over and set up his kingdom. He is not allowed to do that. He's allowed to suffer here. We take that literally. But, He's not allowed to be glorified on this earth. And He's not allowed to rule over this kingdom, but we have to do it in His name." Jesus has already taken over and set up His kingdom. We do not teach that "He is not allowed to do" this. We believe Jesus has already done it. No, we don't, as Dave Hunt insists, "spiritualize away most of the prophesies about the coming of Jesus." We take His own prediction that He would come within a generation very literally. This was pointed out in Chapter 14 of this book. It's Dave Hunt and Tommy Ice who postpone Christ's kingship and thus deny its present manifestation. It is they who deny that He has already set up His kingdom. Jesus is already glorified. Jesus said that He glorified His Father on the earth, having accomplished the work that His Father had given Him to do (John 17:4). Jesus continues by telling us that He "*has been* glorified in" the disciples and that He "is no longer in the world" (vv. 10-11).

The Coming of Christ

Jesus said that He would "come quickly" (Revelation 22:12, 20). It's Dave Hunt who wants to spiritualize the obvious meaning of this verse and other verses that specifically tell us that Jesus would return in judgment to leave Jerusalem desolate within a generation (Matthew 24:34; Revelation 1:1, 3). He will come again to deliver up the kingdom on the last day "when He has abolished all rule and all authority and power. For He must reign until He has put all His enemies under His feet" (1 Corinthians 15:24-25). He will then judge the living and the dead. Dave Hunt mixes these two comings and is thus confused over the issue of eschatology and the timing of certain prophetic events. For Hunt, every eschatological event is yet future.

Hunt then ridicules the idea of the Roman armies surrounding Jerusalem as an outward manifestation of the near fulfillment of Jesus' prophecy that He would come within a generation (Luke

21:20). As was pointed out in a previous chapter, this view is not unique to Christian Reconstruction. Even dispensationalists admit that this is a coming of Christ in judgment. The late Henry Thiessen, who taught at Dallas Theological Seminary, wrote the following about the coming of Jesus in judgment in A.D. 70:

> We may admit that the prophecy concerning the destruction of this city is intimately connected with the predictions concerning our Lord's return in Matt. 24, Mark 13, and Luke 21, and that this event may be called a coming of the Lord in judgment. . . .[2]

Dispensationalists want to insist that there is still a future fulfillment of Matthew 24:1-34. This "double fulfillment" scenario must be read into the text. There is nothing in the text that would warrant such an interpretation. The dispensationalist imposes his theological system on the text.

The Marriage Supper of the Lamb

Hunt continues his summary by attacking a particular interpretation of Revelation 19:7: The marriage supper of the Lamb. Christian Reconstruction does not hinge on any single interpretation of the marriage supper of the Lamb. This is an important point to keep in mind. Dave Hunt did not go to major doctrinal variances to try to prove that Christian Reconstruction is "deviant." Rather, his evaluation of Christian Reconstruction focused on minor texts of Scripture where there has rarely been agreement. Why did Dave Hunt steer the debate away from the essentials of the faith? Why wasn't "deviance" proved by showing how Christian Reconstructionists depart from major doctrines? The answer is simple. Christian Reconstructionists are thoroughly orthodox on *all* major doctrines and *all* minor doctrines.

But what about the "marriage supper of the Lamb"? As with all prophecy, the question of timing is always a consideration. I assume that Dave Hunt believes that the marriage supper of the

---

2. Henry C. Thiessen, *Lectures in Systematic Theology* (rev. ed.; Grand Rapids, MI: Eerdmans, [1949] 1979), p. 346.

Lamb happens during the tribulation, sometime just prior to the millennium. But Robert H. Mounce, a noted premillennialist (non-dispensational), places the marriage supper of the Lamb *after the millennium*. He writes: "John is not saying that the eternal festivities have in fact arrived, but is speaking proleptically [in anticipation] of that period of blessedness which *follows the millennium* (cf. the declaration in 14:8 with the actual fall of Babylon in chaps 17 and 18)."[3] George Eldon Ladd, an historic premillennialist, also states that John is making a "proleptic announcement." But he places the marriage supper of the Lamb "at the coming of Christ when he is united with his church on earth."[4]

Now, if Revelation 19 depicts events in A.D. 70, then the marriage supper of the Lamb has reference to that period of time and not to some yet future event. David Chilton, whose views Dave Hunt is reacting to, offers the following comments on Revelation 19:7:

> *The destruction of the harlot and the marriage of the Lamb and the Bride* — the divorce [of apostate Judaism] and the wedding [of the New Israel] — *are correlative events*. The existence of the Church as the congregation of the New Covenant marks an entirely new epoch in the history of redemption. God was not now merely taking Gentile believers into the Old Covenant (as he had often done under the Old Testament economy). Rather, He was bringing in "the age to come" (Heb. 2:5; 6:5), the age of fulfillment, during these Last Days. Pentecost was the inception of the *New* Covenant. With the final divorce and destruction of the unfaithful wife in A.D. 70, the marriage of the Church to her Lord was firmly established; the Eucharist celebration of the Church was fully revealed in its true nature as "the Marriage Supper of the Lamb" (v. 9).[5]

None of the commentaries I checked on this passage ever said what the marriage supper of the Lamb was. They only described when

---

3. Robert H. Mounce, *The Book of Revelation* (Grand Rapids, MI: Eerdmans, 1977), p. 340. Emphasis added.

4. George Eldon Ladd, *A Commentary on the Revelation of John* (Grand Rapids, MI: Eerdmans, 1972), p. 245.

5. David Chilton, *The Days of Vengeance: An Exposition of the Book of Revelation* (Ft. Worth, TX: Dominion Press, 1987), p. 473.

it would happen. Ladd writes it is "John's custom to proclaim redemptive events which he nowhere actually describes. . . . In the
present pericope John heralds the marriage supper of the Lamb,
but he does not actually describe the event; he merely announces
it."[6] Chilton says that the marriage supper of the Lamb has com-
menced (cf. 2 Corinthians 11:2-3; Jude 3, 24), and he offers an interpretation, something which few commentators even attempt.[7]

But Chilton's interpretation of this passage is not the result of
either a postmillennial eschatology or a Reconstructionist theology. There are probably a number of postmillennialists (both
Reconstructionist and non-Reconstructionist) who would disagree with Chilton's interpretation. Therefore, Dave Hunt's comments are irrelevant to the debate since Christian Reconstruction
is not dependent upon Chilton's interpretation.

The Thousand Years

Hunt continues to engage in extraneous and irrelevant argumentation when he tells us that "we are asked to take comfort by
the fact that Jesus may come in another 100,000 years." Who says
this? He doesn't tell us. Hunt concocts this misrepresentation
from a series of arguments that David Chilton uses to prove that
the length of the thousand year period in Revelation 20 is a very
long period of time. Chilton writes: "My point is this: the term
thousand is often used symbolically in Scripture, to express
vastness; but that vastness is, in reality, much *more* than the literal
thousand."[8] The following quotation will show that Chilton does
not specify the length of the symbolic "thousand years," whether
it's 100,000 or 360,000 years:

> We should see that the "1,000 years" of Revelation 20 repre-
> sent a vast, undefined period of time. It has already lasted almost
> 2,000 years, and will probably go on for many more. "Exactly

---

6. Ladd, *Commentary on the Revelation of John*, pp. 245-46.
7. Chilton's "Eucharistic" interpretation is not unusual. See Geoffrey Wain-
wright, *Eucharist and Eschatology* (New York: Oxford University Press, 1981).
8. David Chilton, *Paradise Restored: A Biblical Theology of Dominion* (Ft. Worth,
TX: Dominion Press, [1985] 1987), p. 221.

how many years?" someone asked me. "I'll be happy to tell you," I cheerfully replied, "as soon as you tell me exactly how many hills are in Psalm 50."[9]

No one knows when Jesus is coming back. As Garry Friesen, a graduate of Dallas Theological Seminary writes, most premillennial teachers hold the opinion that "Christ may return tomorrow or a thousand years from now."[10] Of course, we could say with equal validity that Jesus may return tomorrow or two (three, five, ten) thousand years from now. This view is not unique to the Reconstructionists. Chilton, in a footnote, comments: "Consider the fact that the compilers of *The Book of Common Prayer* provided 'Tables for Finding Holy Days' all the way to A.D. 8400! Clearly, they were digging in for the 'long haul,' and did not expect an imminent 'rapture' of the Church."[11] How many premillennialists of the second century would have dreamed that the return of Christ would be 2000 years off? One older Bible commentary (not Reconstructionist) proposes that if a day is taken for a year,[12] the thousand years

represent 360,000 years, a period which some deem so long as to appear inadmissable. . . . Then, let it be recollected, that Jehu-

---

9. *Ibid.*, p. 199.
10. Garry Friesen, "A Return Visit," *Moody* (May 1988), 1988, p. 31.
11. Chilton, *Days of Vengeance*, p. 497, note 6.
12. Dispensationalists such as Dave Hunt and Tommy Ice should not be surprised at such an interpretation since the hermeneutical methodology that one uses to get this large number is inherent in dispensationalism. For example, a non-existent gap that dispensationalism places between the 69th and 70th week of Daniel 9:24-27 is nearly 2000 years long. "Shortly" is not that the event may occur soon, but when it does, it will be sudden. So then, if I tell you I'll be there shortly, don't hold your breath. Then there are the many "double fulfillments." Joel's prophecy, for example, wasn't *really* fulfilled on the day of Pentecost. There must be a future fulfillment. Peter didn't say it all when he declared that "this is what was spoken of through the prophet Joel" (Acts 2:16). The "this generation" of Matthew 24:34 does not mean the generation to whom Jesus spoke, but a generation nearly 2000 years in the future. Of course, there is the infamous "gap" of innumerable years that C. I. Scofield placed between the first two verses of Genesis 1: "The first creative act refers to the dateless past, and gives scope for all the geologic ages."

vah is described (Ex. 20.6) as 'keeping mercy for thousands,' even for thousands of generations; that he has 'commanded his Word to a thousand generations,' Ps. 105.8; 'and the Scripture cannot be broken,' Jn. 10.35; neither does the Spirit of truth speak in vain and boastful hyperboles; and the length of time thus allotted to the happy condition of the church will appear in no-wise disproportionate to the announcement of other scriptures.[13]

This quotation shows that Christian Reconstructionists are not alone in teaching that it may be some time before Jesus returns. Personally, I do not hold to the "day is a year" interpretation (2 Peter 3:8). Neither do I hold to Milton Terry's assertion that "it may be a million years."[14] No one can dogmatically state how long of a time it might be before Jesus returns.

Again, the belief in an extended period of time before Jesus returns is not unique to Christian Reconstruction since premillennialists hold a similar position. No one knows when Jesus will return.

To show that there is diversity of opinion within postmillennialism, Hunt makes this comment: "I have to give Gary North credit in this little piece here (I've lost it) where he brings it down to the year 2000." Gary North points out that some postmillennialists have held to a "sabbath millennium" where the seven days of creation represent seven thousand years of history, with the seventh day being the sabbath rest, the millennium of Revelation 20. The eighth day, representing the new birth, is the new heavens and new earth. This view is dependent on Bishop Usher's chronology of a 4004 B.C. creation date. According to this view, we are now entering the close of the sixth day (4000 years to the time of Christ plus 2000 years after Christ). The next day, that is, the next thousand year period, will be the millennium.[15] Apparently,

---

13. James W. Lee, ed., *The Self-Interpreting Bible*, 4 vols. (Philadelphia, PA: Keeler & Kirkpatrick, 1896), vol. 4, p. 537.

14. Milton Terry, *Biblical Apocalyptics: A Study of the Most Notable Revelations of God and of Christ in the Canonical Scriptures* (Grand Rapids, MI: Baker Book House, [1898] 1988), p. 451.

15. Gary North, "The Sabbath Millennium," *Biblical Economics Today* (Feb./Mar., 1985), pp. 3-4. Institute for Christian Economics, P.O. Box 8000, Tyler, Texas 75711.

this view was around during the time of the early church fathers. So then, some postmillennialists hold the position that the millennium is tied to the year 2000, while others extend it way into the future. But let's all stay close to biblical reality: *No one knows when Jesus will return.* Let's get on with the work at hand: Leading people to Jesus and showing them how to live in terms of God's Word.

What should the Christian take comfort in? Hunt says it's the rapture. For nearly 2000 years the church did not experience this comfort. No, the comfort is that when we die we will always be with the Lord. Every generation of Christians can rejoice in this truth. "For to me, to live is Christ, and to die is gain" (Philippians 1:21).

Tommy Ice: Summary and Critique

Tommy Ice began his summary by answering a question that I put to Dave Hunt: "Where in Revelation 20 does it say that Jesus will reign on the *earth* for a thousand years?" This was Tommy Ice's answer:

> Gary, Dave said I could tell you the Scripture. It's Revelation 20:6: "Blessed and holy is the one who has a part in the first resurrection; over them the second death has no power, but they will be priests of God and of Christ and *will reign with Him for a thousand years."*

Notice that my question specifically asked where in Revelation 20 does it say that Jesus will reign on the *earth*. There is no mention of Jesus being on the earth in Revelation 20. The passage tells us that those who rule with Him "will be priests of God and of Christ." Scripture says this has already happened: "But you are a chosen race, *a royal priesthood*, a holy nation, a people for God's own possession, that you may proclaim the excellencies of Him who has called you out of darkness into His marvelous light" (1 Peter 2:9). The first chapter of Revelation tells us that "He has made us to be a *kingdom of priests* to His God and Father" (Revelation 1:6; cf. 5:10). God has "delivered us from the domain of darkness, and transferred us to the kingdom of His beloved Son" (Colossians 1:13).

But some might conclude that the text states that the rule is "with Him." Obviously, the saints are on the earth. But Jesus tells us in Matthew 28:20 that Jesus is with us "always, even to the end of the age." Prior to His departure, Jesus said: "For where two or three have gathered in My name, there I am in their midst" (18:20). When Jesus comes again, He will come for us to take us to the place that he has prepared for us. Where is this place? It's heaven (John 14:1-6). Jesus being with us now, as Matthew 28:20 tells us, does not necessitate that He be physically present.

Sudden But Not Soon?

Tommy Ice continues his summary by referring to the suddenness of Jesus' coming:

> In Matthew 24:42-44, Jesus told His disciples, "to be on the alert for you do not know which day your Lord is coming, but be sure of this that if the head of the house had known at what time of night the thief was coming he would have been on the alert and would not have allowed his house to be broken into. For this reason, you be ready too for the Son of Man is coming in an hour when you do not think He will."
>
> Peter was one of those disciples present when our Lord gave this admonition. Just before his death, Peter's final words to believers in 2 Peter 3 were a warning not to be influenced by those who denied that Christ's return would be sudden and cataclysmic. He said, "The day of the Lord will come like a thief." It will be a sudden event, just as were creation and the flood.

There's some question as to whether these verses refer to the Second Coming, that is, the coming of Jesus to deliver the kingdom up to His Father as depicted in 1 Corinthians 15, or in the dispensational system, the rapture. Throughout the gospels, Jesus depicted His coming as being soon—within a generation Matthew 24:34 tells us. Peter was the one who questioned Jesus about the likelihood that John, the beloved "disciple whom Jesus loved," would be alive when Jesus returned. Jesus said, "If I want him to remain until I come, what is that to you? You follow Me" (John

21:22). There is at least the inference here that the apostles believed, with all that Jesus had said previous to this (e.g., Matthew 16:28; 24:34), that He would return in some way within a generation, at least before John died. But, in spite of the assured nearness of Jesus' coming, he tells Peter, "What is that to you?" The emphasis is not on Jesus' coming but on following Him. This same point is stressed in Acts 1:7-8.

What about 2 Peter 3? Is this a description of the period just prior to the dispensationalist's future "rapture"? Or did Peter have his contemporaries in mind? The "mockers" were apostate Israelites who were scoffing at Jesus' prediction that the temple would be destroyed. Peter writes that "in the last days mockers will come with their mocking" (2 Peter 3:3). The fundamental question is, When are the last days? Paul told Timothy "that in the last days difficult times will come" (2 Timothy 3:1). He warns Timothy to "avoid such men as these" (v. 5). How could Timothy have avoided people who would not be around for nearly 2000 years? The writer to the Hebrew Christians says that they are living in the "last days" (Hebrews 1:2). He goes on to show that at His first coming, Jesus was manifested "at the consummation of the ages" (9:26). In his first epistle, Peter writes that while Jesus was "foreknown before the foundation of the world," He "has appeared in these *last times* for the sake of you," that is, for those to whom Peter was writing (1 Peter 1:20). At Pentecost, Peter describes what had happened as a sign that the last days had begun (Acts 2:17). Paul comforted believers by assuring them that the "Lord is near" (Philippians 4:5).

Apostate Judaism was the great persecutor of the church. The book of Acts gives evidence of this (Acts 4:1-22; 5:17-42; 6:8-8:3; etc.). It was only later that Rome turned on the church because of its sole allegiance to one God and the denial that the Roman Caesars were divine. Initially, Rome thought of Christianity as a sect within Judaism. The earliest persecution of the church by Rome was done by Herod Agrippa I. But he was in league with the Jewish leadership: "And when he saw that [killing James the brother of John] pleased the Jews, he proceeded to arrest Peter also" (Acts 12:3). During this period of persecution by the Jews who rejected Jesus, on more than one occasion, Rome intervened in behalf of the church (e.g., Acts 23:12-26:27).

The judgment of those Jews who had rejected their Messiah would be coming on that generation. "Looking forward to the coming destruction of Jerusalem, the writer to the Hebrews warned those tempted to 'draw back' to apostate Judaism that apostasy would only bring them 'a certain fearful expectation of judgment, and fiery indignation which will devour the adversaries' (Hebrews 10:27)."[16] When could they expect this to happen? "For yet *in a very little while*, He who is coming will come, and will not delay" (Hebrews 10:37).

There are other passages that depict the last days as contemporary with the apostolic generation. The early church was living in the last days of the Old Covenant. This is why Jesus' coming is said to be "near" (James 5:1-9; 1 Peter 4:7, 12-13, 17): He would come to remove forever the Old Covenant order with its shadows. Apostate Israel chose the shadows over the substance, Jesus Christ. The passage in 2 Peter 3 must be seen against the backdrop of these verses. The apostate Jews mocked at the idea that their beloved city would ever be destroyed again. They put their trust in the temple, all the while rejecting Jesus' words that something greater than the temple was in their midst. The masterful Bible commentator, John Owen (1616-1683), interprets 2 Peter 3 with the above scenario in mind, and applies it to the generation of Christians and apostate Jews living just prior to God's judgment on Jerusalem:

> It is evident, from sundry places in the New Testament, what extreme oppositions the believing Jews met withal, all the world over, from their own countrymen, with and among whom they lived. They in the meantime, no doubt, warned them of the wrath of Christ against them for their cursed unbelief and persecutions; particularly letting them know, that Christ would come

---

16. David Chilton, *The Great Tribulation* (Tyler, TX: Dominion Press, 1987), pp. 49-50.

in vengeance ere long, according as he had threatened, to the ruin of his enemies. And because the persecuting Jews, all the world over, upbraided the believers with the temple and the holy city, Jerusalem, their worship and service instituted of God, which they had defiled; they were given to know, that even all these things also should be destroyed, for their rejection of the Son of God. After some continuance of time, the threatening denounced being not yet accomplished, — as is the manner of profane persons and hardened sinners, Eccles. viii, 11, — they began to mock and scoff, as if they were all but the vain pretenses, or loose, causeless fears of the Christians. That this was the state with them, or shortly would be, the apostle declares in this chapter, verses 3, 4. Because things continued in the old state, without alteration, and judgment was not speedily executed, they scoffed at all the threats about the coming of the Lord that had been denounced against them.[17]

So then, according to John Owen, 2 Peter 3 is not referring to the last days as a prelude to the yet future "rapture." Rather, these scoffers ridiculed the prophecies given by Jesus of the destruction of the temple and Jerusalem being trodden down by the gentiles within a generation. Owen continues:

(1.) As it was foretold and threatened by Christ. How were believers cautioned to be ready for it with eminent holiness and watchfulness therein! So Luke xxi. 34, 36, "take heed to yourselves; watch, therefore." Why so? "Christ is coming," verse 27. When? "Why, this generation," verse 32. What to do? "Why, to dissolve heaven and earth," verse 25; to dissolve the Jewish church and state. "Watch, therefore; give all diligence." So also Matt. xxiv.42. "Watch, therefore." Oh! on this account what manner of persons ought we to be![18]

Tomorrow or a Thousand Years
But let's take Tommy Ice's approach, agreeing with him that 2 Peter 3 is describing Jesus' final coming. What does this have to

---

17. John Owen, *The Works of John Owen*, 16 vols. (London: The Banner of Truth Trust, [1850-53] 1965), vol. 9, p. 132.
18. *Ibid.*, p. 134.

do with Christian Reconstruction as a "deviant theology?" No one knows when Jesus is returning. It could be tomorrow or a thousand years from now. Dave Hunt and Tommy Ice see no chance for Reconstruction because they believe that Jesus is returning very soon. For centuries prophetic speculators have been predicting that Jesus would return "soon." Hal Lindsey, in his best-selling book *The Late Great Planet Earth*, set a timetable that the rapture would occur in 1981, and the beginning of the millennium in 1988.[19] What if the more reformation-minded Christians had taken this approach to speculating on the Lord's return? Where would the church be today?

Tommy Ice states, "The fact He has not yet returned is not because the Church is to Christianize the world. Rather, as God's word says, it is to be a time of salvation, that is, men coming to Christ in a period of godly living in light of watching and eagerly waiting Christ's coming." But according to dispensational teaching, the millennium will also be a time of evangelism and salvation. Thiessen writes:

> Following the judgment of the nations, the sheep will enter the kingdom (Matt. 25:34-40). They will form the nucleus of the kingdom, together with restored and converted Israel. *But it is evident that multitudes will be born during that age* (Isa. 65:20; Jer. 30:20; Mic. 4:1-5; Zech. 8:4-6), *and these will need to be evangelized.*[20]

The Bible tells us why Jesus has not returned to consummate His kingdom: He has not as yet put all His enemies under His feet (1 Corinthians 15:25). When will this happen? No one knows but God alone. Yes, it is to be a time of salvation, and Christians should be living godly lives. This is the very thing Christian Reconstructionists have been saying. Tommy Ice connects godly living with Jesus' Second Coming. That's fine. But as I've already

---

19. Hal Lindsey, *The Late Great Planet Earth* (Grand Rapids, MI: Zondervan, 1970). p. 54. For a critique of a number of Lindsey's failed prophecies, see Samuele Bacchiocchi, *Hal Lindsey's Prophetic Jigsaw Puzzle: Five Predictions that Failed!* (Berrien Springs, MI: Biblical Perspectives, 1987), pp. 8-57.

20. Thiessen, *Lectures in Systematic Theology*, p. 398.

stated, there are a number of motivators for holy living. Jesus said, "If you love Me, you will keep My commandments" (John 14:15). This verse applies to every generation no matter what the circumstances.

Tommy Ice says that the "Reconstructionist's point of view in prophecy is deviant because it insists that our Lord delays His coming, that Christ cannot return for at least a thousand years, most likely more." Obviously, from man's perspective, the Lord has delayed His *final* coming.[21] We have 2000 years of church history to prove it. Will He delay it for another 2000 years? No one knows. The *Moody* article cite above states very clearly that premillennialists have taught that Jesus could return tomorrow or a thousand years from now. So then, Tommy Ice's objection must be leveled against premillennialists who disagree with him.

Who are the Mockers?

In his concluding remarks, Tommy Ice links us with the mockers in the first century. He states: "The sad fact of the matter is that this is the same perspective put forth by the mockers in the last day in 2 Peter 3." We're not mocking saying, "Where is the promise of His coming?" We don't know when He's coming. If there is any mocking, it's leveled against those who make certain predictions when the Bible explicitly tells us "of that day and hour no one knows, not even the angels of heaven, nor the Son, but the Father alone" (Matthew 24:36). If Jesus' return is as sudden and unexpected as Tommy Ice says, then why the preoccupation with it?

Ice tells us that "control of the last thousand years of world history [i.e., the earthly millennium] belongs to the risen Christ." Who has been in control of world history for the last 2000 years? Satan? If he has been in control, where is his earthly throne? Why is he able to rule the world without being physically present while Jesus must be physically present? Jesus commended the Roman

---

21. In Acts 1:7-8, Jesus informs us that God has set the times and seasons. There is no delay and there is no imminency. The time of His coming is none of our business. It's a "secret thing" (Deuteronomy 29:29).

Centurion because he believed that Jesus could heal his slave even
at a distance (Luke 7:2-10). Dare we say that Jesus cannot rule at
a distance?

The Reign of Christ

Tommy Ice tells us that Jesus "will rule directly upon planet
earth with His brethren." He doesn't offer any biblical evidence
for this. Revelation 20 certainly doesn't say this. There is no verse
in the New Testament that explicitly states that Jesus will reign on
the *earth* for a thousand years. Revelation 20 specifically mentions
the whereabouts of Satan, but it says nothing about where Jesus
is. Since the Bible in other places states that Jesus' throne is in
heaven, we have no right to import into the text what we may
hope is there, namely, the earthly reign of Christ.

The coming of Jesus to the earth is described by Walvoord as
being depicted in Revelation 19:11-21. But there Jesus returns on a
horse. The Bible very clearly states that Jesus "will come in just
the same way as you have watched Him go into heaven" (Acts
1:11). The dispensational literalist has a real problem here:

> In this vision John sees a white horse upon which Christ is
> seated. Premillennialists see the Second Coming of Christ in
> these verses. But such an interpretation violates the statement of
> the angels in Acts 1:11, to the effect that Christ will return "in the
> same way" that the disciples "saw him go" into heaven. John him-
> self was among those who saw Christ ascend. Hence there can be
> but one conclusion: this passage makes no reference whatsoever
> to the Second Coming of Christ. Christ did not ascend on a white
> horse; He will not return on one. Since this vision shows Jesus
> sitting upon a white horse, the Second Coming simply is not in
> view here.[22]

Revelation 19 depicts Jesus coming in judgment. The figures are
not meant to be taken literally. John sees these events in a vision.

---

22. Martin G. Selbrede, "Revelation 19:11-20:10: A Postmillennial Analysis,"
in Loraine Boettner, *The Millennium* (rev. ed; Phillipsburg, NJ: Presbyterian and
Reformed, [1957] 1984), p. 390.

The scene represents a warrior waging war on his enemies and winning the victory over all his adversaries. Revelation 19 is fulfilled when Jesus came in judgment upon apostate Jerusalem in A.D. 70. Matthew 24 is its parallel.

The Exaltation of Christ

Lastly, Tommy Ice tries to prove his point that Jesus *must* reign on the earth for a thousand years by deduction rather than exegesis. Ice writes:

> Since Christ's first coming as a time of humiliation was spent immediately and physically upon the earth, then it would be a reduction of Christianity to say that He will not even be present during His exaltation, His glorious kingdom. No, Christ will be present. May He come quickly. Maranatha.

Scripture plainly teaches that Jesus has already been exalted. Is He not sitting at His Father's right hand? Compare Tommy Ice's view of a future exaltation with the Word of God.

> [Jesus], although He existed in the form of God, did not regard equality with God a thing to be grasped, but emptied Himself, taking the form of a bond-servant, and being made in the likeness of men. And being found in appearance as a man, He humbled Himself by becoming obedient to the point of death, even death on a cross. Therefore also *God highly exalted Him, and bestowed on Him the name which is above every name, that at the name of Jesus every knee should bow, of those who are in heaven, and on earth, and under the earth, and that every tongue should confess that Jesus Christ is Lord, to the glory of God the Father* (Philippians 2:6-11).

Jesus has been "exalted to the right hand of God, having received from the Father the promise of the Holy Spirit" (Acts 2:33). Jesus is now "both Lord and Christ" (v. 36). Now, who teaches a reduction of Christianity? Dave Hunt and Tommy Ice who say that Jesus' exaltation is yet future, or Christian Reconstructionists who believe the Bible when it says that "God highly exalted Him"?

Conclusion

Millennial issues are central to the theologies of Tommy Ice and Dave Hunt. Their summary statements make this clear. Their dispute, therefore, is with a larger portion of the body of Christ. Millions of Christians today do not hold the narrowly focused eschatological position outlined by these two representatives of dispensational premillennialism. The debate over Christian Reconstruction will continue, but it will be carried on with those who do not define orthodoxy so narrowly. This debate has shown that Christian Reconstruction is far from deviant. Tommy Ice and Dave Hunt had to go out of their way to find things to disagree with, and these turned out to be misrepresentations.

CONCLUSION

The spirit of the reformation rests on the Latin phrase *ecclesia semper reformanda*, an ever reforming church. As fallible men and women, we see through a glass darkly, and so as Christians we should always be submitting our views of what we believe the Bible teaches to the Bible itself. This process should never stop.

Our understanding of Scripture is not always accurate. This fault does not lie with the Bible, however. God's Word is no more true today than when it was first penned. It is and always will be God's inscripturated inerrant and infallible Word to His church. The problem lies with finite, fallible, and fallen sinners like ourselves.

The pre-reformation period of the sixteenth century is a testimony of how easily the church can become corrupted in the areas of doctrine and morals. As Dave Hunt has been quick to tell us, we should mount a campaign for a return to biblical Christianity. But what road do we take? In some cases, Dave Hunt has done the church a service. But in other instances, he is not well-informed and has needlessly disrupted the church. A fresh study of Scripture is needed to put the church on the right road. This may mean discarding long-cherished doctrines that have no foundation in the Bible.

One of the important lessons that emerges from the debate over Christian Reconstruction is this: Anyone who sets out to critique another theological system needs to get his facts straight. This has been a constant problem throughout this particular debate.

Consider the following:

• Dave Hunt has not distinguished between the Calvinistic theology of the Christian Reconstructionists and the often undefined charismatic theologies of the other groups he criticizes. The

231

simple fact that Christian Reconstructionists are Calvinists—a fact very easy to discover—is enough to expose the absurdity of many of Hunt's assertions, such as the supposed links to the Manifest Sons of God and Positive Confession theology. Hunt never even mentions that Reconstructionists are Calvinists.

• Hunt gives absolutely no historical context for understanding different millennial positions, and Tommy Ice states explicitly (and falsely) that premillennialism was *the* position of the early Church. Both attempt to create the impression that other millennial positions are unorthodox. This is unfair.

• Despite repeated denials and explanations, critics of Christian Reconstruction continue to claim that we want to establish the kingdom of God by our own efforts. How many times does it have to be said before people will listen? How many books must we write before our critics will believe us?

The problem, however, runs deeper than the many specific misrepresentations. The problem is with the entire approach to cult research. I'm not saying that Hunt's work and the work of numerous cult-research groups have no value; much of it has a great deal of value. What I am saying is that Dave Hunt, for example, sometimes sees connections between movements and ideas that don't have any connection with each other. He implied during the debate, for example, that Rev. Kenneth Gentry, a Presbyterian minister, is teaching the same things as the Manifest Sons of God. This conclusion is based on the fallacy that similarity of language is equivalent to similarity of idea: If you *sound like* the Manifest Sons of God in a single point of theology, then you must be teaching what they teach. Hunt does not attempt to put Gentry's statements in the context of the rest of his article, much less Gentry's other writings. Hunt never raises the question of how a Calvinist pastor could also be a "manifest son."

Another area of concern is the way that Hunt (and many others) have become the *de facto* protectors of orthodoxy. Who gave these "cult experts" the authority to declare people heretics? This might sound like an unfair question. After all, don't Protestants believe that even the common believer has the right to examine what the leadership says? Yes, Protestantism teaches that. But Protestant-ism has always recognized the authority of the *church* to test and approve the orthodoxy of ministers and teachers. Heresy is not a term to be bantered about casually.

The point is this: Kenneth Gentry has received several years of seminary education, as have nearly all Christian Reconstruction-ist writers, and has been rigorously examined by a presbytery of the Presbyterian Church in America, declared orthodox, and or-dained to the ministry. Now, Dave Hunt comes along and charges him with holding heretical views. He has every right to do this, if he does it responsibly and follows the correct procedure. But did Hunt follow the correct procedures? Did Hunt approach Gentry's presbytery with his concern? Has Hunt filed charges of heresy against Gentry? Did Hunt follow the steps outlined in Matthew 18? And why didn't Gentry's colleagues in the PCA pick up on his supposed heresy when they examined him for ordination? If Gentry is such a heretic, how did he slip by his examiners? With his shotgun approach, Hunt hits many targets that need to be hit, but he is also attacking some genuinely orthodox, godly men. The issue is not Rev. Gentry himself; Hunt's charge is too absurd even to be con-sidered worthy of investigation. But Hunt's irresponsible charges might forever tarnish the reputations of godly and orthodox men.

I am not saying that Reconstructionists are above criticism. No man is above criticism, even from the simplest of God's peo-ple. Indeed, it is often the simplest of God's people who discern falsehood most readily. Our point is that everyone deserves a fair, responsible, and *charitable* hearing; we don't forget 1 Corinthians 13 when we engage in critical analysis. The other point is that Hunt has failed to give Christian Reconstruction a fair hearing.

The underlying point of this discussion is that evangelical and fundamentalist Christians and churches need to develop proce-dures for dealing with disagreement. Matthew 18 is the starting point, and there is no good reason for circumventing the require-ments of that passage. Even if the sin is public, one should first approach the sinner individually, then with other believers. Horace L. Fenton, Jr., gives an example of how this could work in a situation when a person is accused of heresy for his published statements. Dr. Anthony Campolo, a Christian professor, had been accused of making heretical statements in one of his books. Others were drawn into the controversy to defend and to accuse Campolo. As Dr. Fenton describes it:

> The situation deteriorated, threatening to become a knock-down, drag-out fight. Opinions may still differ as to whether such a tragedy was completely averted. Nevertheless, the debate was tempered by those who were concerned with both the doctrinal issues and the threat of disruption in the body of Christ. A panel of three highly respected Christian leaders was asked to meet with Campolo and with his critics to help all concerned understand the issues, and to minister constructively both to the accused and the accusers.[1]

But what if the person accused of heresy or some other sin will not listen to a rebuke, even from a group of prominent Christian brothers? How do conservative churches, divided as they are, enforce a sentence of excommunication? The only answer at this stage of church history is for everyone to recognize the right of other churches to decide who is orthodox and who is a heretic. Thus, since several orthodox denominations have determined that the distinctives of Christian Reconstruction—theonomy and postmillennialism—are orthodox (though not necessary) teachings, critics should give Reconstructionists the benefit of the doubt. Again, this doesn't mean that Reconstructionists cannot be criticized; it means that critics should exercise care. This is a very imperfect way to deal with heresy. Who decides, after all, whether the church itself is orthodox? But as long as the churches remain in the present state of division, there is really no other responsible and God-honoring solution.

Finally, there is the issue of emphasis. In the final analysis, Dave Hunt's disagreement with Reconstructionists comes down

---

1. Horace L. Fenton, Jr., *When Christians Clash: How to Prevent and Resolve the Pain of Conflict* (Downers Grove, IL: InterVarsity Press, 1987), p. 73.

to the two "E's": eschatology and emphasis. Reconstructionists, he claims, don't put enough emphasis on heaven or on suffering. That may be true, and it should be corrected in order to avoid distortions. But someone is not a heretic simply because he emphasizes one thing more than another (though a distorted emphasis can *lead* to heresy). None of us is able to emphasize everything that needs to be emphasized. We all have particular gifts and interests. Each of us has limited time and energy. But if our emphasis is biblical, it is reconcilable with the emphases and interests of other Christians. That's what it means to be a member of the Body of Christ.

Where do we go from here? This is not an easy question to answer. A lot of damage has already been done. A plethora of newsletters have reached my desk broadcasting to the world that Christian Reconstruction is "heretical." The research is poor and the reasoning borders on the absurd.

Here is what I propose:

All those who have written on the subject of Christian Reconstruction should reassess their evaluations in the light of *The Reduction of Christianity* and *The Debate over Christian Reconstruction.* It is the duty of all those who have the desire to critique Christian Reconstruction to read the literature of Christian Reconstructionists before any additional evaluations come forth from the pens (or computers) of self-styled heresy hunters. Finally, there are a number of prominent authors who owe a good number of Reconstructionists an apology and a retraction.

Appendix A

THE ABOMINATION OF DESOLATION:
AN ALTERNATE HYPOTHESIS
by James B. Jordan

As a result of my studies in Leviticus for my forthcoming book *Touch Not, Taste Not,* I have come to the tentative conclusion that the abomination of desolation spoken of in Daniel 9 and Matthew 24 is none other than apostate Judaism, and that the Man of Sin spoken of in 2 Thessalonians 2 is the apostate High Priest of Israel. In this essay I wish simply to set out the bare bones of an argument for this hypothesis, and float it out as "bread upon the waters" to see what the Christian community thinks of it.

I am taking for granted the fundamental preterist position as set forth by Jay Adams in *The Time is at Hand*[1] and by David Chilton in *Paradise Restored*[2] and *Days of Vengeance.*[3] On Matthew 24, my taped lectures, available from Geneva Ministries, Box 131300, Tyler, TX 75713, can be consulted for details. With this in mind, let us turn to Daniel 9:26-27.

> 26. Then after the 62 weeks, the Messiah [Jesus] will be cut off [excommunicated by the religious rulers of Israel] and have nothing [the cross, Phil. 2:7]; and the people of the Prince [the enthroned Christ] Who is to come will destroy the city [Jerusalem] and the sanctuary [Temple]. And its end will come with a flood [like Noah; like the threats of Deut. 28; like the locust flood

---

1. (Phillipsburg, NJ: Presbyterian and Reformed, 1970).
2. (Fort Worth: Dominion Press, 1985).
3. (Fort Worth: Dominion Press, 1987).

of Joel]; even to the end there will be war [the Jewish War of 66-70 A.D.]; desolations are determined.

27a. And He [Messiah the Prince] will confirm a covenant [by fulfilling the Old Covenant as the New Covenant] with the many [the church] during one week [the 70th week]. But in the middle of the week He will put a stop to sacrifice and grain offering [by dying on the cross, and thereby ending the sacrificial system].

Now we come to the statement that "on the wing of detestable things, or abominations, comes one who makes desolate, even until a complete destruction, one that is decreed, is poured out on the one who makes desolate" (v. 27b). In the past, I have taken the wing as a reference to the eagle, and thus to invading armies (e.g., Is. 10:5, 12, 24-27; Hab. 1:8). Rome's imperial standard was the eagle, but the Bible also symbolizes Edom with the eagle (Jer. 49:16; Obad. 4; Dan. 11:41). The Romans and Idumeans together managed to destroy the Temple. The Idumeans (Edomites) invaded the Temple and filled it with human blood. The Romans sacked it. I understood the last phrases of the verse to be saying that in time the Romans would also be destroyed.

There is a problem with this view. Those who ignore the Idumean invasion of the Temple cannot deal with Jesus' statement in Matthew 24 that the abomination of desolation stood in the holy place. Luke's parallel statement that Jerusalem would be surrounded by armies (actually a reference to the Idumean-Zealot conspiracy that let the Edomites into the Temple) is not equivalent: surrounding Jerusalem is not the same as standing in the Temple. Only the Idumeans stood in the Temple.

But is this enough? The other passages in Daniel to which Jesus alludes indicate that counterfeit worship was set up in the Temple, and that this was the abomination of desolation. Prophesying of Antiochus Epiphanes, Gabriel (?) tells Daniel that he will "desecrate the sanctuary fortress, and do away with the regular sacrifice, and they will set up the abomination of desolation" (Daniel 9:31; 1 Maccabees 1:41-61). At the end of Daniel, the preincarnate Christ (?) tells him that "from the time that the regular sacrifice is abolished and the abomination of desolation is set

up, there will be 1290 days" (Daniel 12:11). In my opinion this also
has to do with Antiochus, the 1290 days being thrice 430, but days
instead of years (Exodus 12:40), while the 1335 days of the next
verse go back to the 45 years between the Exodus and the Con-
quest of the land (Deuteronomy 2:14; Joshua 14:6-10). The oppression of Antiochus will be worse than that of Egypt, but much
shorter. Blessed is he who endures to the end and sees the land re-
conquered. All this is a type of the New Covenant, of course.

With this in mind, though, it certainly seems that the mere
presence of wicked Edomites and Zealots in the Temple is not
enough. We need to have a cessation of true sacrifices and an implementation of counterfeit ones. And of course, that is exactly
what happened. With the death of Christ, the sacrificial system
came to an end. Any sacrifices offered after the cross were simply
abominations. The High Priest, who presided over such abominable sacrifices, was just like Antiochus.

The whole of Old Testament theology points us to this. The
"wing of abominations" goes back to Numbers 15:37-41, where
every Israelite was commanded to wear a blue tassel, called a
wing, on his garments. ("Corner" is literally "wing.") This was the
"wing of holiness," to remind Israel to obey the law (v. 40).
Naturally, an apostate Israelite would no longer have "wings of
holiness" but "wings of abominations." Their leader, the High
Priest, would be the preeminent example of this.

A full study of the "wing" motif must await the future. I want
to call your attention, however, to the wings of the cherubim, on
which God sat enthroned. The wings on the garments of the
Israelites meant that they, too, were cherubim, and were to guard
God's holiness. The High Priest, described in Ezekiel 28:11-19 as
the true spiritual King of Tyre, is called a cherub. Counterfeit
cherubic wings carrying a counterfeit Ark to a counterfeit Temple
are pictured in Zechariah 5:5-11, and this is relevant background
to the destruction of Jerusalem because these also are wings of
abomination. Notice also that apostate Jerusalem in Revelation
18:2 is said to be a "dwelling place of demons and a haunt of every
unclean spirit, and a haunt of every unclean and detestable *bird*."

The idea of abomination is thoroughly Levitical. Unclean food was called abominable, or literally detestable, because you were to spit it out. If they ate detestable food, they would become detestable, and God would spit them out. This is clearly set out in Leviticus 11:43, 18:28, and 20:23; see also Revelation 3:16. This was all symbolic of sin, of course. It meant that God would spit out the people if they corrupted themselves with idolatry, since the unclean animals were associated with idols and with the idolatrous nations. (Compare Paul's "table of demons.")

False worship is idolatrous worship. When the Jews rejected Jesus and kept offering sacrifices, they were engaged in idolatry. The fringes of their garments became "wings of abominations." This was the "wing of abominations" that took place in the Temple. It is why the Temple was destroyed.

A full picture of this is provided in Ezekiel 8-11. I shall not expound the passage, but simply direct you to it. There you will see that when the apostate Jews of Ezekiel's day performed the sacrifices, God viewed them as an abomination. He called the holy shrine an "idol of jealousy, that provokes to jealousy" (8:3). The Jews had treated the Temple and the Ark as idols, and so God would destroy them, as He had the golden calf. Ezckiel sees God pack up and move out of the Temple, leaving it empty or "desolate." The abominations have caused the Temple to become desolate. Once God had left, the armies of Nebuchadnezzar swept in and destroyed the empty Temple. (When we remember that Ezekiel and Daniel prophesied at the same time, the correlation becomes even more credible.)

This is what happened in Matthew 24. Jesus had twice inspected the Temple for signs of leprosy (Lev. 14:33-47; the two so-called cleansings of the Temple in John 2 and Matthew 21). Jesus had found that the Temple was indeed leprous, and as the True Priest He condemned it to be torn down, in accordance with the Levitical law. "And Jesus came out from the Temple [leaving it desolate; God departing] and was going away [compare Ezekiel], when His disciples came up to point out the Temple buildings to Him. And He answered and said to them, 'Do you not see all these things? Truly I say to you, not one stone here shall be left upon another which will not be torn down'" (Matt. 24:1-2).

(Note that the counterfeit Ark is removed from Israel right after a description of house-leprosy in Zechariah 5:4. The message in Zechariah was that when God's Temple was rebuilt, wickedness would be removed. This is a type of the New Covenant: When the Church was established at Pentecost, God sent leprosy into the Temple, and it became a seat of wickedness.)

With this background we can interpret Daniel 9:27b much more clearly: "And on the wing of abominations [apostate Jewish clothing of the High Priest] will come one who makes desolate [the apostate High Priest], even until a complete destruction, one that is decreed, is poured out on the one who makes desolate [at the destruction of Jerusalem in A.D. 70]." Thus, verse 27 is simply an explanation of verse 26. Verse 26 says that the Messiah will be sacrificed; verse 27 explains that this ends the sacrificial system. Verse 26 says that the Roman invasion will desolate the Temple and that it is determined. Verse 27 says that wrath will be poured out on the apostate Jews and their High Priest, whose actions desolated the Temple, and that this is decreed.

This correlates magnificently with 2 Thessalonians 2, as follows:

3. Let no man in any way deceive you, for it [the Day of the Lord] will not come unless the apostasy [of the Jews] comes first, and the man of lawlessness is revealed, the son of destruction [the apostate High Priest, prince of the Temple, no longer a man of God's law but a man of lawlessness, no longer a son of Abraham but a son of destruction].

4. Who opposes and exalts himself against all that is called God and every object of worship, so that he takes his seat in the Temple of God, displaying himself as being God. [The High Priest had opposed Christ and God, and thus had opposed the true meaning of all the worship objects in the Temple. "The scribes and Pharisees have *seated* themselves in the *seat* of Moses," Matthew 23:2. Those who reject God make themselves God, Genesis 3.]

6. And you know what restrains him now, so that in his time he may be revealed. [The Church and her evangelism in Palestine created fence-sitters who were restraining apostate Judaism. An example is Gamaliel, Acts 5:33-42.]

7. For the mystery of lawlessness [the apostate Jewish counterfeit of the Pauline Gospel Mystery] is already at work; only he who restrains will do so until he is taken out of the way. [The Church would be removed from Jerusalem before her destruction; also possibly this means that the fence-sitters like Gamaliel would either be converted to Christianity or would be de-converted to a whole-hearted adoption of apostate Judaism, and in either event would stop restraining. Josephus records that the Zealots and Edomites slew one such restrainer, Zechariah the son of Berechiah or Baruch, in fulfillment of Matthew 23:35. After the removal of this restrainer, all hell broke loose.[4] Since Jesus had mentioned this man by name, possibly it is he who is particularly referred to here, as one they "know."]

8. And then that lawless one will be revealed whom the Lord will slay with the breath of His mouth and bring to an end by the appearance of His coming. [I believe that the "breath of His mouth" refers to Gospel preaching, which slew apostate Israel, as Chilton points out in his liturgical remarks throughout *Days of Vengeance*. The "appearance of His coming" refers to Daniel 7:13 and to Jesus' prophecies in Matthew 26:64, that the High Priest would "see" the Son of Man "come" to the Father to receive His Kingdom. When the fact of that "coming" becomes apparent ("appears"), the Jews will be without excuse, and will be destroyed. Note: the "coming" is not the Second Coming, nor is it a "coming in wrath upon Jerusalem," but is the event predicted in Daniel 7:13 and shown in Revelation 5. Christ came to the Father at the ascension, and this was "shown" to Israel for forty years. When Israel rejected this "second chance," they were destroyed.]

9. The one whose coming is in accord with the activity of Satan [the High Priest as son of Satan, not of Abraham; "You are

---

4. See Josephus, *Jewish War* 4:5:4.

of your father, the Devil," John 8:44], with all power and signs and false wonders [see Chilton and Josephus on the situation in Jerusalem just before the end].

10. And with all the deception of wickedness for those who perish because they did not receive the love of the truth so as to be saved. [This clearly describes the situation of apostate Judaism.]

11. And for this reason God will send upon them a deluding influence so that they might believe what is false. [Compare Romans 1:21-32 and 1 Kings 22:19-23.]

12. In order that they all may be judged who did not believe the truth but took pleasure in wickedness.

Now, just because these events were fulfilled in A.D. 70 does not mean that they are irrelevant to us. Churches can also apostatize, and Christ warned the Seven Churches that they too could be destroyed if Christ departed from them. They would be "desolate" and their worship would be "abominable" (Rev. 2-3). The destruction of the Temple and of its Jerusalem-culture, as portrayed in the remainder of Revelation, was thus a warning to the Seven Churches: If you do the same thing, God will do this to you. Thus, the principles are still in force, and serve to warn us today: If our churches depart from Christ, He will destroy both them and our society, which grew up around them.

Appendix B

THE PLACE OF ISRAEL
IN HISTORIC POSTMILLENNIALISM

This is one of the most anti-semitic movements I've seen since
Adolph Hitler.[1]
— Hal Lindsey

The purpose of this appendix is two-fold. First, to show that
the Church addressed the question of Israel's future before the
nineteenth century. Second, in the course of proving this, it will
be shown that the postmillennial view is not anti-Semitic; on the
contrary, historic postmillennialism gives the Jews a very prominent place in prophecies of the latter-day glory of the Church.
Postmillennialism denies, however, that the Jews can be members
of God's people apart from their conversion to the Messiah. The
Jews will be saved, the postmillennialist teaches, only by faith, repentance, and entrance into the life of the Body of Christ. As Iain
Murray says, "Puritans did not believe that there are any special
and unfulfilled spiritual promises made to Israel *apart from* the
Christian Church."[2]

In addition to this appendix, a third complementary appendix
has been added. In Appendix C, a letter from a Jewish Christian
pastor, who identifies himself as a postmillennial Christian
Reconstructionist, is included in this book to answer some of the

1. Hal Lindsey, "The Dominion Theology Heresy," #217. Hal Lindsey Tape
Ministries, P.O. Box 4000, Palos Verdes, California 90274. As of June 21, 1988,
the tape was still available.
2. Iain Murray, *The Puritan Hope: Revival and the Interpretation of Prophecy* (London: Banner of Truth Trust, 1971), p. 77.

244

charges made by those who say that Christian Reconstruction is anti-Semitic.

The Jews in Prophecy

During the April 14, 1988, debate, Tommy Ice claimed that in the 1800s the Church addressed the question of "what to do with Israel," a concern that contributed to the rise of dispensational premillennialism. Ice's comment seems to imply that the Israel issue had not been raised prior to this time. Whether Ice meant to imply this or not, it is an important question, and bears some examination. As will be shown below, the nineteenth century was not the first time the question of the place of Israel in prophecy was raised. In fact, Reformed postmillennialists were deeply concerned with the future of Israel already in the late *sixteenth* century. Generally, the focus of interest was Romans 11, where postmillennialists found prophesied a future conversion of the Jews to Jesus Christ.

More seriously, it has been alleged that the "dominion/kingdom" theology of David Chilton, Gary North, and other Reconstructionists is anti-Semitic. One writer goes so far as to associate postmillennialism with anti-Semitism. The *Report from Concerned Christians*, a publication of Concerned Christians of Denver, Colorado, claims that Chilton's book, *The Days of Vengeance*, "closely parallels Identity Theology," a theology that claims that the Anglo-Saxon and Germanic races fulfill all the prophecies of the Old Testament. With astonishing disregard for consistency or intelligibility, the same report claims that "The cornerstone of kingdom/dominion doctrine replaces Israel with the Church," a Church that, of course, includes hundreds of thousands of Asians, Africans, South and Central Americans, *and* Jews! How one can teach that Old Testament prophecy is fulfilled both in the Anglo-Saxon race and in the international Church is left unexplained. Apparently, the one common denominator between "dominion" and "identity" theology is, according to the Concerned Christians of Denver, that both are anti-Semitic.[3]

---

3. "Christian Anti-Semitism: Kingdom/Dominion Doctrine: The Dire Consequences of Replacing Israel," *Report from Concerned Christians*, March/April 1988. This *Report* is available from Concerned Christians, P.O. Box 22920, Denver, Colorado, 80222.

In the Spring 1988 issue of *New Hope Notes*, the author of an article with the title "Political Power: Battle for the Soul of the Church," writes this about postmillennialism:

> Postmillennialism, then, does not respect the promises God made to the Jews; those promises have been abrogated—nullified because of perfidy [treachery]; repealed because of treason—the betrayal of Messiah. Anti-Semitism is a stalking phantom which often preys upon postmillennial believers—not always, but quite frequently (p. 9).

The author offers no evidence for this claim. If the premise is true, that the promises to Israel have been abrogated, then no ethnic group has them. Why then aren't postmillennialists anti-Italian, anti-German, anti-Spanish, anti-Chinese, anti-Japanese, and anti-Irish, since none of these ethnic groups has the promises? Anti-Semitism has very little to do with the promises being abrogated. No, the reasons for anti-Semitism must be found elsewhere.

Anti-Semitism, along with other forms of racism, is the unforgivable sin of the twentieth-century West. Generally, however, anti-Semitism is left undefined. The two articles just mentioned seem to define an anti-Semite as anyone who denies that Israel should be the "most honoured of all nations," or says a bad word about things Jewish, or suggests that the suffering of the Jews is God's judgment upon their unbelief, or believes that the Church is the New Israel made up of Jews and Gentiles (John 10:16; Romans 11:24; Galatians 3:28-29; Ephesians 2:13-16; 3:4-6), or believes that the Israeli state begun in 1948 has nothing to do with biblical prophecy. Obviously, this usage of "anti-Semitism" is so broad as to be virtually meaningless, since the great majority of Christians *do* believe that the Church, made up of Jews and Gentiles, is the New Israel. Even dispensationalists, moreover, deny that 1948 was a significant date on the prophetic calendar. Charles L. Feinberg, writing in the October 1955 issue of *Bibliotheca Sacra*, the theological journal of Dallas Theological Seminary, stated emphatically that "the present return to the land is not the fulfillment of the Abrahamic Covenant."[4]

A more precise definition would be to describe anti-Semitism as a form of racism that includes attributing evil exclusively to a particular race and judging the dignity and worth of a person on the basis of his race.[5] An anti-Semite considers individual Jews to be evil simply because they are Jews, and/or views the Jewish people as the source of all earthly evil. According to this definition, the Identity Movement is thoroughly anti-Semitic, since it claims that Satan "has a literal 'seed' or posterity in the earth commonly called the Jews today."[6] This is anti-Semitism in its worst form, and it is ugly and unChristian. Biblically, Satan's seed is not limited to a particular race, but includes all those who serve the ruler of the kingdom of the air, whatever their ethnic background, including unbelieving Jews in Jesus' day (John 8:44).

It is ironic that at one time dispensationalism itself was charged with being associated with Nazism, while today the theological opponents of dispensationalism receive similar charges.[7] Such charges were nonsense when levelled against dispensationalists, and they are nonsense when levelled *by* dispensationalists against postmillennialists. It is probably too much to hope that such tactics will cease to be a part of theological debate within the Body of Christ.

Historical Evidence

Theodore Beza, John Calvin's successor in Geneva, taught, according to English theologian Thomas Brightman, that the world would "be restored from death to life again, at the time when the Jews should also come, and be called to the profession of the Gospel." Martin Bucer, the reformer of Strasbourg and per-

---

4. Charles L. Feinberg, "The State of Israel," *Bibliotheca Sacra*, 112 (October 1955), p. 319.

5. Technically speaking, the Jews are not a race. Rather, they constitute an ethnic grouping.

6. Doctrinal Statement of Beliefs, Kingdom-Identity Ministries, P.O. Box 1021, Harrison, Arkansas, 72602.

7. On the charges against dispensationalism, see Charles Ryrie, *Dispensationalism Today* (Chicago, IL: Moody Press, 1965), p. 12.

haps the continental Reformer who had the most direct influence on English Puritanism, wrote in a 1568 commentary on Romans that Paul prophesied a future conversion of the Jewish people. Peter Martyr, Bucer's associate in Strasbourg, agreed.[8]

In England, the place of the Jews in prophecy was a prominent issue already in the seventeenth century, and, significantly, this was most true among the generally postmillennial English Puritans and Scottish Presbyterians. Iain Murray summarizes the seventeenth-century concern for Israel in this way:

> The future of the Jews had decisive significance for them because they believed that, though little is clearly revealed of the future purposes of God in history, enough has been given us in Scripture to warrant the expectation that with the calling of the Jews there will come far-reaching blessing for the world. Puritan England and Covenanting Scotland knew much of spiritual blessing and it was the prayerful longing for wider blessing, not a mere interest in unfulfilled prophecy, which led them to give such place to Israel.[9]

This emphasis fits neatly into the postmillennialist position: The latter-day glory of the Church will be inaugurated by the conversion of the Jews to Christ; this is what Paul meant when he said that the conversion of the Jews would be "life from the dead" (Romans 11:15). There were other views of Paul's prophecy in seventeenth-century England. One school of interpretation claimed that Romans 11:26 ("all Israel shall be saved") referred not to a future dramatic conversion of the Jews but to the gradual conversion of the Jews throughout history. It is significant that this view was "almost uniformly rejected by English and Scottish exegetes of the Puritan school." They favored the postmillennial view described above.[10]

---

8. Quotations from J. A. DeJong, *As the Waters Cover the Sea: Millennial Expectations in the Rise of Anglo-America Missions, 1640-1810* (Kampen: J. H. Kok, 1970), p. 9.

9. Murray, *Puritan Hope*, pp. 59-60.

10. *Ibid.*, p. 64.

Calvinist Theologians on Israel

Murray's book provides abundant documentation of the post-millennial concern for Israel, of which we can cite only a small portion. Already in the 1560 Geneva Bible and in Peter Martyr's commentary in Romans (English publication, 1568), this view was advanced. Scottish theologian Charles Ferme, writing sometime in the late sixteenth century, argued that Paul indicated that "when the fulness of the Gentiles shall have been brought in, the great majority of the Israelitish people are to be called, through the gospel, to the God of their salvation, and shall profess and own Jesus Christ, whom, formerly, that is, during the time of hardening, they denied."[11]

In a 1635 letter the Scottish theologian Samuel Rutherford expressed a wish to live to see the conversion of the Jews:

> O to see the sight, next to Christ's Coming in the clouds, the most joyful! Our elder brethren the Jews and Christ fall upon one another's necks and kiss each other! They have been long asunder; they will be kind to one another when they meet. O day! O longed-for and lovely day-dawn! O sweet Jesus, let me see that sight which will be as life from the dead, thee and the ancient people in mutual embraces.[12]

Clearly, Rutherford, a postmillennialist, found a place for Israel in prophecy, and, just as clearly, it was an important element in his view of prophecy, second only to the Second Coming of Christ.

William Perkins, a leading Puritan teacher and writer, taught that there would be a future national conversion of the Jews. Similarly, Richard Sibbes wrote that "The Jews are not yet come in under Christ's banner; but God, that hath persuaded Japhet to come into the tents of Shem, will persuade Shem to come into the tents of Japhet." Elnathan Parr's 1620 commentary on Romans espoused the view that there would be two "fullnesses" of the Gentiles: one prior to the conversion of the Jews and one following:

---

11. Quoted in *ibid.*, pp. 64-65.
12. Quoted in *ibid.*, p. 98.

"The end of this world shall not be till the Jews are called, and how long after that none yet can tell."[13]

Speaking before the House of Commons in 1649, during the Puritan Revolution, John Owen, a postmillennial theologian, spoke about "the bringing home of [God's] ancient people to be one fold with the fulness of the Gentiles . . . in answer to millions of prayers put up at the throne of grace, for this very glory, in all generations."[14] Owen even believed, as he explained in his popular 1677 book, *Israel Redux*, that the Jews would someday return to the land of Palestine.[15]

Creeds and Confessions

Councils of the English and Scottish churches also addressed the question of Israel. The Westminster Larger Catechism, Question 191, displayed the same hope for a future conversion of the Jews. Part of what we pray for in the second petition, "Thy kingdom come," is that "the gospel [be] propagated throughout the world, the Jews called, the fullness of the Gentiles brought in." Similarly, the Westminster *Directory for Public Worship* directed ministers to pray "for the Propagation of the Gospel and Kingdom of Christ to all nations, for the conversion of the Jews, the fullness of the Gentiles, the fall of Antichrist, and the hastening of the second coming of the Lord."[16] In 1652, a group of eighteen Puritan ministers and theologians, including both Presbyterians and Independents, affirmed that "the Scripture speaks of a *double conversion* of the Gentiles, the first before the conversion of the *Jews*, they being *Branches wild by nature* grafted into the *True Olive Tree* instead of the *natural Branches* which are broken off. . . . The second, after the conversion of the Jews."[17] In the American colonies, the *Savoy*

13. All quotations from DeJong, *As the Waters Cover the Sea*, pp. 27-28.

14. Quoted in Murray, *Puritan Hope*, p. 100.

15. Peter Toon, *God's Statesman: The Life and Work of John Owen* (Grand Rapids, MI: Zondervan, 1971), p. 152.

16. Quoted in DeJong, *As the Waters Cover the Sea*, pp. 37-38.

17. Quoted in Murray, *Puritan Hope*, p. 72. Interestingly, some of this same language—the phrase "double conversion of the Gentiles" in particular—was used by Johann Heinrich Alsted, whose premillennial *The Beloved City or, The Saints Reign on Earth a Thousand Yeares* (1627; English edition 1643) exercised great influence in England. See De Jong, *As the Waters Cover the Sea*, p. 12.

Declaration (1658) included the conversion of the Jews in its summary of the Church's future hope:

> We expect that in the latter days, Antichrist being destroyed, the Jews called, and the adversaries of the kingdom of his dear Son broken, the churches of Christ being enlarged and edified through a free and plentiful communication of light and grace, shall enjoy in this world a more quiet, peaceful, and glorious condition than they have enjoyed.[18]

Clearly, the conversion of the Jews was part of a postmillennial view of prophecy.

Prayer for Israel's Conversion

Because they believed that the Jews would be converted, Puritan and Presbyterian churches earnestly prayed that Paul's prophecies would be fulfilled. Murray notes that "A number of years before [the Larger Catechism and Westminster Directory for Public Worship] were drawn up, the call for prayer for the conversion of the Jews and for the success of the gospel throughout the world was already a feature of Puritan congregations."[19] Also, among Scottish Presbyterian churches during this period, special days of prayer were set aside partly in order that "the promised conversion of [God's] ancient people of the Jews may be hastened."[20]

In 1679, Scottish minister Walter Smith drew up some guidelines for prayer meetings:

> As it is the undoubted duty of all to pray for the coming of Christ's kingdom, so all that love our Lord Jesus Christ in sincerity, and know what it is to bow a knee in good earnest, will long and pray for the out-making of the gospel-promises to his Church in the latter days, that King Christ would go out upon the white horse of the gospel, conquering and to conquer, and make a conquest of the travail of his soul, that it may be sounded that the

---

18. Quoted in DeJong, *As the Waters Cover the Sea*, p. 38.
19. Murray, *Puritan Hope*, p. 99.
20. Quoted in *ibid.*, p. 100.

kingdoms of the world are become his, and his name called upon
from the rising of the sun to its going down. (1) That the old off-
casten Israel for unbelief would never be forgotten, especially in
these meetings, that the promised day of their ingrafting again by
faith may be hastened; and that the dead weight of blood removed off them, that their fathers took upon them and upon their
children, that have sunk them down to hell upwards of seventeen
hundred years.[21]

Puritan Independent Thomas Goodwin, in his book, *The Return of
Prayers*, encouraged people to pray even when they failed to see
their desires realized. Among the things for which the Church
should pray were "the calling of the Jews, the utter downfall of
God's enemies, the flourishing of the gospel." Goodwin assured his
readers that all these prayers "will have answers."[22]

Eighteenth-Century America

Jonathan Edwards, a postmillennialist's postmillennialist,
outlined the future of the Christian Church in his 1774 *History of
Redemption*. Edwards believed that the overthrow of Satan's kingdom involved several elements: the abolition of heresies and
infidelity, the overthrow of the kingdom of the Antichrist (the
Pope), the overthrow of the Muslim nations, and the overthrow of
"Jewish infidelity":

However obstinate [the Jews] have been now for above seventeen
hundred years in their rejection of Christ, and however rare have
been the instances of individual conversions, ever since the destruction of Jerusalem . . . yet, when this day comes, the thick
vail that blinds their eyes shall be removed, 2 Cor. iii.16. and
divine grace shall melt and renew their hard hearts . . . And
then shall the house of Israel be saved: the Jews in all their disper-
sions shall cast away their old infidelity, and shall have their
hearts wonderfully changed, and abhor themselves for their past
unbelief and obstinacy.

---

21. Quoted in *ibid.*, pp. 101-102.
22. Quoted in *ibid.*, p. 102.

He concluded that "Nothing is more certainly foretold than this national conversion of the Jews in Romans 11."[23]

Nineteenth- and Twentieth-Century Reformed Theologians

This view continued to be widely taught throughout the nineteenth and into the twentieth century. Robert Haldane, an early nineteenth-century Swiss Reformed preacher, preached through the book of Romans in Geneva in 1816. On Romans 11:26, he made this comment:

> The rejection of the Jews has been general, but at no period universal. This rejection is to continue till the fulness of the Gentiles shall come in. Then the people of Israel, as a body, shall be brought to the faith of the Gospel.[24]

The great Princeton theologian Charles Hodge found in Romans 11 a prophecy that "the Gentiles, as a body, the mass of the Gentile world, will be converted before the restoration of the Jews, as a nation." After the fullness of the Gentiles comes in, the Jewish people will be saved: "The Jews, as a people, are now rejected; as a people, they are to be restored. As their rejection, although national, did not include the rejection of every individual; so their restoration, although in like manner national, need not be assumed to include the salvation of every individual Jew." This will not be the end of history, however; rather, "much will remain to be accomplished after that event; and in the accomplishment of what shall then remain to be done, the Jews are to have a prominent agency."[25]

John Brown, a nineteenth-century Scottish theologian, wrote this in his commentary on Romans:

---

23. Jonathan Edwards, "History of Redemption," *The Works of Jonathan Edwards*, 2 vols. (Edinburgh: Banner of Truth Trust, [1834] 1974), vol. 1, p. 607.

24. Robert Haldane, *The Epistle to the Romans* (London: Banner of Truth Trust, 1958), p. 541.

25. Charles Hodge, *A Commentary on Romans* (London: Banner of Truth Trust, [1864] 1972), p. 374.

The apostle [Paul] contrasts the former state of the Gentiles with their present state, and the present state of the Jews with their future state. The past state of the Gentiles was a state of disobedience—their present state, is a state of gracious salvation. The present state of the Jews is a state of disobedience—their future state is to be a state of gracious salvation.[26]

The reason for God's rejection of the Jews and for their future restoration is to display both the total depravity of men—both Jew and Gentile—and the pure and sovereign grace of salvation.[27]

Southern Presbyterian theologian Robert L. Dabney included under the category of "unfulfilled prophecy" the "general and national return of the Jews to the Christian Church. (Rom. xi: 25, 26)."[28]

This same view was taught in the present century by some of the leading Reformed theologians. John Murray of Westminster Theological Seminary, for example, wrote this comment on Romans 11:26:

> If we keep in mind the theme of this chapter and the sustained emphasis on the restoration of Israel, there is no alternative than to conclude that the proposition, "all Israel shall be saved", is to be interpreted in terms of the fulness, the receiving, the ingrafting of Israel as a people, the restoration of Israel to gospel favour and blessing and the correlative turning of Israel from unbelief to faith and repentance. . . . The salvation of Israel must be conceived of on a scale that is commensurate with their trespass, their loss, their casting away, their breaking off, and their hardening, commensurate, of course, in the opposite direction.[29]

---

26. John Brown, *Analytical Exposition of the Epistle of Paul the Apostle to the Romans* (Edinburgh: Oliphant, Anderson, & Ferrier, 1883), p. 417.

27. *Ibid.*, pp. 418-419.

28. Robert L. Dabney, *Lectures on Systematic Theology* (Grand Rapids, MI: Zondervan, [1878] 1972), p. 838.

29. John Murray, *The Epistle to the Romans*, 2 vols. (Grand Rapids, MI: Eerdmans, 1968), vol. 2, p. 98.

Conclusion

Many more examples of the postmillennial concern for the conversion of Israel could be cited, but we have sufficient evidence before us to permit us to come to several conclusions. First, the preterist interpretation of prophecy and postmillennial eschatology does not imply that the Jews have no place in God's plan in history. Owen and Edwards, both of whom emphasized the importance of the destruction of the Jerusalem Temple in A.D. 70, also believed in a future conversion of national Israel. Historically, it has been the amillennial position that denies a future large scale conversion of Jews.[30]

Second, postmillennial writers were concerned with the issue of Israel for centuries before dispensationalism made its appearance. It is patently false to imply that dispensationalism was the first view of prophecy to deal with the question.

Third, the concern for the Jews among postmillennialist writers makes anti-Semitism unthinkable.

The reader interested in further evidence for these conclusions is directed to J. A. DeJong's *As the Waters Cover the Sea* and Iain Murray's *The Puritan Hope*.

---

30. E.g., William Hendriksen, *Exposition of Paul's Epistle to the Romans* (Grand Rapids, MI: 1981), pp. 377-82; and Anthony A. Hoekema, *The Bible and the Future* (Grand Rapids, MI: Eerdmans, 1979), pp. 143-47.

Appendix C

TO THOSE WHO WONDER IF
RECONSTRUCTIONISM IS ANTI-SEMITIC
by Steve M. Schlissel

Greetings in our Messiah. I must say that when I was told that reconstructionists are being accused of being anti-semitic, I was somewhat taken aback. Why would anyone, aware of the hopes, let alone the principles, that guide and motivate reconstructionists regard them as anti-semitic?

Perhaps it is because they have encountered certain reconstructionists who are, in fact, anti-semitic. Indeed, there are some who have written things about the Jewish people, especially their history, which ought to be regarded as stupid (at least), but even then not necessarily anti-Jewish. In any event, it would be wrong to extrapolate from the one to the many. That would be, of course, an example of prejudice and bigotry of which, I am sure, most dispensationalists would not like to be guilty.

After all, having at one time been a missionary with one of the largest and oldest dispensational Jewish mission organizations in the world, I have met more than one dispensational anti-semite. But I do not, therefore, conclude that all dispensationalists and their system are anti-semitic. That is clearly not the case. It is the custom of Christian gentlemen to judge by the best of a class, not the worst; to focus on principles in controversy, not persons.

But that we may present a more positive case in the hope that we may put to death the notion that reconstructionism is anti-semitic, consider me, if you please. I was born and raised as a Jew in a city of 2,000,000 Jews. I was circumcised the eighth day, at-

256

tended Hebrew School, became Bar Mitzvah at 13 years of age, went to shul (synagogue), attended Passover seders all my life (still do each year, with my still unbelieving Jewish family), and have the highest regard for Jewish culture and community. I am, in a word, a Jew! (It may be of passing interest to you that one of my brothers returned to Israel under provisions of law there encouraging Jews to return. He has been there more than ten years and, of course, has served in the military.)

My Jewishness has never been an issue nor an obstacle in my fellowship with Christian reconstructionists. The opposite has been the case. On the other hand, my Jewishness was often seemingly the only thing that mattered in fellowshipping with dispensationalists. On being introduced by dispensationalists to others, it was almost invariably noted that I was Jewish. Not so with Reformed folk.

After my eyes were opened, by the grace of God, to the Messiahship of Jesus our Lord, I attended militantly dispensational congregations. I was nurtured on books by Charles Ryrie, Dwight Pentecost, Hal Lindsey — in short, my fare was from the table prepared by the Moody-Dallas school of theology. It should be noted that I still admire my "instructors" for their deep commitment to Christ, their sincere piety, and their diligent efforts to glorify God. While I no longer subscribe to their theology, I never forget that I, too, was once an ardent dispensationalist.

Now, however, I am what you might call "a rock-ribbed Calvinist," one of the variety which believes that *Covenant* is the motif which alone faithfully serves as an organizing principle of all Scriptural data; Covenant as opposed to *Dispensation*. I believe that the Law of God continues in force as explained in the Westminster Confession of Faith, that all areas of life are to be lived in joyful subjection to it and that the world will one day recognize this, by the sovereign power of the Holy Spirit of God (i.e., I am a Postmillennialist). Yet, no Christian who knows me would for a moment entertain the suggestion that I am anti-semitic.

I am a minister in the Christian Reformed Church in North America. In addition to a Jewish pastor, our local church has another Jewish Elder, and more than one fourth of our membership is Jewish.

As a minister, I have had numerous opportunities to speak in Reformed and Presbyterian churches not only in the Northeast, but also in the South, Midwest, Southwest, and Canada. In these churches I have presented what seems to me to be the Biblical posture for the church to take toward the Jewish people. This position was summarized by a person dear to the heart of every reconstructionist, John Calvin, in his *Institutes* (IV, XVI, 14).

> (S)alvation depends on God's mercy, which He extends to whom He pleases [Romans 9:15-16]; . . . there is no reason for the Jews to preen themselves and boast in the name of the covenant unless they keep the law of the covenant, that is, obey the Word.
>
> Nevertheless, when Paul cast them down from vain confidence in their kindred, he still saw, on the other hand, that the covenant which God had made once for all with the descendants of Abraham could in no way be made void. Consequently, in the eleventh chapter (of Romans) he argues that Abraham's physical progeny must not be deprived of their dignity. By virtue of this, he teaches, the Jews are the first and natural heirs of the gospel, except to the extent that by their ungratefulness they were forsaken as unworthy — *yet forsaken in such a way that the heavenly blessing has not departed utterly from their nation.* For this reason, despite their stubbornness and covenant-breaking, Paul still calls them [i.e., unbelieving Israel, SMS] holy [Rom. 11:16]. . . . (D)espite the great obstinacy with which they continue to wage war against the gospel, we must not despise them, while we consider that, for the sake of the promise, *God's blessing still rests among them.* Emphasis added.

Those hearing a debate between postmillennial reconstructionists and premillennial dispensationalists might be interested to know that the existence of the State of Israel was a concern much discussed by *postmillennialists* before William Blackstone (author of the famous late 19th-century Christian Zionist tome *Jesus is Coming*) was old enough to be bar mitzvah!

An article in the *British and Foreign Evangelical Review* in 1857 asked the question in its title: "Will the Jews, as a Nation, be Restored to their own Land?" This question was answered affirmatively; the (unsigned) article concluded that Scripture taught that the Jews must be restored to their land if certain prophecies would be fulfilled. But contra dispensationalism, the article asserted, "*The condition of the restoration . . . is repentance, true religion.* But it is agreed on all hands—with exceptions that need not detain us—that the Jews, as a nation, *will* be converted to Christianity, at some time yet future. The condition *then* will be complied with" (p. 818).

This excerpt highlights the difference between the attitude of the reconstructionist and the dispensationalist toward the nation of Israel. Dispensationalists believe that the Jewish people have a title to the land that transcends virtually any other consideration, including unbelief, rebellion, and hatred toward Christ and His church. Consequently, anti-zionism is equated with anti-semitism.

The reconstructionist, on the other hand, makes a distinction. He believes that the Jewish people may exercise the title only when they comply with the condition of repentance and faith. He has nothing against Jews living in "eretz yisrael" per se, but he recognizes that the far more significant question is Israel's faith. In light of this, it might be appropriate to ask which theological system has the true and best interests of the Jew close to its heart? If one's heart's desire and prayer to God for Israel agrees with the inspired Apostle's as recorded in Romans 10, can he thereby be called anti-semitic?

It is of more than passing interest that the above-mentioned article refers to the Jewish people as "a standing miracle, an ever-existing monument of the truth of prophecy." The author also maintained that, "the Jews, as a nation, *will* be converted to Christianity. . . . This is so clearly taught in the eleventh chapter of the Epistle to the Romans that one could scarcely deny it and retain his Christian character" (p. 812). Yet, he felt compelled to offer this disclaimer in a footnote: "It is proper for (the author) to state emphatically that he has no sympathy whatever with any Millenarian (i.e., Premillennial) theory, and that he considers all such ideas, and especially such as involve the personal reign of our Savior (from earthly Jerusalem), as merely carnal and Judaizing."

As early as 1847 the great Dr. David Brown (of Jamieson, Faussett & Brown fame) wrote of his conviction that the Jews would one day again possess the Land of Israel. But he labored carefully to emphasize the point that whatever occupation of the land they may enjoy outside of Christ, that would *not* be the fulfillment of the promised restoration. Dr. Brown, in his mature years wrote a most stimulating, and characteristically irenic book on the subject. Both dispensationalists *and* reconstructionists would profit from reading *The Restoration of the Jews: The History, Principles, and Bearings of the Question* (Edinburgh: Alexander, Strahan & Co., 1861).

Now, whatever any individual Christian reconstructionist might say, either from ignorance or honest disagreement, it can hardly be maintained that reconstructionism itself is anti-semitic. Calvin's position (as excerpted above) is mine, and I am a "reconstructionist." I can testify that while not every reconstructionist would agree with my position, my views on this issue are not only *accepted* within the reconstructionist world as being perfectly consistent with the system, but sought out.

This being the case, I think it would be best to bury the charge of anti-semitism in the sea of disproved contentions. If you should meet or read a reconstructionist who is, in fact, anti-semitic, please put him in touch with me. And as for me, if I should meet a dispensationalist who really believes that the church's efforts to reach the Jews with the Gospel will be successful, I'll be sure to send him to you so that you can convince him of the futility of his optimism!

It seems to me that this is what has occurred: Some dispensationalists have accepted the unbelieving Jewish expectations of the Messianic Kingdom as correct. They have, thereby, taken sides with Rabbinical Judaism against Christ's "Judaism," or Kingdom. They then cite the existence of the State of Israel as proof of their assertions, define themselves as the true protectors of the Jews, and, with the arrogance that so often accompanies such pragmatic paternalism, declare that all those who don't agree with their theology are, in principle, anti-semitic. Hogwash (i.e., non-kosher argumentation).

I trust this letter has served to provoke more careful thinking about this most important subject. To be sure, the last word has not been said. It is my judgment that the interpretation of prophecy requires more patience and care than most other areas of theology. This being the case, we are more faithful servants of Christ and the church when we allow latitude in this area, all other areas being orthodox. In this way, it may be that our efforts may turn toward more productive cooperation in achieving what we both desire: glory to God through the conversion of sinners, both Jewish and Gentile.

Steve M. Schlissel
Messiah's Christian Reformed Church
Brooklyn, New York

"Magnify the Lord with me; let us exalt His name together" (Psalm 34:3).

SCRIPTURE INDEX

OLD TESTAMENT

263

NEW TESTAMENT

NAME INDEX

275

SUBJECT INDEX

281

What Is Christian Reconstruction?

Is Christian reconstruction a deviant theology? Best-selling author Dave Hunt thinks it is. But author Gary DeMar contends otherwise.

In this insightful and stimulating audio cassette program Mr. Hunt, along with pastor Tommy Ice debate Mr. DeMar and author/theologian Dr. Gary North.

This four (4) tape package includes two cassettes from the live debate between these four men on April 14, 1988 and two single cassettes from the nationally broadcast "Point of View" radio program. The first single cassette features Gary DeMar and Dave Hunt on "Point of View," interviewed by Kerby Anderson. The second single tape features Gary DeMar, interviewed by Mr. Anderson on "Point of View."

This program will demonstrate the distinctives of Christian reconstruction and how it differs from the system of theology known as dispensationalism. All the key Scripture passages and fundamental questions are addressed, and answered.

Perfect for personal use or for group discussions.

Tapes 1 & 2: The entire two-hour debate held in Dallas, Texas, featuring Gary DeMar, Gary North, Dave Hunt, and Tommy Ice. Moderated by Kerby Anderson.

Tape 3: Gary DeMar discussing his best-selling book, *The Reduction of Christianity* on "Point of View" radio show. Interviewed by Kerby Anderson.

Tape 4 : Gary DeMar and Dave Hunt debate the issue of Christian reconstruction on "Point of View" radio show. Interviewed by Kerby Anderson.

All four cassette tapes are attractively packaged in a durable vinyl album. The retail price is $24.95 and can be ordered from your local Christian bookstore.

If it is not available in your bookstore you may order directly from the publisher by sending $24.95 plus $3.00 postage and handling. Please include your street or delivery address as all orders are shipped via United Parcel Service.

Send your order to:

Dominion Press
Post Office Box 8204
Fort Worth, Texas 76124